PENGUIN HANDBOOKS

THE INLAND NAVIGATOR

Bryan Marsh was born in 1932 and educated at the Lancaster Royal Grammar School. He worked in architecture for several years before taking up professional mountaineering and establishing a climbing school in the Lake District. He retired from climbing in the mid-sixties and returned to an earlier passion for boating after a holiday on the English canals. Since then he has explored most of the inland waterways of Britain and Ireland. At present his time is divided between writing and seasonal work on Windermere as skipper of a passenger vessel.

Bryan Marsh is the author of the Penguin Handbook *The Good Boat Guide*, and has revised and updated L. T. C. Rolt's classic history and account of the rivers and canals of Britain, *Navigable Waterways*, also published by Penguin.

Bryan Marsh

THE INLAND NAVIGATOR

The essential companion to canal and
river cruising in the British Isles

PENGUIN BOOKS

Penguin Books Ltd, Harmondsworth, Middlesex, England
Viking Penguin Inc., 40 West 23rd Street, New York, New York 10010, U.S.A.
Penguin Books Australia Ltd, Ringwood, Victoria, Australia
Penguin Books Canada Limited, 2801 John Street, Markham, Ontario, Canada L3R 1B4
Penguin Books (N.Z.) Ltd, 182–190 Wairau Road, Auckland 10, New Zealand

First published by Viking 1985
Published in Penguin Books 1986

Copyright © Bryan Marsh, 1985
All rights reserved

Made and printed in Great Britain by
Richard Clay (The Chaucer Press) Ltd,
Bungay, Suffolk
Typeset in Monophoto Photina

CONTENTS

LIST OF TEXT FIGURES

LIST OF MAPS

INTRODUCTION

For the great majority of people in Britain, holidays as we know them today – in the sense of several continuous days away from work – were practically unheard of until mid-Victorian times, and even then were limited to the enjoyment of mostly local activities such as fairs and outings in the countryside. The more fortunately placed – as regards wealth and leisure – had for decades made a practice of visiting the fashionable spas and seaside resorts, and this was made increasingly easier with the coming of the railways in the 1830s and their subsequent rapid growth: by 1870 more than 15,000 miles of track had been laid, and this figure grew to exceed 20,000 by 1890. The establishment of a widespread, speedy and convenient passenger transport system in turn encouraged the growth of what was then an embryo tourist industry; seaside fishing villages blossomed into holiday resorts, and previously remote and relatively unknown areas of the country became easily accessible. These developments were aided and encouraged not only by rising national prosperity, but also by a steady increase in middle-class occupations, which provided at least a section of the populace with both the money and a certain degree of free time to indulge in holidays away from home.

Boating as a leisure activity, apart from messing about in small craft on local rivers and lakes, had previously been a privilege of the well-to-do, especially favoured by those who owned country houses situated near inland waters, and this state of affairs – perhaps contrary to expectations – remained largely unaffected by the spread of railways except in two areas of the country: the Norfolk Broads and the Thames Valley.

The Norfolk Broads constitute a physical oddity that occurs nowhere else in Britain. Contained within a compact area of East Anglia lying between Norwich and the coast and measuring roughly twenty-two by seventeen miles, they consist of five interconnected rivers which together form a navigable system with outlets to the North Sea at Great Yarmouth and Lowestoft. The term 'Broad' refers to the characteristic small, shallow lakes – of which there are many – dotted around the area, and which, in most cases, are accessible from the various rivers. These lakes were originally formed, it has been suggested, through inundation of ancient peat diggings by the sea during the thirteenth century. From the seventeenth century onwards improvements were made to the rivers to bring them up to navigable standards, and they supported considerable local trade up to about the time of the First World War. The establishment of a national railway network eventually led to their decline, as with most other commercial waterways, but also resulted, in the case of the Broads, in the foundation of a tourist industry based mainly upon boats and boating.

The hiring out of craft of sufficient size to provide reasonably comfortable accommodation, on a weekly basis (or longer), probably dates back to the 1870s, for by the mid 1880s a thriving hire-boat business was in existence on the Broads, excellently served by the Great Eastern Railway from the London termini of Liverpool Street and St Pancras. A contemporary guide to the Broads, published about 1887, lists no fewer than thirty firms hiring out sailing craft varying in size from a two-ton lug-rig 'camping boat' to a thirty-ton wherry (the wherry was at that time the commercial workhorse of the area) which, suitably converted, provided comfortable and spacious accommodation for up to twelve persons. Professional crews could be engaged for all types of craft, and were compulsory on the larger ones. A few steam-powered craft were also available, but none of these were for hire on a self-steer basis, for hirers could not be expected to possess the expertise necessary for the safe working of the boilers and machinery. Interestingly enough, the author of the guide referred to above chartered such a craft for the cruise on which he based the descriptive accounts of the area – at the outset stating, somewhat apologetically, that 'Our chief motive for taking the voyage by steam is its quickness.' And relatively quick it must have been for those days – in spite of a broken propeller shaft and an unfortunate occurrence when the boat ran out of coal!

The widespread use of the internal combustion engine over the past sixty years or so has perhaps induced us to forget that even in Edwardian times the choice lay between sail and steam as a means of propulsion for the larger inland craft; the semi-diesel engine was first fitted to a commercial narrowboat in 1912, and it was only after the First World War that both oil and petrol engines for boat propulsion began to appear in significant numbers. The consequence was, of course, that mechanically propelled craft were simply not available for hire on a self-steer basis until the period between the two world wars, and even then on a very small scale.

But to return to our author on his Broads cruise in the steam yacht *Lily*. It is interesting to compare this power-driven charter boat with the hire craft available to us today:

Here she is, the *Lily* – somewhat like a launch in hull, but broader in the beam in proportion to her length. She is 30 ft long and 7 ft 6 ins. beam. Forward in the peak is a small American cooking-stove; so that the man who drives the engine, which comes next, can keep one eye on the dinner which is preparing, and the other on the machinery. A cabin amidships makes a snug dining and bedroom combined, 9 ft long, 7 ft wide, and 5 ft 9 ins. high. It contains innumerable lockers for the thousand-and-one articles to be used on the voyage. Long seat-lockers fold down at night, forming ample sleeping accommodation for four persons. Large stern-sheets, with lockers all round, forming seats, fill up the space between the cabin and the stern.

It is noticeable that the author says little about the accommodation for the 'driver', although from events described later in the book it would seem likely that he did not share the comfort of the main cabin with the 'gentlemen', but instead slept in the fore-peak, probably with his head on the cooking stove and his feet against the boiler! The author goes on to advise his readers that the trip may be undertaken with equal ease in a sailing vessel:

Indeed, most persons would prefer being under sail, so as to obviate the incessant vibration caused by the throbbing of the propeller, and also the unpleasantness of the smoke.

Such was the typical power-driven hire craft of Victorian times – a far cry from the huge wide-beam fibreglass cruisers of today, with their powerful diesel engines and every modern convenience from refrigerator to double-bedded stateroom.

The present-day Broadlander would very likely have felt much more at home in the accommodation provided by the large converted wherries of the period, besides avoiding 'the unpleasantness of the smoke'. These wherries were rather similar in shape to a sailing barge, and carried a single huge sail on a stout mast positioned well towards the bow. Their equipment was fairly comprehensive, and included several items no longer to be found in hire craft inventories, but typical of those days:

A wherry is divided into three compartments – viz., bedroom, saloon, and kitchen. The bedroom and saloon are under one roof, and occupy nearly two-thirds of the length of the vessel. The fore-part, or bows, is left clear as a promenade deck; then comes the ladies' bedroom, occupying the whole width of the craft (some 10 ft), and about 10 ft of its length; next this is the saloon, 20 ft long, nicely carpeted and painted, &c., with a large dining-table in the centre, and, at the after end, the crowning glory – a piano. After dark, with the lamps lighted, and the merry party gathered around this instrument, many a happy hour is passed away ...

Next the saloon, with a serving-door leading into it, is the kitchen, fitted with a neat American range, which is presided over by the skipper, who, besides being sailing-master is also cook and steward. The dirty work is performed by the 'crew' – a lad of sixteen or seventeen years of age. All washing-up, potato-peeling, fish-cleaning, &c., falls to his lot.

This, of course, would be taken entirely for granted in an age when domestic servants formed part of every household above a certain income level. Today the Norfolk Broads are one of the most popular boating areas in Britain, with many thousands of registered craft, both privately owned and for hire, of all types, shapes and sizes, and, in spite of the consequent overcrowding, to many people the attraction of the area shows no sign of diminishing – indeed, some would give this as a reason for its continued popularity.

No other inland waters in Britain were, at that time, quite so well suited as the Broads for this type of boating holiday (with the possible exception of certain of the English Lakes, notably Windermere, but this magnificent stretch of water was the almost exclusive preserve of the wealthy owners of private yachts, either sail- or steam-driven, and was already an established centre for important sailing regattas), for the fact that the whole cruising area of the Broads is on one level eliminates the necessity for manhandling large sailing craft through locks. This is probably why that ancient and much-loved river navigation, the Thames, never approached the popularity of the Broads for cruising holidays until well into the era of the marine internal combustion engine. The section of the Thames between Teddington and Oxford contains no fewer than thirty-two locks in a distance of ninety-four miles – that is, one lock to approximately every three miles of river, the six-and-a-half-mile reach at Wallingford being the longest stretch of water on one level. Nevertheless, from mid-

Victorian times onward the Thames grew rapidly in popularity as a venue for pleasure-boating, as distinct from holiday cruising. A Thames guide of 1886 featured advertisements offering for hire 'Steam Launches and Boats of every description to Let by the Day, Week, Month, or Year'. These were the years, right up to the First World War, when weekend boating on the river reached its peak; contemporary photographs show the much-frequented Boulter's Lock at Maidenhead jammed with craft ranging from passenger steamers to small skiffs and punts, the ladies elegantly dressed and the men sporting straw boaters and striped blazers. Small boats outfitted for camping could be hired for a few days or longer, and by this means it was possible to undertake a leisurely trip down river from Oxford, leaving the boat at a yard near London, whence it would be returned to Oxford by train. The Great War put an end to all that, and although boating on the Thames revived during the 1920s the really tremendous increase in activity did not occur (as with all other sections of the inland waterways) until the advent of fibreglass craft in conjunction with the affluence of the 1960s and 1970s.

The Norfolk Broads and the Thames together form only a small fraction of the total mileage of navigable inland waterways in this country; by far the greater proportion is made up of canals and navigable rivers, and even includes the wide drainage dykes of Lincolnshire and the Fens. Most of these waterways form an interconnected system spreading over much of England and a part of Wales; a system, moreover, that had been substantially completed by the time of the building of the first railways during the 1830s. These were all commercial navigations, built to serve the growing industrial power of England, and busy with boat traffic of all kinds until railway competition caused their gradual decline, which continued throughout Victorian times and ultimately resulted in their commercial extinction in the face of road transport. In spite of the possibilities presented by the extensive nature of the system, the canal network as a whole could in no way fulfil the genteel expectations of the Victorian holiday-maker. The commercial traffic was far too heavy (even on the Thames there was bad blood between pleasure-boaters and professional boatmen), there were too many locks, and although long stretches of canal traversed open – and, quite often, beautiful – countryside, all too frequently the waterways entered the back doors of grimy industrial towns thick with canalside factories and warehouses. Besides which, as we have already seen, there were at that time no craft suitable for long-distance cruising, other than camping punts and skiffs, and perhaps chartered steam launches of dimensions compatible with the narrow-gauge locks of the Midlands canal system.

So the Victorian and Edwardian pleasure-boaters – with a few exceptions such as Temple Thurston, who travelled the inland waterways in the horse-drawn narrowboat *Flower of Gloster*, and published an account of his adventures in 1912 – shunned the canals entirely, preferring instead the romantic peacefulness of the rivers and broads of East Anglia, or the fashionable crowds of boaters and onlookers at Henley and Maidenhead. Following a brief revival during the Great War, commercial traffic on inland waterways continued its slow decline, and as profits fell the companies sought ways by which their operations could be rendered more economical – notably, through use of the internal combustion engine. By the end of the 1920s the once-famous steam narrowboats had all been converted to diesel power, and henceforth canal transport was to be increasingly dominated by the motor boat. But in parallel with these events there occurred a phenomenon of ominous import for the future of inland waterways: the rapid development of the motor vehicle and a corresponding growth in the construction of new roads. While the semi-diesel engine was too bulky and inconvenient for use in pleasure-craft, the compact and relatively inexpensive petrol engines used in the new breed of small cars proved ideal, after suitable conversion, for powering river cruisers, and it was not long before small motor boats began to appear on the canals.

This change in attitude towards the canals as regards their use for pleasure-boating is probably not unconnected with the beginnings, in the 1930s, of what we now call 'activity' holidays: the involvement of people in pursuits requiring the acquisition of physical skills, including those associated with pony-trekking, canoeing, climbing, skiing, and many other outdoor activities. It was during the 1930s that widespread interest in hill walking and rambling first got under way, encouraged by the cheap and convenient accommodation provided by the Youth Hostels Association, and the foundation, on a nationwide scale, of rambling, climbing, cycling and camping clubs. These were relatively inexpensive pursuits, and therefore available to a great many people; comparatively few, at that time, could afford the expense of owning a boat suitable for cruising holidays, although the boating enthusiast could always book holiday hire craft on the Broads and the Thames – and many did, year after year. Then, in 1935, hire cruisers appeared on the canal system for the first time, based at Christleton on the outskirts of Chester, and run by the Inland Cruising Association (to become well known, twenty years later, as Inland Hire Cruisers Ltd). These operations, which included boat-building, were apparently successful until closed down by the outbreak of war in September 1939. Revived after the war, the company continued in business from its base on the Shropshire Union Canal at Christleton until it was finally dissolved in 1972.

Wartime necessity again brought an increase in waterborne traffic, but this could not be sustained, and after 1945 the inexorable decline continued. In 1948 the canal system and certain river navigations were nationalized and placed under the aegis of the British Transport Commission which, with various administrative changes from time to time, continued up to 1963, when the Commission was abolished and its interests transferred to the newly established British Waterways Board. Meanwhile, in spite of post-war austerity and shortages of all kinds, two more hire fleets sprang into being on the canals. First on the scene was the Canal Cruising Company Ltd, based at Stone on the Trent and Mersey Canal just a few miles north of Stafford. Faced with the problem of finding suitable craft, the company bought ex-commercial narrowboats (in fact, unpowered seventy-foot boats known as 'butties', which in their working lives had been towed by horse or motor boat), cut them in half, and fitted new stern ends. The provision of cabin accommodation and the installation of suitable motors and propellers, together with tiller-steering, completed the conversion. This solution proved to be the right answer, for the sturdy hulls had been built for canal conditions in the first place, and their shape was well suited for conversion to cabin spaces. Thus a pattern evolved that was to be widely adopted in the future, for nowadays almost all canal hire craft are built on lines derived from the hull shape of working boats.

The second new hire company to start up after the war was Canal Pleasurecraft, operated from Stourport at the southern end of the Staffordshire and Worcestershire Canal. Its approach to boat design was radically different from that employed by the Stone company, and had more in common with the type of craft used by the Inland Cruising Association, for the boats were built of marine plywood on lines akin to the river cruisers of the Thames and the Broads, but modified in detail to the more exacting demands of canal usage. Of these three pioneer hire operators, only one – the Canal Cruising Company – now remains in business, as Canal Pleasurecraft was absorbed by another hire firm in 1978.

During the early post-war period, changing attitudes towards the use of canals for pleasure-cruising were brought into sharp focus largely through the efforts and inspiration of one man, the late L. T. C. Rolt. In company with his wife, Tom Rolt had cruised the inland waterways in the converted narrowboat *Cressy* during the last few weeks of peacetime and the early years of the war, and had related their experiences in his book *Narrow Boat*, published in 1944. Such was the power of his writing that he fired others with his own enthusiasm, soon gathering about him a group of people equally concerned with the waterways and their future, and from these small beginnings the Inland Waterways Association (IWA) was born in 1946. As a campaigning body the Association was extremely success-ful from the start, and it is no exaggeration to say that without its influence the navigable waterways as we know them today would largely have ceased to exist. The aims of the IWA were – and still are – to exert pressure on central government and other authorities in order to secure the retention, restoration and development of water-ways and to encourage their fullest recreational and commercial use – often in the face of indifference, intransigence and sometimes out-right hostility on the part of the authorities. The IWA did not win every battle, however, and it remains a tragedy that one of the most important was lost when the public right of navigation on those waterways administered by the British Waterways Board was removed under the 1968 Transport Act, although the Association continues to press for its restoration.

As commercial traffic on the canals continued to dwindle after the Second World War, so there began a slow but steady upsurge of interest in the potential of waterways for pleasure purposes; the number of cruising clubs, and their membership, began to grow, and canal societies were formed to look after the interests of particular canals and, in some cases, to promote the restoration of derelict waterways. With the growing affluence of the 1960s and 1970s there came a tremendous increase in boat ownership, largely due to the introduction of mass-produced fibreglass (glass-reinforced plastic, or GRP) boats, together with the disappearance, almost overnight, of the last of the big carrying fleets. This occurred after the exceptionally severe winter of 1962–3, when the canals froze over for many weeks, thus sounding the death knell for commercial narrowboat traffic in general; the British Waterways Board (BWB) ceased trading and disposed of its fleet, and although some private companies struggled on for a few years, by the early 1970s it was all over and the canal network became, like the Thames and the Broads, a venue devoted almost solely to pleasure-cruising.

During the 1960s the number of hire operators and hire craft gradually increased until quite suddenly, in the early 1970s, there occurred a spectacular boom; by the end of the decade about 150 firms and over 1,500 boats were in operation, mostly on the BWB waterways. At the outset there was a tendency for some hire operators to equip their fleets with GRP cruisers, but in the hands of novices these are not really suitable for canals, and were gradually phased out in favour of steel narrowboats, the hulls of which, as has been already noted, are ideal for canal work. Today these craft constitute the great majority of canal hire boats (but not private craft); on the Thames and the Broads the revolutionary techniques of GRP construction led to the adoption of the wide-beam (up to twelve-foot) fibreglass cruiser as the mainstay of the hire fleets, and similar craft are now based on the Caledonian Canal in Scotland and on the waterways of Eire and Northern Ireland. Almost all hire craft are now fitted with compact, reliable and safe diesel engines that are easy to operate and require no technical knowledge on the part of the hirer, while the boats themselves are fitted out in general to an unprecedented degree of luxury, including central heating, showers and baths, and galleys resembling modern kitchens, with full-size gas cookers, refrigerators and stainless steel sinks.

These developments reflect the tremendous popularity of inland boating today, and with good reason. Never before has the holiday-maker had available such a wide-ranging variety of inland waters, nor such an overwhelming choice of craft. Inland boating possesses a peculiar charm – very likely to do with the intimate connection between land and water, seeing town and countryside from a different and unusual viewpoint, the opportunity of gaining an appreciation of the colourful history of our inland waterways, and – not least of all – the sheer pleasure and satisfaction to be derived from navigating river, lake and canal with competence and safety. Such is the attraction of holiday cruising that it appeals to all: be they canal narrowboat enthusiasts or river cruiser devotees, hardened long-distance navigators or leisurely family groups, all will find their own enjoyment on our inland waterways.

It is for such people that this book has been written; and if in the search for that enjoyment its contents prove to be of some value, then its purpose will have been served.

B.M.

Ambleside
The Lake District
Summer 1983

CHAPTER ONE

THE NEW HIGHWAYS

The beginnings of inland waterborne transport on any significant scale may be traced back to early medieval times, for it was only after the onset of the Middle Ages that social and political developments in Britain created the conditions of stability necessary for the steady growth of commerce. However, the all-important means whereby commercial expansion is achieved – namely, a satisfactory transport system – was sadly lacking; the carriage of merchandise by land was at best an uncertain affair, for the excellent paved roads constructed during the Roman occupation of Britain had long since fallen into disrepair. Not that these roads had ever formed a comprehensive network in any of the Roman-occupied countries, as they were built primarily as military highways linking the principal towns and cities only, leaving other settlements to be served by unmade tracks, pathways, and drovers' roads, and these were mostly impassable in bad weather conditions. As a result it was only to be expected that navigable rivers would be used for the carriage of goods whenever this was feasible, and indeed up to the Middle Ages the larger rivers of England had been utilized in this way. River channels, at that time largely unobstructed by bridges and often subject to tides that reached far inland, were rendered periodically suitable for navigation by large vessels when water depths were increased by the backing-up of land water by flood tides and winds; the inconvenience to river traffic of waiting upon tide and wind was accepted as inevitable in the days of sailing ships, and was no different, of course, from similar delays at sea ports and harbours.

Long though this situation lasted, it could not remain unaffected by the changes set in motion during the Middle Ages, some of which were to create a conflict of interest between shipping merchants and those who sought to use rivers for purposes other than navigation. For example, the establishment of riverside mills using water as a source of power entailed the construction of weirs to provide the head necessary for the wheel-race, thus causing a total obstruction to navigation. Again, the increasing demands on food production led to the building of special weirs in which fish were trapped or netted, and the erection of bridges in an effort to improve overland communications often rendered a stretch of river impassable through lack of headroom and constriction of the channel.

Such was the position, in broad terms, until inevitably the interplay of events turned full circle and the growth of trade created a renewed demand for the benefits of river navigation. As any substantial improvements would certainly entail modifications to existing weirs, the mill owners and the fishing interests so bitterly opposed the reopening of through navigation that little was done for a long time, but gradually the opposition was mollified and the necessary work carried out, thus marking the start of what might be called the 'modern' era of inland navigation.

The problem facing the advocates of river improvement was, quite simply, how to overcome the difference in water levels created by a weir; the solution adopted was the invention variously called a flash lock, staunch, navigation weir or water gate (the now-familiar pound lock was to appear at a later date). Flash locks differed in detail according to region and date of construction, but a common type consisted of two horizontal beams set one above the other and spanning an opening in the weir; the upper beam was removable, while the lower formed a fixed 'sill' on the river bed. On the upstream side, vertical timbers called 'rimers' rested against the horizontal members and supported long-handled boards called 'paddles'. The method of operation was tedious, to say the least: first, the paddles were withdrawn by means of the attached handles, followed by the rimers, and finally the upper horizontal beam was removed. Downstream craft would then be carried down on the fall of water, which might be considerable, while upstream traffic would wait until the current had subsided to the point where boats could be hauled into the upper reach by a fixed winch provided for that purpose. Rather surprisingly, navigation weirs of the paddle and rimer type, together with later versions – the water gate and the Fenland staunch – survived until modern times, and examples of the latter were even being built as late as the nineteenth century, in spite of the fact that the pound lock had first been constructed some 260 years earlier. This anachronous situation arose not from economic necessity, but out of the continued opposition of mill owners, who feared that the operation of pound locks would further interfere with their precious water supplies.

Against this background of prejudice and ill-will the further improvement of river navigations made slow progress until the construction of the Wey Navigation in the mid seventeenth century – an engineering feat significant not only for the number of pound locks employed, but mainly on account of the length of artificial channel excavated: almost half the total length of the entire navigation. This notable achievement proved to be a landmark in the development of engineering concepts, and foreshadowed the great works of river improvement carried out during the first half of the eighteenth century, when the gradually quickening tempo of the Industrial Revolution created renewed pressure upon transport facilities. In response to these demands the Aire and Calder Navigation was opened to traffic in 1703, followed thereafter by a spate of river improvement schemes, among them the Kennet and Avon Navigation, Bristol Avon and Medway in the south; and in the north the Mersey, Irwell, Douglas and Weaver, culminating in what was probably the most outstanding of them all: the Calder and Hebble Navigation. This welter of activity signalled the emergence of civil engineering as a recognized profession, and already the first of the great engineers – Thomas Steers, John Smeaton, and William Jessop – had established their reputations; they were soon to be followed by many others, for by 1760 Britain stood on the threshold of the Canal Age.

By the middle of the eighteenth century the Industrial Revolution had gathered sufficient momentum to create the conditions necessary for its own further development, and the time had arrived for men of vision to take decisive action if their ambitions for the expansion of trade and industry were to be realized. Ingenuity and invention were not lacking – coke-fired smelting techniques and the steam engine had by this period been in use for many years, and the rich mineral deposits of the Midlands pointed to a prospect of unlimited prosperity – but in the absence of cheap and efficient transport the stimulus to growth would be severely inhibited. Although the improvement of river navigations had contributed greatly towards communications in certain areas of the country, constraints imposed by the geographical distribution of river basins ensured that a nationwide network based on similar methods was clearly out of the question. Nor could the problem be solved by deepening, extending and connecting headwater streams and tributaries, as this would merely result in the elimination of the vital water supply. But quite apart from these considerations, the crucial requirement was for a system of water-ways that would serve industry at its own workplace: in and around the mineral areas of the Midlands and the North. The implications of this were obvious: the new navigations would have to consist of artificial channels, or cuts, connecting the various industrial centres, and provided with adequate means of water supply. Stated baldly, the concept appears simple, but it is easy to overlook the fact that the enormous task of excavation and construction would have to be done without the use of any powered machinery: the brawn of men and animals would have to suffice.

The first canal proper – as distinct from improved river navigations – was the Newry Canal in Northern Ireland, completed in 1745 to provide through navigation from the inland Lough Neagh to the Irish Sea at Carlingford Lough; after an interval of twelve years the Sankey Canal, connecting the Lancashire town of St Helens to the River Mersey, was opened, and it was really this event that inaugurated the era of canal-building in Britain, although it was destined to be over-shadowed by an undertaking which has since become historically celebrated as the archetype of English canals: the Bridgewater.

Perhaps influenced by the example of the neighbouring Sankey Canal, the Duke of Bridgewater conceived the idea of a canal link between his coal mines at Worsley and retail outlets in Manchester – an idea which came to fruition in 1761 with the completion of the waterway through to Stretford. The engineering works associated with the project were on a scale unprecedented at that time in England, an achievement due to the close cooperation between the Duke, his agent John Gilbert, and a hitherto unknown engineer, James Brindley. Certainly the widespread interest aroused by the construction of the Bridgewater Canal was responsible for the ex-plosion of enthusiasm for canal-building which followed, and Brindley found his services much in demand. Once the necessary techniques had been proven and the idea shown to be viable, caution was thrown to the winds and a scheme devised which was breath-taking in its implications: no less than the linking of the major rivers of England by means of a 'cross' of canals, with the Trent and Mersey Canal – or 'Grand Trunk', as it was first called – forming the backbone of the system. To this backbone would be joined the Staffordshire and Worcestershire Canal (connecting the Trent and Mersey Canal to the

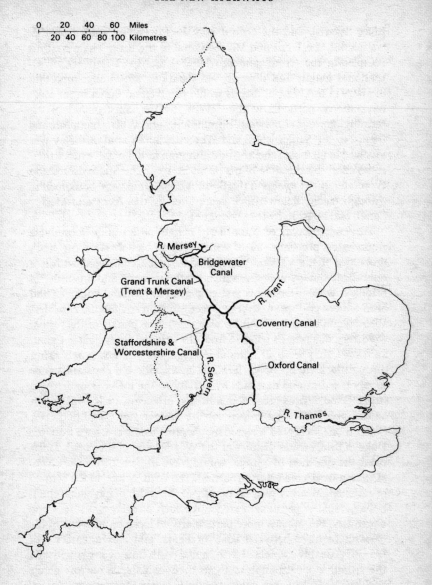

The canals of the 'cross'

River Severn), and the Oxford and the Coventry Canals (together connecting the Trent and Mersey Canal to the River Thames), thus completing the 'cross' and providing a transport network of exceptional length and diversity. In addition, the vitally important industry of the West Midlands would be given an outlet to the river navigations, particularly the Severn, by the construction of the Birmingham Canal between Birmingham and Wolverhampton and thence to the Staffordshire and Worcestershire Canal. Brindley was involved in all these schemes, and although he did not live to see their completion, by the time of his death in 1772 the Staffordshire and Worcestershire Canal and the Birmingham Canal were both open to through traffic, followed five years later by the Trent and Mersey Canal, and in 1790 by the Oxford Canal.

The construction of these early canals posed quite formidable engineering problems, all of which had to be solved as the work proceeded if the various projects were to be completed within a reasonable time, and it says much for the tenacity and ingenuity of Brindley, who, prior to his first engagement as canal engineer had been a mere craftsman, that he successfully overcame the considerable difficulties with which he was faced. The canals of the 'cross' were very different in concept from the original Bridgewater Canal: for a start, they were all 'summit level' canals – that is, canals rising through locks to an upper level, or levels, where a constant water supply is fed in and descends by gravity to the lower pounds. At a stroke Brindley was presented with two problems, neither of which he had previously had to face, for the Bridgewater Canal had been built on one level with a water supply provided by drainage from the Duke of Bridgewater's mines at the Worsley end of the canal. Moreover, the question of 'gauge' would have to be settled before construction work could start in earnest. The term 'gauge' in the context of canal engineering refers generally to the width of navigable channel available at permanent structures such as bridges, tunnels and aqueducts, but applies more particularly to locks on account of the close fit required between boat, or boats, and lock chamber. For reasons probably connected with capital costs, time, water supply and the primitive construction methods then available, a narrow gauge was adopted, and this subsequently became the standard for all Midland canals. The dimensions of narrow-gauge lock chambers were fixed at about seventy-five feet by seven feet, six inches, thus giving rise to the emergence of the commercial 'narrowboat', or 'longboat', with overall length and beam of approximately seventy feet and seven feet respectively.

In his layout of the actual line of the first canals, Brindley adopted a method known as 'contour cutting', in which the canal followed a particular land contour for as long as practicable before rising or falling to a different level as circumstances dictated. It will be appreciated that this technique is hardly conducive to economy in the length of cut required, and in fact resulted in the necessity for certain extremely tortuous sections of canal – notably on the Oxford – to be straightened at a later date in order to reduce passage times.

Meanwhile, even as work proceeded on the canals of the 'cross', other projects had been completed and further canal construction put in hand; by 1790, for example, the original Bridgewater Canal had been extended through to Runcorn and a connection effected with the Mersey; the Loughborough Navigation (River Soar), Thames and Severn, Chesterfield, Birmingham and Fazeley, and Erewash Canals were all in existence, and work was proceeding on the Stourbridge and the Dudley Canals, while the first of the trans-Pennine water-ways – the Leeds and Liverpool Canal – was slowly struggling towards completion. Assisted by the growth of waterway communications during the period 1760 to 1790, the pace of the Industrial Revolution quickened, and thus provided an even greater stimulus to canal-building, eventually culminating, during the early 1790s, in that astonishing increase in the number of projects now dubbed 'canal mania', which, after an explosive beginning, slowly ran down and finally petered out some forty years later in the face of railway competition.

This was the period during which Brindley's successors – among them Thomas Telford, John Rennie, and William Jessop – secured their reputations by the engineering of the great works of canal construction: Pontcysyllte aqueduct in the Vale of Llangollen, the Lune aqueduct at Lancaster, the Caledonian Canal, the long tunnels at Blisworth and Braunston on the Grand Junction Canal (now the Grand Union Canal), the Birmingham and Liverpool Junction Canal (now part of the Shropshire Union system) with its lofty embankments and deep cuttings, to mention just a few. But the general excitement and enthusiasm for canal promotion sometimes overrode common sense and led to the building of routes through quite unsuitable terrain, the Rochdale Canal being a case in point. Opened to through traffic in 1804, it traversed the Pennines from the Bridge-

water Canal at Manchester to a junction with the Calder and Hebble
Navigation at Sowerby Bridge, a feat involving the construction of
ninety-two locks in a total distance of thirty-two miles, and – in spite
of the knowledge then available – it was given an exceptionally short
summit pound. To make matters worse, it was a broad-gauge canal
with lock dimensions suited to the commercial craft of the Lancashire
plain – that is, about seventy-two feet by fourteen feet – a wholly
unnecessary extravagance, as vessels of these dimensions were
unable to pass the locks of the Calder and Hebble Navigation, which
would only accommodate craft not exceeding fifty-seven feet, six
inches in length. Even more absurd in this respect was the Huddersfield Narrow Canal, crossing the Pennines to the south of the
Rochdale, for in addition to the heavy lockage the canal was built to
the standard narrow gauge of the Midlands system, whereas the
Huddersfield Broad Canal, with which it joined on the Yorkshire side,
employed Calder and Hebble gauge, thus limiting through traffic to
shortened narrowboats of about fifty-seven feet in length. These
examples, which are by no means isolated, shed some light upon the
attitudes of the time: an ingrained provincialism of outlook and
consequent indifference to the need for a common approach to the
overall viability of a national, as opposed to a local or regional,
waterways system. The creation of the canal network as we know it
today was also influenced by factors beyond the control of individual
companies: inflation, economic slump and lack of profitability. Faced
with such difficulties, quite grandiose schemes might come to nothing
or be altered to the point where they bore little resemblance to the
original concept, as was the case with what is now called the
Llangollen, or Welsh, Canal.

This beautiful rural waterway is all that remains of a scheme (the
Ellesmere Canal) to connect the Mersey at Ellesmere Port with the
Severn at Shrewsbury, a scheme that was conceived during the period
of 'canal mania' and which reflected the bubbling optimism of
the times. However, financial difficulties caused by inflation forced the
proprietors to reconsider their plans, resulting in abandonment of the
proposed route of the main line via the Alyn Valley and the substi-
tution of an alternative line between Frankton and the Chester Canal
near Nantwich. The northernmost section of the new canal between
Ellesmere Port and Chester had already been constructed, and a
connecting link extended towards the Montgomery Canal, but the
southern section never did reach Shrewsbury as intended. That

portion of the original main line between Frankton and the Vale of Llangollen was built as planned, and contains the major engineering works associated with the project: Pontcysyllte and Chirk aqueducts, and Whitehouses and Chirk tunnels; the aqueducts are really magnificent structures, and Pontcysyllte is reckoned to be Telford's greatest single achievement. Finally, a feeder branch from the northern end of Pontcysyllte to the River Dee at Llantisilio was constructed to provide the canal with water, as use of the proposed supply reservoirs had been lost with the abandonment of the original line to the north. As completed, the project differed considerably from the vision of its originators; instead of an arterial link between two great river navigations it became a predominantly rural waterway, important in its own fashion but in the end unable to keep going because of the lack of traffic. Unlike so many of its kind, however, the Llangollen Canal survived, on account of its use as a water channel connecting the River Dee to reservoirs at Hurleston near Nantwich, and for many years has been probably the most popular cruising route in the entire canal network.

The closing decade of the eighteenth century witnessed the completion of the remainder of 'first generation' canals and their subsequent extensions: Dudley Canal No. 2 and the Wyrley and Essington Canal in the Birmingham Canal Navigations system; the Warwick and Birmingham Canal, together with its southern counterpart, the Warwick and Napton Canal, opening a through route to the Oxford Canal at Napton Junction; the Peak Forest and the Ashby Canals; the Derby and the Nottingham Canals, and the adjoining improvements to the River Trent by construction of Cranfleet and Beeston cuts; the Leicester Navigation, a continuation of the improvements to the River Soar above Loughborough; and the isolated but important canals around Swansea and Cardiff serving the industrial and mining areas of South Wales, and the Basingstoke and the Andover Canals in the south of England.

The majority of canals completed before 1800 had been promoted before the onset of 'canal mania', so we may conveniently regard the turn of the century as marking the commencement of the 'mature' phase of canal-building. Since the early days of the Bridgewater Canal, engineering techniques had become increasingly sophisticated; for instance, 'cut and fill' – whereby the spoil removed from cuttings was used for the raising of embankments, thus allowing a more direct line to be followed – had largely supplanted the old 'contour cutting' method, although the latter was employed in the construction of the Leicester summit section of the Grand Union Canal as late as 1814. Tunnelling techniques had similarly improved, to the extent that Telford's 'new' Harecastle Tunnel, opened in 1827, took only three years to build as against the eleven years required for Brindley's original bore.

Success and confidence fed upon one another, and the opening years of the nineteenth century saw the completion of a veritable spate of canal projects, among them the Stainforth and Keadby, Sheffield. Huddersfield, Rochdale, and Cromford Canals; the Stratford, Worcester and Birmingham, Kennet and Avon Canals – and, most importantly, the Grand Junction Canal linking the industrial Midlands with London, and providing for the first time an alternative to the old route via the Oxford Canal and the then unimproved upper Thames. Canal projects in the west of England had from the start been associated with an idea of connecting the Bristol and the English Channels, and although this remained an unfulfilled dream it did give rise at about this time to the construction of several canals, such as the Bridgwater and Taunton, Chard, Grand Western, and – further to the west – the Bude Canal. Tub boats, resembling rectangular boxes and towed in trains, were used extensively on these waterways, and their special requirements gave rise to some quite remarkable engineering works: inclined planes (carefully graded slopes fitted with tram rails upon which the tub boats were hauled, either on wheeled cradles or on their own permanently attached wheels) were commonly used to overcome differences in level, an established technique employed on the earlier tub boat canals of industrial Shropshire. An additional feature of these western canals, and one not widely used elsewhere, was the vertical boat-lift, some types of which were of strikingly original design.

Among the schemes completed during this period were some that had been in gestation for decades, their construction delayed by financial stringency, engineering problems and other factors: the Worcester and Birmingham line took twenty-four years all told, the Lancaster twenty-seven (it never did effect a water junction with the main network, goods being transhipped by tramway across the River Ribble), and, most amazing of all, the Leeds and Liverpool Canal with a grand total of forty-six years from commencement to completion – fifty-one if we include the eventual connection with the Bridgewater Canal at Leigh in Lancashire. But by the 1840s it was nearly all over.

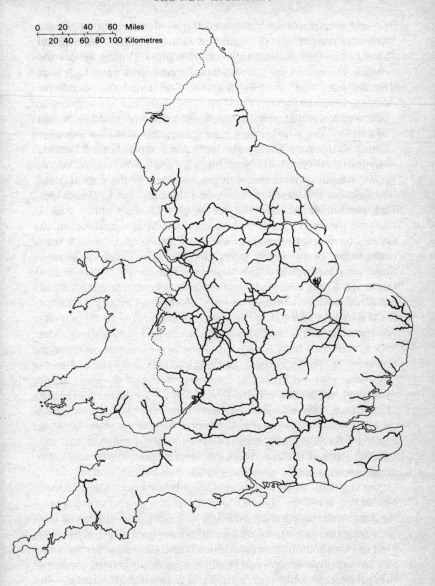

0 20 40 60 Miles
20 40 60 80 100 Kilometres

The inland waterways system of England and Wales in the mid nineteenth century

Myopic administrative policies combined with mounting pressure from the competition of expanding railway interests were putting many canal companies into severe difficulties. During the previous decade the last of the narrow-gauge canals had been built – the Birmingham and Liverpool Junction Canal, and the Macclesfield Canal – while the Oxford Canal Company had rather belatedly decided to straighten and improve the northern section of their line between Braunston and Hawkesbury. The proprietors of the Birmingham Canal Navigations (BCN) also authorized much-needed improvements to their system at about this time, and Telford was called in to make necessary recommendations, resulting in the eventual construction of the 'new' main line from Birmingham to Deepfields, a scheme which included the spectacular Galton Cutting with its elegant cast-iron road bridge, now preserved as a national monument. Further extensions to the BCN, intended to reduce traffic congestion, followed some years later: the Tame Valley Canal, and a long overdue bypass of the hopelessly constricted Dudley Tunnel, achieved by the construction of Netherton Tunnel, impressive in its size and provided with two towpaths illuminated by artificial light.

Meanwhile, the last of the major improvements to the old river navigations had taken place: in the north-east the Aire and Calder Navigation had been connected to the River Ouse at Goole by the opening of the Knottingley and Goole Canal in 1826, and in the following year a difficult and dangerous stretch of the lower Severn was bypassed by the construction of the Gloucester and Sharpness Ship Canal. This enterprising scheme proved to be the forerunner of a great project which came to fruition sixty-seven years later: the Manchester Ship Canal, Britain's largest artificial waterway.

But in spite of all eleventh-hour attempts to postpone the inevitable, from about the 1830s onwards canal transport in general entered upon a period of slow decline. Competition from other modes of transport placed the canal network in its true perspective as a commercial undertaking weighed down by inefficiencies that arose from many causes, any one of which might have been a severe handicap but in combination ultimately proved fatal. Canal companies strove for monopolistic control and maximum dividends instead of rational cooperation in what was, after all, a nationwide enterprise – but perhaps that is expecting too much from the entrepreneurial thinking of the day. But whatever their failings in that respect, many companies were certainly short-sighted when it came to the conservation of their principal asset, the 'track', for what should have been a continuous reassessment and upgrading of the waterways consisted – with certain exceptions – merely of essential maintenance. In some instances water supply became a critical factor in determining the amount of traffic that could be carried, and all too often the inadequacy of supply would stop all movement for quite long periods. The situation was further worsened by the totally unnecessary breaks in gauge, which either reduced the size of craft to that accommodated by the narrowest gauge (hence the permanent adoption of the narrowboat on such broad-gauge canals as the Grand Junction), or created the necessity for transhipment, which simply increased costs. Some canals, too, had never really shown an adequate return on the capital invested (especially the rural lines) and were abandoned at a relatively early date, while others, such as the Rochdale and the Huddersfield, driven at immense cost through entirely unsuitable country, were able to maintain a local industrial traffic at both ends, but never achieved viability as through routes. On the other hand certain canals, through a combination of wise management and favourable circumstances, were successful in retaining, or even increasing, their trade. Outstanding in this respect was the BCN, which, serving a highly concentrated industrial complex, sustained a vigorous short-haul traffic until the middle of this century. Many canal interests were eventually absorbed by railway companies, and although some were quietly abandoned, on occasion the new owners found it advantageous to maintain the waterway as a going concern. Finally, however, the introduction of the motor vehicle and the social upheavals of two world wars brought about the end of commercial activity on the canal system; last-minute attempts to improve the 'track', such as the modernization programme carried out on the Birmingham–Napton section of the Grand Union Canal during the 1930s, were of little avail, and the surviving remnants of the long-distance commercial narrowboat fleets ceased trading in the early 1970s.

Today the movement of goods by inland waterways, apart from a few working narrowboats operated by enthusiasts, is virtually restricted to the old river navigations – the Aire and Calder and the Sheffield and South Yorkshire systems, Rivers Trent and Ouse, Gloucester and Sharpness Ship Canal, River Weaver, River Thames, and the Manchester Ship Canal – which between them carry vessels ranging in size from motor barges to ocean-going liners.

In spite of its great age combined with many years of neglect, the main canal network still exists, and indeed is being steadily extended through the efforts of volunteer working parties devoted to the task of restoring long-derelict waterways. So what has been a loss on the one hand has proved ultimately to be a gain on the other, for there are now available many hundreds of miles of waterways on which to cruise the length and breadth of the country – an asset which will continue to bring pleasure to the increasing number of waterway enthusiasts.

CHAPTER TWO

THE ANATOMY OF INLAND NAVIGATIONS

THE 'CUT'

The immense undertaking of building a canal was always preceded by the comparatively modest task of carrying out a visual inspection of the country through which the line would have to pass. This preliminary survey by the engineer, done on horseback in those days, was absolutely essential in determining the best line for the 'cut' as well as providing the proprietors with some rough idea of probable costs, and also in ascertaining whose land would have to be crossed – a matter involving financial compensation. Once the engineer had made his recommendations, a team of assistants would make a detailed survey and the route would then be laid out on the actual ground, but only after the consent of Parliament had been obtained and agreement reached with the landowners concerned (or powers of compulsory purchase invoked).

When all these details had been settled, the work of excavation could begin, using large gangs of labourers whose employment on canal projects earned them the title of 'navvies', a term usually understood as being an abbreviation of 'navigators'. These gangs were hired by the local contractor responsible for a short section of the line, as in those days there were no large contracting organizations such as there are now. All the work was done by hand, using pick, shovel and wheelbarrow, and might be assisted by the employment of horses and mules to cart away spoil and bring in building materials by means of temporary plate tramways and wagon roads. The excavated bed of the 'cut' having been consolidated and the towpath built up, sometimes with a protective facing wall of masonry or brick if necessary, on a hardcore foundation of broken stone and brick finished with a wearing surface of gravel or other suitable material, the waterproof lining of the canal would be tamped into place. This lining, which might be anywhere from a few inches up to several feet thick, depending on the nature of the ground, consisted of clay 'puddle', an invention credited to James Brindley, and an essential feature of construction in preventing water leakage through the bed of the canal. Natural clay will absorb water and thus allow it to pass, but once the clay has been suitably worked up, or 'puddled', it becomes totally impervious. Following this stage the length of completed 'cut' would be supplied with water, so becoming available as an additional means of transport in connection with the works, and commercial boats would even begin trading if this was justified by the length and the situation of the finished section.

Such was the sequence of operations in the construction of a typical 'contour' canal of the early period, and although using similar techniques to a large extent, the procedures of later projects were governed to a degree by the added complications of 'cut and fill'. As previously mentioned, this method was employed when the line of a canal cut across contours instead of along them, necessitating the excavation of cuttings through ridges and the raising of artificial embankments across valleys. Both these operations require that the finished ground slope should be stable, a condition that relied heavily upon the experience of the engineer, as the science of soil mechanics was virtually unknown at that time. Material from cuttings was used for embankment construction, and might not always be suitable; it could, for instance, produce when tipped a slope whose 'angle of repose' was so low as to require an inordinate amount of fill if the designed width of channel at the correct level was to be obtained. Particularly obdurate in this respect were the great embankments of the Birmingham and Liverpool Junction (Shropshire Union) Canal, Shelmore bank especially suffering so many earth slips that the final opening of the canal was delayed by many months. Nor were the cuttings on this same canal free from trouble either, for Telford (the engineer) had chosen too high an angle of slope, with the result that falls of earth and rock were frequent and still plague the canal to this day. However, these are isolated examples of faults that were, for the most part, avoided; the massive embankments at Burnley on the Leeds and Liverpool Canal and others – such as those on the Macclesfield Canal – bear witness to the empirical skills of the canal engineers.

The first requirement for the efficient working of any canal must be an adequate water supply, for any shortcomings in this respect will sooner or later lead to a breakdown in the flow of traffic. Summit level canals are particularly vulnerable to loss of water through lockage, which, in the case of heavily trafficked routes, may reach serious proportions and even lead to temporary closure of the canal in question. Moreover, even in a country with high average annual precipitation such as Britain, the constancy of rainfall (and snowfall, which is heavily relied upon for the filling-up of reservoirs) is by no means assured, as exemplified by the drought conditions of the mid 1970s. Water storage in the form of reservoirs is therefore essential to the maintenance of water supply during periods of low rainfall when the smaller feeder streams may well dry up, but it is essential that water stored in this manner be conserved as much as possible if the waterway is to remain open. Reservoirs are most often sited above the level of summit pounds, to which water is supplied by gravity through a feeder channel fitted with an arrangement of sluices to control the flow; the reservoir itself is positioned in a suitable catchment area containing sufficient natural streams to provide an adequate supply of water to the reservoir under normal conditions.

Sometimes a stream may be fed directly into the summit pound – for this too can be considered a form of reservoir – an idea readily apparent to the first canal engineers, who stressed the necessity for maximum length of summit pound for this very reason, although it must be admitted that in practice they did not always follow their own precept. Sheer area of reservoir or length of summit pound has, however, its own drawbacks: loss of water by evaporation may be very considerable, but although unavoidable may be more than offset by the increased volume of water storage; the summit level of the Leeds and Liverpool Canal, for instance, was not only lengthened but also deepened at the construction stage expressly to provide such additional storage. Rivers too may be utilized as a source of water supply, though usually at a level below that of the summit pound, an arrangement that is particularly effective where heavy lockage occurs, such as on the Grand Union Canal in its descent from the Chilterns at Tring summit to Uxbridge, a section fed by several small rivers which augment the water supply for lockage purposes.

In addition to water supplied from reservoirs, streams and rivers, extensive use of underground sources has been made by means of pumping, especially in the case of the Birmingham Canal Navigations, which, due to their situation on a natural plateau, are particularly liable to considerable water loss through the heavy lockage involved in the several connections to the surrounding Midlands system. Here the problem was partially solved by the installation of pumping stations, some of which served a dual function by keeping mine workings free of water; at one period the Birmingham network boasted no fewer than seventeen pumping stations and six reservoirs, all of which were required in order to maintain the intensive traffic. Other notable examples of pumping stations are situated on the Kennet and Avon Navigation, where the Claverton water-powered pump and the Crofton steam-powered pump have both been restored to working order. Wind-driven pumps have also been used, mostly in East Anglia and the Fens, although for a rather different purpose: that of land drainage in areas subject to excessively high water tables. On canals, pumps are also employed to return used water to a higher level at lock flights – two such instances occur at Buckby and Braunston on the Grand Union Canal – while temporary pumps have been used in recent times to help overcome water shortage caused by drought.

The water in all canal pounds has to be maintained at a predetermined level and not allowed simply to fill up the pound, as this might well have disastrous consequences. Any excessive rise in water level could result in erosion of the banks through overtopping, not to mention the danger of a spectacular burst caused by increased hydrostatic pressure. In this latter connection it is interesting to note the situation on the northern section of the Bridgewater Canal where the waterway traverses the South Lancashire coalfield. Over the years mining subsidence has necessitated the continual raising of the canal embankment in order to maintain the water level, but of course this implies a parallel increase in water depth and a consequent dangerous build-up of hydrostatic pressure, a threat which in this case is averted by the simple expedient of filling up the bed of the canal to the same degree that the embankment is raised, thus ensuring a constant water depth. This must be the only example in the country of a canal whose maintenance, instead of being dependent upon dredging, actually involves the opposite!

The water levels in canal pounds are maintained by means of weirs, the lips of which are set at the desired level of the pound. Weirs are of two types: bypass weirs, which discharge to lower levels of the canal, and overspill weirs, which discharge excess water out of the canal altogether.

Bypass weirs, or by-washes, are, as the term implies, situated at locks, and allow excess water to drain away to lower pounds. The most common type consists of either an open channel or an underground culvert, placed roughly parallel with the lock chamber and having an inlet from the upper pound adjacent to the head of the lock, with a lower outlet discharging through, or just beyond, the abutment at the lock tail. A different, and rather attractive kind of bypass weir may be found on the section of the Staffordshire and Worcestershire Canal south of Aldersley Junction. This is the well-weir, which, as the name implies, consists of a vertical shaft, circular in plan like a well, with the rim of the shaft forming the weir lip. The weir is located close by the head of the lock, and is surmounted by a dome-shaped iron cage to prevent blockage of the culvert by floating debris. On occasion, locks themselves may be used as weirs, in which case both top and bottom gates have top rails set somewhat lower than usual so that excess water may spill through the lock to the pound below. When negotiating this type of lock, craft should be kept well clear of the 'downstream' side of the gates to avoid the danger of flooding by any water coming over the gate tops.

Overspill weirs are designed to prevent the water in canal pounds from exceeding a certain predetermined level and possibly causing damage through overtopping the banks. The weir, built of masonry, brick or concrete, is positioned at the side of, and parallel to, the channel, and is several yards in length with a lip set at the desired maximum water level. Behind the lip the weir back slopes away to an open leat, which discharges to a watercourse.

River weirs are usually built of concrete or masonry, and may be constructed for a variety of purposes, but their navigational function is to create a depth of channel sufficient for the passage of craft, which negotiate the change in level by means of a lock positioned in the artificial cut alongside the weir. All river weirs are potentially very dangerous − more so if water levels are high and the current is running strongly – and all craft should keep well away from them, even if they are guarded by safety barriers (and some are not).

FLOOD SLUICES, STOP-PLANKS, AND PILING

The weirs of some navigable rivers, of which the Thames is a notable example, are fitted with large vertically operated sluices for the purpose of water control, and these are drawn at times of high water levels to prevent flooding. At Richmond, on the tidal section of the Thames, a curious arrangement of guillotine gates, suspended between the spans of the footbridge, are lowered when the river is at half tide in order to maintain navigable depth upstream to Teddington, and at these times the adjacent lock has to be used. When the river exceeds half-tide level the gates are raised and craft may proceed in the main channel. The Grand Sluice on the Witham Navigation at Boston fulfils a somewhat similar purpose, but in reverse, for it is used to prevent flood tides, which are commonly higher than normal river levels, from backing further up the navigation. On the River Nene the locks themselves are used as sluices for the purpose of flood control; the lower ends of the chambers are fitted with guillotine gates which are normally left in the raised position, and in times of flood the top mitre-gates are fastened back to allow water to flow straight through the lock chamber. When this happens all river traffic, of course, is halted.

The problems caused by too much water entering canal pounds are mainly dealt with, as previously mentioned, by the use of overspill weirs, but in times of very severe flooding an additional remedy is available in the form of the flood sluice. This consists basically of a culvert built into the canal bank and fitted with a paddle operated by rack and pinion gearing. Like the overspill weir, the flood sluice discharges into a convenient watercourse. This type of sluice has a double function, as it is also used to drain off sections of canal for inspection and maintenance of the bed; in this respect some canals have their beds fitted with large plugs which are withdrawn by means of attached chains.

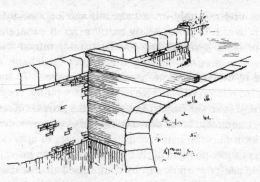

Fig. 1 Use of stop-planks

But before any water is let out of a canal pound, the ends of the section to be drained must first be sealed off, and this is done by means of stop-planks, or stop-gates, which in effect form a coffer dam against the head of water remaining in the rest of the pound. They are also used to seal off the damaged length of canal in the event of a bank burst. Stop-planks are sturdy lengths of timber or reinforced concrete, and may be seen stacked at intervals alongside canals, sometimes in small brick or timber structures, or even in special compartments built into bridge abutments. To form the coffer dam they are lowered horizontally into position with their ends secured in vertical slots cut into the masonry of bridge bases, lock mouths, or specially built 'narrows' in the canal. That is the usual method employed in forming this type of coffer dam, but on the Bridgewater Canal is to be found a different arrangement in which the planks are permanently fixed together, forming a kind of heavy door which is lowered into the slots by a hand-operated crane positioned specifically for that purpose. The stop-gate is a more sophisticated type of temporary dam, and consists of a single hinged gate, or a pair of mitre-gates, positioned in length-ened bridge-holes and in 'narrows'. In the event of a burst, stop-gates, which are normally held back against the channel walls, may close automatically under the resulting pressure of water, and are often used in situations where a burst is likely to have serious consequences – as would be the case, for instance, on high embankments.

Bank erosion, caused by the breaking wash of craft moving at excessive speed, has long been of major concern to waterways authorities, and not only on canals, but also on heavily trafficked rivers such as the Thames. Along many miles of canal the original masonry or brick bank-walling has been undermined and washed down into the channel, leaving the unprotected bank extremely vulnerable to further erosion. Measures to prevent this have in the past included reinforced concrete piling, timber piling, concrete-filled sandbags and even the encouragement of the growth of reeds at the sides of the channel to break down boat wash, but nowadays the most common form of canal bank protection consists of interlocking galvanized steel sheet-piling of fairly light gauge, driven into place using a hand-held pile-driver powered by compressed air. For major engineering works such as are involved in the construction of bridges and in remedial work made necessary by mining subsidence, interlocking steel piles of heavy channel section are used, and are driven in by large diesel- or steam-powered pile-drivers.

LOCKS

The pound lock is of ancient origin and was first built in Europe during the fourteenth century, but it was not until some 200 years later that it was used in this country – on the Exeter Canal – and its adoption made possible the construction of the summit level canals of the Canal Age. Other methods of transferring craft between pounds have been employed in the past, as we shall see, but the rugged simplicity of the pound lock ensured its survival long after other more complex arrangements had disappeared. There are several types of lock, all of which, even though their respective structures show considerable differences, work on a principle best explained by reference to the straightforward single chamber lock.

In essence this consists of a rectangular brick or masonry box (these are the most common materials, although locks have been constructed of timber planking, iron sheet, concrete, steel piling and steel plate) sunk into the ground between two pounds and fitted with gates at both ends. The bottom of the chamber is approximately level with the bed of the lower pound, while the bed of the upper pound abuts the top of a thick retaining wall that extends vertically from the bottom of the chamber. This retaining wall, known as a 'sill', is topped by a

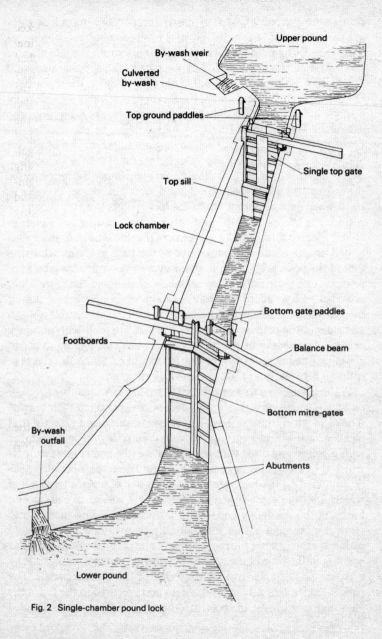

Upper pound

By-wash weir

Culverted
by-wash

Top ground paddles

Single top gate

Top sill

Lock chamber

Bottom gate paddles

Footboards

Balance beam

Bottom mitre-gates

By-wash
outfall

Abutments

Lower pound

Fig. 2 Single-chamber pound lock

single gate, or a pair of gates, of massive proportions (most lock gates are constructed of oak, although steel has been used in a number of instances), hung from the lock side wall and restrained against water pressure from the upper pound by a rebate in the opposite side wall. The bottom of the gate is similarly held by a rebate in the top surface of the sill. At the bottom end of the lock a pair of gates (occasionally a single gate), mitred on their meeting surfaces, are hung from the side walls and restrained by a V-shaped rebate in the shallow sill below them. These 'mitre-gates', as they are called, have a combined width greater than that of the lock chamber and thus, when closed, wedge together forming a shallow 'V' on plan, hence the necessity for the mitres and the shaped sill rebate. The 'V', of course, in order to resist water pressure from inside the lock, points towards the upper pound. The heel posts of the gates are rounded at their outer ends to enable them to rotate in a lined groove in the side-wall masonry called a 'hollow quoin', and are supported at the base in a cup, while the tops of the posts are held in position by a metal strap. Long balance beams – extensions of the top members of the gate structure – are provided both to afford sufficient leverage when opening or closing the gates and to assist in counterbalancing their considerable weight. The sides of the pounds adjacent to the lock are built with masonry or brick abutments which taper inwards towards the lock mouths and are often fitted with steel or timber fenders to minimize the effects of collision between boat hulls and the lock structure.

Water is admitted to, and drained from, the lock chamber through an arrangement of sluices – or 'paddles', to give them their correct name – of which there are two basic types: ground and gate. Ground paddles consist of underground culverts connecting the lock chamber with a pound and fitted with a sliding plate (the paddle) by means of which the culvert may be opened or closed. The actual operating gear is positioned on the lock side and may be one of several types, all of which fulfil the same function: to provide a means of raising and lowering the paddle by converting a circular winding motion into vertical movement, either mechanically or hydraulically. The gate paddle is exactly what the name implies, and consists of a rectangular opening in the base of the gate below normal water level covered by a sliding plate similar to that employed in the ground paddle. The paddle gear in this case is mounted on posts secured to the top of the gate and is operated in most instances by means of an extended spindle bar.

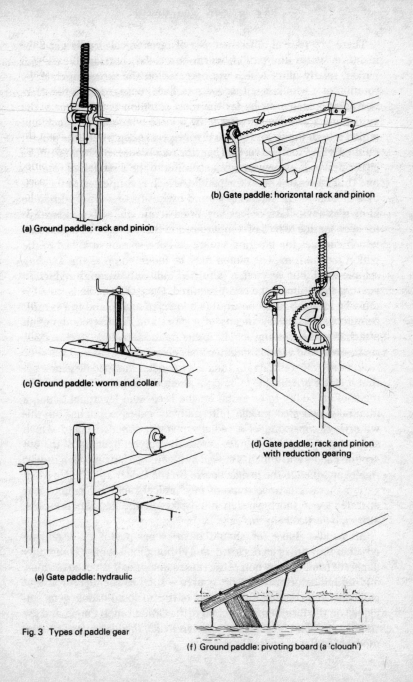

(a) Ground paddle: rack and pinion

(b) Gate paddle: horizontal rack and pinion

(c) Ground paddle: worm and collar

(d) Gate paddle; rack and pinion with reduction gearing

(e) Gate paddle: hydraulic

Fig. 3 Types of paddle gear

(f) Ground paddle: pivoting board (a 'clough')

There are several different types of mechanical paddle gear, for instance, worm and pinion, worm and collar, horizontal rack and pinion, nearly all of which are operated on the same principle: by rotation of a windlass (either loose or fixed) engaged with the gear-operating spindle, but by far the most common type of gear is the vertical rack and pinion worked by a loose windlass. The rack and pinion is both simple and effective: rotation of a cog wheel (the pinion) meshed with a toothed vertical bar (the rack) causes the latter to move either upwards or downwards according to the direction of rotation and thus raises or lowers the paddle, which is connected to the rack by a steel bar. The pinion is wound by means of a cranked handle known as a windlass, or lock key, fitted at one end with a square eye (or eyes, for due to lack of standardization there is more than one size) which engages the tapering square end of a spindle attached to the pinion mechanism. The pinion may be mounted on to the winding spindle itself, but very often is turned indirectly through reduction gearing to minimize the effort required. Once the paddle is raised it must be locked in position until it is lowered again, and this is most commonly effected by means of a pawl and ratchet combination attached to the winding spindle; other methods include steel wedges, rack pawls, and various spanner-like devices.

So many different arrangements of paddles and paddle gear exist that it is not practicable to describe them all, but mention should be made of an oddity to be found on the Leeds and Liverpool Canal: a manually operated paddle (alternatively called 'cloughs' on this waterway) consisting of a radially pivoting wooden board which slides through ninety degrees across the culvert opening of the top ground paddle and which is moved by means of a long wooden handle rigidly attached to the paddle board. On the Calder and Hebble Navigation there is a novel type of mechanical rack and pinion gear operated by a short wooden handspike on the capstan principle, although vertically in this case.

All paddles have (or should have) some means of displaying whether they are open or closed, and although this is most commonly apparent from the position of the rack, sometimes it is not so obvious, and an indicator of some sort is used – such as the metal rod that emerges from the top of the casing of the enclosed paddle gear employed on the Birmingham section of the Grand Union Canal, and the small triangular pointer that moves vertically in a slot on a particular model of enclosed hydraulic gear.

Hydraulic paddle gear is a comparatively modern innovation, and only in fairly recent times has it been introduced on the canal system, mostly as a replacement for damaged or worn-out mechanical gear. At present it is used solely in conjunction with gate paddles, and in this form consists of a steel cylinder containing a manual pump mounted on the balance beam and connected by small diameter pipes to a piston assembly set vertically above the gate paddle, the two being joined together by a steel bar in the usual manner. From the axis of the cylinder protrudes a tapered square spindle on to which fits the standard windlass; as the latter is wound the pump pressurizes the oil-filled assembly and moves the piston (and thus the paddle) up or down according to the direction of rotation. The big locks of river navigations such as the Thames, Trent and Severn, together with the Yorkshire commercial system, are fitted with electrically powered hydraulics, although these are operated only by the official lock-keepers. Out of hours the Thames locks may be worked by boat crews, but with the power switched off and the gear turned by hand.

There is a type of single chamber lock that employs a gate arrangement which is not hinged in the usual way but slides vertically in an overhead frame: the so-called 'guillotine' gate. In this case no paddles are required in conjunction with the gate as the latter fulfils this role, initial movement of the gate allowing water to flow beneath it. Gates of this type are always tedious to work, as the effort required to move

Fig. 4 Guillotine gate

the great weight of the gate is necessarily diminished by the use of reduction gearing, but only at the expense of a large increase in the number of windlass turns required. Conversely, the slow movement lessens the turbulence created by the too sudden opening of such a large area of gate.

Side pond locks

To reduce loss of water through lock operation some locks were built with what are called 'side ponds'. These are brick or masonry open chambers built into the ground alongside the lock and connected to it by a side paddle. Water conservation is effected by transference of water between the lock chamber and the side pond: opening the side paddle when the lock chamber is full will transfer about half a lock of water to the side pond, all movement ceasing when the levels equalize, whereupon the side paddle is closed, leaving the water stored in the side pond. The remainder of the lock water is then discharged

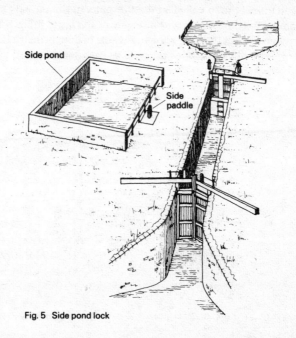

Fig. 5 Side pond lock

to the lower pound in the usual way through the bottom paddles. When proceeding uphill the side paddle is first opened to discharge the side pond water into the lock chamber; when levels equalize the side paddle is closed and the lock filled in the normal way from the upper pound. By this means about half a lockful of water is conserved each time the lock is used. A variation on the side pond theme is to be found on the paired locks of the Trent and Mersey Canal in the Cheshire flight and at Hillmorton locks on the northern Oxford Canal, where a connecting side paddle allowed one lock to act as side pond to the other, and vice versa. Regrettably, these side paddles are no longer in use.

Staircase locks

Where a consistently steep drop in ground level had to be overcome, the problem was solved in many instances by building 'staircase' locks. These staircase, or 'riser', locks take the form of a monolithic structure enclosing two or more chambers connected by joint gates (that is, without intermediate pounds), the top gate of one chamber being the bottom gate of the chamber above. Water for lockage is supplied in either of two ways: by transference of water directly through the chambers by means of the usual ground and gate paddles, or by means of side paddles connecting the chambers to large side ponds. Staircase locks operated by the first method are very wasteful of water as well as being rather tedious to work in some circumstances, notably when the staircase is set against you, as you will then have to empty or fill every chamber except the one that you first enter, depending upon your direction of travel. Conversely, if the staircase is set for you, then the first chamber only will have to be emptied or filled, as the case may be.

Except for the topmost chamber, which receives its water from the upper pound, the chambers of side pond staircase locks are always filled from the side ponds themselves; likewise, all chambers above the lowest, which empties into the lower pound, discharge into the side ponds. Adjacent chambers in the staircase are not connected by paddles directly (as they are in the other type of staircase lock), but instead are each fitted with side paddles leading to a common side pond, the water level of which is coincident with that of the lower of

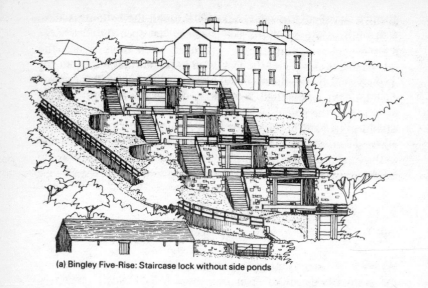

(a) Bingley Five-Rise: Staircase lock without side ponds

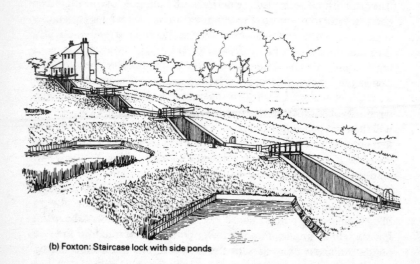

(b) Foxton: Staircase lock with side ponds

Fig. 6 Staircase locks

the two chambers when it is full and that of the upper chamber when it is empty, thus permitting craft to pass from one chamber to the other.

The unique flight of three locks at Bratch on the Staffordshire and Worcestershire Canal is something of a curiosity, as at first sight it appears to be a hybrid, incorporating features of both types of staircase lock just described. In fact it is not a staircase lock at all, for each chamber is provided with its own top and bottom gates, and as we have seen, the distinguishing feature of a staircase is the common gate between adjacent chambers. The illusion of a staircase is created by the fact that the bottom gates of the two upper chambers are set only a few feet away from the top gates of the chambers below them, which has been made possible by positioning the intervening pounds not in line with the flight in the usual manner, but roughly at right-angles to it, extending through and beyond the towpath abutments.

Stop-locks

Occasionally one will meet up with locks having a very short rise or fall – usually of the order of about six inches – close to canal junctions. These are 'stop-locks' and were originally constructed to prevent the free flow of water between the two canals; usually the one of later build had to make a concession to the existing canal by effecting a junction at a slightly higher level, thus ensuring that no water would be lost to the new canal once the junction had been made. The stop-lock at King's Norton on the Worcester and Birmingham Canal, however, provided for a change of level on either side of the lock by employing vertically rising guillotine gates, which, of course, is the simplest method of coping with reversing water flows. The gates are still there, but are now permanently raised to maintain a common level between the Worcester and Birmingham Canal and the northern Stratford Canal.

Flood-locks and tidal doors

When river-cruising the newcomer to inland waterways may be somewhat surprised to find certain locks with their gates open at both ends. These are 'flood-locks', placed at the upstream end of an artificial cut to prevent an abnormal rise in its level when river levels rise. At such times the gates are closed and the lock functions normally, but when the river and the canal levels are about equal the gates are fully opened and water is allowed to pass freely through the lock. The object of all this is to maintain the water in the canal at, or about, a predetermined level, otherwise flooding and damage may result – considerations which apply in other contexts such as tidal locks and basins.

Depending upon the relationship between the level in the basin, canal or river and the mean height and range of tide in the adjoining tideway, the tidal lock may have merely the usual set of gates at each end or it may be fitted with an additional set of gates pointing in the opposite direction, thus permitting use of the lock at or near high tide, while at the same time maintaining the level of the basin or waterway. A modern application of this principle occurs at Barmby Marsh in Yorkshire, where the lock at the confluence of the Rivers Derwent and Ouse has been built with radial sector gates designed to withstand water pressure from each side. Sometimes a single set of gates, or flood doors, are employed as protection against unusually high tides and tidal surges, an example being Eastham locks at the Mersey entrance to the Manchester Ship Canal.

INCLINED PLANES AND LIFTS

In the construction of canals, locks are not the only possible solution to the problems presented by changes in ground levels, and from an early date it became apparent that they could not be the perfect answer in every situation; moreover, they are inevitably wasteful of water and time. To overcome these deficiencies, two alternatives were adopted – the inclined plane and the boat lift.

Inclined planes are railways laid on a carefully graded and constant slope connecting upper and lower levels of a canal. There were three methods of transporting craft on a plane: first, by floating the boats in massive caissons supported on bogies; secondly, by carrying them 'dry' on wheeled cradles; and thirdly, by fitting wheels to the boats themselves. Twin sets of rails were used to accommodate ascending and descending traffic, with the caissons, cradles and wheeled craft connected by cable to a winding drum, often steam-powered (although other forms of power were used, including water wheels and counterweights), on the counterbalance principle. The water-filled caissons, of course, balanced each other exactly regardless of the craft and loads being carried, and the motive power was required only to overcome inertia and friction; considerably more power was needed to move the cradles if the load was being hauled against the slope. The wheeled cradle type of plane was used for the transportation of tub boats – small, rectangular, tank-like vessels, usually towed in strings – which were widely used at one time both in the industrial and mining area of Shropshire between Newport and the Severn, and in the West Country.

The only remaining complete example of an inclined plane may be seen at Blists Hill, near Coalport, where the Ironbridge Gorge Museum Trust have restored the Hay incline to working order (but not the steam winding engine). This incline, opened in 1793, formerly connected the southern end of the Shropshire Canal (not to be confused with the Shropshire Union Canal) to the Coalport Canal, which ran for three-quarters of a mile at low level parallel to the Severn. Wheeled cradles were used on the incline, which has a vertical rise of 207 feet in a horizontal distance of about 1,000 feet – the equivalent of no less than twenty-seven locks.

Probably the most famous of all the inclined planes was that built at Foxton in Leicestershire at the beginning of this century. It was constructed to bypass the flight of ten staircase locks on what is now the Leicester section of the Grand Union Canal, and remained in use for almost eleven years before being closed to traffic; its final end came during the 1920s, when it was dismantled and sold for scrap. The Foxton incline was of the caisson type, and consisted of two huge steel tanks fitted with guillotine gates at each end and mounted on multiple bogies running on sets of rails supported on a mass concrete foundation. The caissons were connected by cable to a steam-powered winding drum and operated on the counterbalancing principle, one ascending as the other descended, the total lift being about seventy-

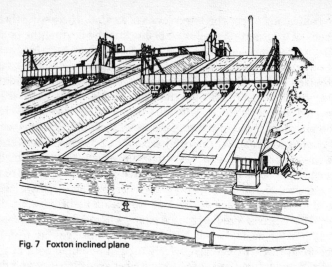

Fig. 7 Foxton inclined plane

five feet on a plane length of 307 feet. Over recent years much work has been done by volunteers in clearing undergrowth and tidying up the site in general, revealing the base to the engine-house, the upper part of the concrete slab forming the incline and the brick walling of the upper docks.

In addition to inclined planes, vertical boat lifts were employed during the nineteenth century, notably on the Grand Western Canal in Devon, but none have survived except that built at Anderton in 1875 to connect the Trent and Mersey Canal with the River Weaver fifty feet below. The structure consists of a massive iron framework from which are suspended two caissons, each large enough for a pair of narrowboats and fitted with guillotine gates at both ends. Originally the lift was hydraulically operated, with power supplied by a steam engine, but steam was replaced by electricity in 1903, and five years later large counterbalance weights were substituted for the hydraulic system. The Anderton lift is a truly impressive example of Victorian engineering and is still in use today, providing one of the most unforgettable experiences associated with inland cruising.

TUNNELS

The inherent difficulty – and often, impossibility – of supplying very short summit pounds with sufficient water meant that narrow transverse ridges obstructing the line of a canal could not be crossed by simply building flights of locks to lift the waterway over the hill; nor, in most cases, could the problem be solved by excavating a deep cutting, for the amount of work entailed would have been prodigious, and the increased costs could only be aggravated by subsequent continual expenditure on the maintenance of the cutting slopes. Even at the time of the earliest canals it was obvious that the solution lay in tunnelling, not least because the technique was ready to hand in the expertise of the mining industry, but the total absence of powered machinery and the dreadfully dangerous working conditions ensured that the first tunnelling projects were costly, slow and restricted in bore.

Once the necessity for tunnelling had been settled (after examining – and rejecting – all other possible solutions, including diversion of the route, construction of lock flights, open cutting and the like), the line of the proposed tunnel would be marked out over the surface of the ridge, and the level of the canal at both ends of the bore carefully determined. Vertical shafts were then sunk at intervals along the line down to canal level, and from these (and from the tunnel portals) headings were driven along the axis of the tunnel in both directions until the bores met – hopefully, in a straight line throughout. However, this was not always achieved, and some tunnels are noticeably kinked as a result, particularly those at Saltersford and Barnton on the Trent and Mersey Canal near Northwich, which were among the earliest to be built. The vertical shafts, which had provided both access to the headings for men and materials and the means of removing spoil to the surface, were for the most part filled in upon completion of the bore, but some were left open to provide ventilation, in which case the brickwork of the shafts was continued up above ground level to form stubby 'chimneys'. Excellent examples of these may be seen between Stoke Bruerne and Blisworth on the main line of the Grand Union Canal, where the road over Blisworth Hill follows the line of ventilation shafts connecting with the 3,075 yard-long Blisworth Tunnel beneath.

The variability of geological strata caused many headaches for tunnel engineers, and in some cases delayed completion of the works by many years: a section of Blisworth Tunnel had to be abandoned at one stage and a new line of bore selected due to the unstable nature of the ground, as a result of which the tunnel was opened some five years after the rest of the canal had been built; Standedge, the longest tunnel on the canal system at 5,698 yards, took fourteen years in all to construct, mainly due to difficulty in boring through the Pennine limestone; and Cowley Tunnel on the Shropshire Union Canal, with an original projected length of 690 yards, finished up a mere eighty-one yards long because of a series of collapses during construction. Where solid rock was encountered the bore was left unlined, but otherwise the tunnel section was lined in brickwork of varying thickness according to the nature of the strata, provision being made for drainage of ground water and springs at intervals. Many tunnels were built without towpaths, and some were extremely restricted in bore (aggravated in certain instances by later subsidence), so that the resulting one-way traffic eventually caused unacceptable delays. For this reason Brindley's tunnel under Harecastle Hill was supplemented in 1827 by Telford's 'new' tunnel, which contained a towpath. Later ones were generally of increased section to accommodate two-way traffic.

In the case of horse-drawn craft, the negotiation of tunnels without towpaths was a particularly tedious and exhausting business. While the horse was being led over the top of the hill the boat crew would propel the boat through the tunnel by 'legging', by pulling on chains or pegs attached to the walls, or by shafting. The first method entailed the use of a plank laid across the fore-end of the boat on which two men lay while pushing with their feet against the walls. Professional leggers were employed at Blisworth Tunnel by the Grand Junction Canal Company from 1827, and their services were only dispensed with following the introduction of steam tugs in 1871. At the turn of the century steam tunnel tugs were in use on many canals, where they continued to work for the next thirty years or so until they were finally made redundant by the growing number of self-propelled working boats. At Harecastle, both tunnels had deteriorated by the early 1900s due to mining subsidence – Brindley's to such an extent that it had to be closed, and subsequently an electric tug that pulled itself along on a cable was put into service in the 'new' tunnel where it worked until 1954, when the present ventilation fans were installed. All the tugs are now long gone, and in most cases boat crews are left to exercise their own good sense in negotiating tunnels safely, although during the summer months traffic in Harecastle Tunnel is regulated by tunnel-keepers, and at Preston Brook (also Harecastle when the keepers are off duty) permitted entry times are displayed on each portal.

AQUEDUCTS

Just as tunnelling provided a means of overcoming obstacles rising above the line of a canal, so did the construction of aqueducts enable waterways to pass over obstacles lying at a lower level, such as roadways, rivers, valleys and even other canals. The first canal aqueduct to be built in this country was that at Barton, near Manchester. Opened in 1761, it carried the Bridgewater Canal over the navigable River Irwell, and was remarkable for its time, being about 600 feet long overall in three spans allowing headroom of thirty-eight feet to the river; the masonry trough was lined with puddled clay and provided a channel eighteen feet wide and four and a half feet deep. So robust was the structure that it lasted in good condition for 130 years until it was demolished during the construction of the Manchester Ship Canal, when it was replaced by the present swing aqueduct.

The original Barton aqueduct, with its massively simple outlines, set the pattern of aqueduct construction for many years, although later designs tended towards the blending of ashlar masonry with architectural features in the classical style then prevalent. Outstanding in this respect are the aqueducts at Avoncliffe and Dundas on the Kennet and Avon Canal, both designed by Rennie, who was also responsible for the magnificent structure carrying the Lancaster Canal high above the River Lune at Lancaster and thought by many to be the finest masonry aqueduct in this country. There is a splendid masonry aqueduct at Chirk on the Llangollen Canal, where the latter crosses the valley of the Ceiriog. The structure is built in ten spans with a total length of 600 feet and a height of seventy feet, and is unusual in that the bottom of the trough is formed of iron plates securely bonded into the side wall masonry, thus constituting both a structural cross-tie and a relatively lightweight watertight bed.

The construction of Chirk aqueduct began in 1796 under the supervision of Telford, its designer, but the previous year had seen the start of work on the most spectacular of all aqueducts: that spanning the Vale of Llangollen at Pontcysyllte, again designed by Telford. The main principle of its construction closely followed that established by the building of Telford's aqueduct at Longdon-upon-Tern on the Shrewsbury Canal, where the channel was formed by a cast-iron trough 186 feet long supported on iron bearers. The sheer height of Pontcysyllte – something over 120 feet where it crosses the River Dee – ruled out the use of a cast-iron supporting structure, and the trough was therefore carried on eighteen masonry piers braced by cast-iron arches. The trough itself is 1,007 feet long, with an approach embankment at the southern end almost 100 feet high. The cross-section of the trough measures about twelve feet in width and five in depth, and the towpath is cleverly placed within the overall width but above water level so as not to diminish the cross-sectional ratio (see p. 142). Pontcysyllte took ten years to build and was finally opened in November 1805. Without doubt it was the greatest engineering achievement of its time and stands today as an impressive memorial not only to its creators, but also to the Canal Age in Britain.

The Barton Swing Aqueduct was the last major aqueduct to be built, and, like the Anderton Lift, is a remarkable example of Victorian engineering ingenuity. The old masonry aqueduct carrying the Bridgewater Canal over the Irwell was far too limited in headroom and span to accommodate the deep-sea shipping which would use the Manchester Ship Canal, at that time being constructed over the course of the Irwell, and a new fixed aqueduct at the level of the Bridgewater was out of the question for similar reasons. As the Ship Canal required an air draught of seventy-five feet, an early scheme proposed an elevated aqueduct to suit that dimension with access at each end provided by vertical boat-lifts, but this was rejected as being too slow in operation to cope with the heavy traffic on the Bridgewater Canal. Instead, a swinging-span aqueduct was built, the structure of which is 235 feet long, twenty-four feet wide and thirty-three feet high, with a trough width and depth of eighteen feet and seven feet respectively. To reduce operating time, and to save water, the aqueduct trough and the canal itself are closed off by separate hinged doors at both ends and the whole structure, weighing about 1,500 tons, is swung while full of water; it is hydraulically driven and pivots through ninety degrees on a central island in the Ship Canal, thus leaving unlimited headroom for shipping.

BRIDGES

Of all the many different types of structure associated with the inland waterways none shows such variety of form, size and construction as do bridges – which is not surprising, as bridge-building reaches back to ancient times and reflects in many ways the developments in engineering techniques that have accompanied the changing modes and patterns of land transport over the centuries. A considerable number of river bridges were built originally by, or under the auspices of, the Church, which during medieval times was in a more powerful position than most other institutions to undertake the necessary organizing and financing of the works. The fifteenth-century stone bridge over the Great Ouse at St Ives still bears evidence of the Church's interest, for its delightful form and setting is enhanced by a tiny chapel built into the east parapet. Abingdon Bridge on the Thames also dates from the fifteenth century and it too was built by the Church, as was Culham Bridge a short distance downstream. Financed by Sir Hugh Clopton, the well-known Clopton Bridge across the Avon at Stratford is of similar age and was a monumental work for its time as it had an original length of about 1,000 feet, although this has since been much reduced. During the Middle Ages packhorse bridges became common, and although many spanned insignificant rivers and streams some were of considerable size, such as Essex Bridge over the Trent near Great Haywood, which has fourteen arches in a length of 100 feet.

The expansion of waterborne traffic resulting from canal-building in the latter half of the eighteenth century was taken into account in the design of new river bridges by providing bigger spans for navigation arches, which were made possible by improvements in civil engineering techniques. Like certain aqueducts of the period, many of the contemporary stone bridges were built with architectural details in the classical manner, such as Richmond and Henley bridges on the Thames. Chertsey Bridge, dating from 1785, is a relatively plain structure but of stylish proportions, and in this respect is reminiscent of bridges built about that time by the canal engineers. Developments in iron-making during the eighteenth century led to the extensive use of both wrought and cast iron for bridge-building, beginning with the famous Iron Bridge spanning the Severn near Coalbrookdale, the first of its kind in the world. More sophisticated use of iron followed in the construction of suspension bridges, notable examples being those over the Thames at Marlow, Hammersmith and Chelsea (the Albert Bridge) and, most impressive of all, I. K. Brunel's Clifton Suspension Bridge across the Avon Gorge at Bristol. To the materials used in the bridges of the eighteenth and nineteenth centuries were later added steel and reinforced concrete, the latter exemplified in the numerous motorway bridges of modern times, but the most intensive period of bridge-building remains that which took place in the thirty years or so following the opening of the first railways in 1830, when about 25,000 railway bridges and viaducts were constructed, many over navigable waterways.

Canal bridges

By far the most common type of bridge to be found on canals – and one that gives them much of their character – is the single-arch bridge of brick or stone, beneath which the towpath is carried on a projection of the abutment. Most of these bridges are roughly similar in size, having been built to carry what are now minor roads or to provide farmers with access to their properties ('accommodation' bridges),

Fig. 8a Typical brick accommodation bridge

and many have a characteristic hump-backed shape caused by a steep rise to the crown in order to provide sufficient headroom for navigation. Occasionally the bridge span includes no towpath, as on some brick bridges built across the tails of locks on the Staffordshire and Worcestershire Canal, but in other cases of similar nature provision for towing-lines has been made by fitting twin cast-iron cantilevered bridge-decks with a central gap left between them. Over the years many brick and stone bridges suffered considerable wear from the rubbing of towing-lines and consequently were fitted with iron guards to protect the outer angles of the abutments, but even these were not immune to the filing action of grit carried in the rope fibres, as may be seen from the deep grooves worn in the ironwork. A particularly pleasing form of traditional canal bridge is that known as a 'roving', 'turnover' or 'changeline' bridge, built to carry the towpath from one side of the canal to the other (this was done to alter periodically the direction of pull on the horse), in some cases by returning one of the bridge ramps in on itself in a graceful curve so that the towing-line was taken *under* the bridge arch and thus did not need to be cast off. Some very fine examples of the roving bridge, constructed in masonry, are situated on the Macclesfield and Lower Peak Forest Canals. Canal cuttings are sometimes crossed by bridges at high level, often with impressive effect, as may be seen at Woodseaves Cutting on the Shropshire Union Canal, but undoubtedly the most striking is the elegant Galton Bridge, a cast-iron structure 150 feet long spanning the deep Galton Cutting at a height of seventy-five feet above the main line of the Birmingham Canal Navigations at Smethwick. Cast iron was widely used for all types of bridge during the nineteenth century, including some very graceful single-span towpath bridges

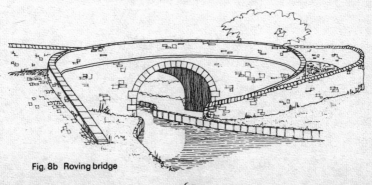

Fig. 8b Roving bridge

produced at Horseley Iron Works, many of which are still in existence at various places in the Midlands and are to be found in numbers around the Birmingham Canal Navigations. In that same area the less elegant structures of the modern motorway network cross the old canal system at many points, notably in the complex known as 'Spaghetti Junction', where the elevated decks of the M6 and its approach roads stride over the meeting place of three canals.

Lift and swing bridges

Problems of finance induced many canal companies to make savings on construction costs at every opportunity – even at the expense of navigational efficiency – and it is largely this parsimony that accounts for the considerable number of wooden movable bridges scattered throughout the waterways system. They consist of two main types: the lift bridge – or drawbridge – and the swing bridge. Of the former, the most common design utilizes a bascule structure in which the hinged bridge-deck is lifted by its attachment to a pair of massive overhead beams pivoted on vertical posts and provided with balancing counterweights. The bridge-deck is usually raised by pulling down on a chain suspended from the weighted arms, but on occasion – particularly where a minor road is involved – bridges are fitted with

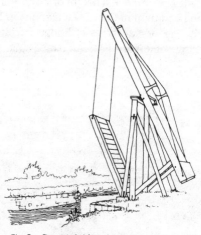

Fig. 8c Bascule bridge

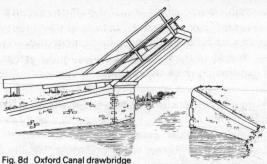

Fig. 8d Oxford Canal drawbridge

a hand-winding mechanism operated by windlass. Probably the best-known bascule bridges are those on the Llangollen Canal, but examples may also be found on other waterways such as the northern Stratford and Caldon Canals and the Northampton Arm of the Grand Union Canal. A different type of drawbridge is employed on the southern Oxford Canal, consisting of a hinged bridge-deck to which heavy counterbalance arms are attached at an upward angle. By depressing the arms until they are horizontal the deck is correspondingly raised to the open position. Plank Lane lift bridge carries a busy road over the Leigh branch of the Leeds and Liverpool Canal and is hydraulically operated by a bridge-keeper; it is one of the few of this type now in use, the most famous of which, of course, is Tower Bridge spanning the Pool of London.

Swing bridges of the manually operated kind may be found on several waterways, including the Leeds and Liverpool, Peak Forest, Macclesfield and Lancaster Canals. The bridge-decks are cantilevered

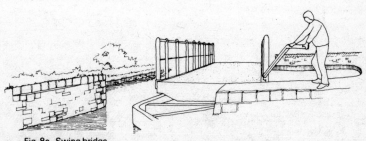

Fig. 8e Swing bridge

from a turntable mounted on one of the abutments and if in good condition are fairly easy to operate, but in cases where the bridge-deck has sagged on its bearings the use of a crowbar may sometimes be necessary, in spite of the leverage provided by the extension of the handrail featured on most swing bridges. Where swing bridges are few and far between their operation can provide exercise and interest for boat crews, but otherwise may prove irksome, as on the beautiful sixteen-mile pound of the Leeds and Liverpool Canal between Gargrave and Bingley, in which distance there are no fewer than twenty-four bridges of this type. Larger swing bridges are usually worked by keepers, and may be either manually or hydraulically operated. Both types may be seen on the Gloucester and Sharpness Canal and on the wide commercial waterways of Yorkshire; the road bridges spanning the River Weaver in Cheshire and the Manchester Ship Canal at Barton are hydraulically powered on account of their massive size and weight, in part due to the large span required over navigations frequented by sizeable deep-sea vessels.

CHAPTER THREE

BOATS
AND THEIR EQUIPMENT

Not so many years ago the great majority of inland waterways craft
available for hire on a self-steer basis were motor cruisers, constructed
of moulded GRP (glass-reinforced plastic, otherwise known as 'fibreglass'), marine ply or wood, and powered by inboard petrol or diesel
motor, or by outboard motor; only a handful of canal hire companies
departed from convention by offering craft whose design was based
on the traditional working narrowboat of the Midlands canal system.
Since then, this situation has drastically altered. Starting about the
late 1960s, canal hire companies progressively re-equipped and enlarged their fleets by building or purchasing steel-hulled narrowboat-
type craft, fitted with diesel engines and tiller-steered, until these now
form the bulk of hire craft based on the canal system and certain of
its associated rivers. This revolution in canal pleasure-craft design has
not, however – with a few exceptions – made any impact upon the
hire fleets of the Norfolk Broads and the River Thames, where wide-
beam motor cruisers have traditionally been the mainstay of operations for many years. The hire fleets based on the waterways of
Scotland, Northern Ireland and the Irish Republic are also mostly
equipped with modern wide-beam motor cruisers, although on the
Grand Canal in the Irish Republic narrowboats have been in service
since 1976.

STEEL-HULLED NARROWBOATS

Hulls: their layout and fittings

There are now many boat-builders offering for sale purpose-built and standard narrowboats, most of which are designed on similar principles and vary only in detail – although it is often the careful attention to detail that distinguishes the excellent from the indifferent and the downright poor. While varying in length from about thirty to seventy feet, all narrowboats have certain common features that are imposed by necessity rather than through choice: width of beam, draught, overall height above water level and – to a lesser degree – cross-sectional shape of the superstructure above gunwale level. All these are factors that are influenced by the forms and dimensions of the various engineering fixtures associated in particular with the canal system. Lock gauges impose limitations on length and width of hull, and tunnels, lifting and fixed bridges – especially bridges featuring an arched opening with a low springing point – demand careful attention to the design of boat superstructures and to their overall height above water level, while the shallowness of many canals places a premium on minimal water draught. (The height above water level of the uppermost fixture on a boat is known as its 'air draught'.) Modern narrowboats have an air draught sufficiently restricted to cope with most situations, and in spite of this still manage to provide a minimum headroom of six feet throughout the cabin accommodation. Boatbuilders tend to keep water draught as shallow as possible – consistent with other factors – and in practice the draught of narrowboats is usually one foot nine inches to two feet, which may usefully be referred to as 'standard draught'.

The various constraints upon design, together with other considerations, result in a hull that is almost rectangular in cross-section with a beam not exceeding six feet ten inches and a length which is usually proportional to the amount of accommodation it is intended to provide. The majority of this type of hire craft are between thirty-five and fifty feet in length, although, as already noted, the full range of lengths varies from about thirty to seventy feet. Typically, a hull is of welded construction in mild steel plate, with three-sixteenths- or quarter-inch-thick sides and a quarter-inch-thick flat bottom, and tapers slightly inwards towards the chine. Hull sides are fitted with flat

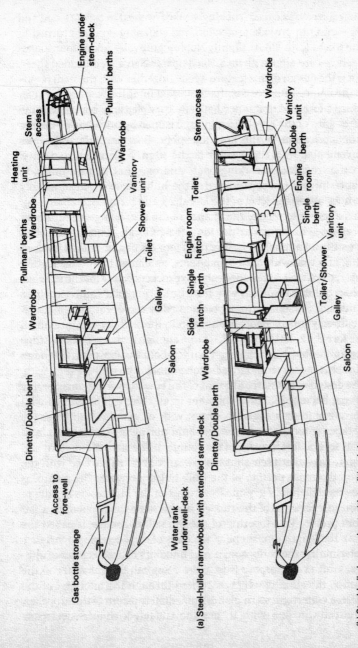

Engine under stern-deck

'Pullman' berths

Stern access

Heating unit

Wardrobe

'Pullman' berths

Vanitory unit

Wardrobe

Toilet

Shower unit

Wardrobe

Galley

Saloon

Dinette/Double berth

Access to fore-well

Gas bottle storage

Water tank under well-deck

(a) Steel-hulled narrowboat with extended stern-deck

Wardrobe

Vanitory unit

Double berth

Stern access

Engine room

Toilet

Engine room hatch

Single berth

Vanitory unit

Single berth

Toilet/Shower

Side hatch

Galley

Wardrobe

Saloon

Dinette/Double berth

(b) Steel-hulled narrowboat with traditional short counter

Fig. 9 Steel-hulled narrowboats

section steel strips called 'rubbing strakes' welded to the fore-end and stern section to provide protection and stiffening, and are turned in at the top to form flat or slightly sloping gunwales about four inches wide. Bows are almost always raked upwards in a well-defined sheer, and it is the design of this feature which, together with the stem profile and the choice of curve for the bow section of the 'top strake', can produce a fore-end that is aesthetically very pleasing; conversely, the general lines of the whole boat may be ruined by uncaring or incompetent fabrication of the bow assembly. Bow sheer is sometimes complemented by a slight sheer at the stern, a feature also derived from the traditional working boat, and one that can do much to enhance further the appearance of the hull. The stem-head usually protrudes above the level of the fore-deck and is rounded off to a fair radius in order to reduce the chance of the bow being caught under projections – in particular the top gates of locks. Immediately abaft the stem-head a small triangular flush fore-deck extends for a few feet, ending at a well with fixed bench seats, an almost invariable feature of this type of craft. Often the seats have lockers below for the stowage of loose equipment such as windlasses, mooring spikes and hosepipes, and this space is sometimes supplemented by a forepeak locker accessible either by hinged doors opening on to the well-deck or by a hatch in the fore-deck. If the forepeak is large enough it may serve as storage space for gas bottles or may contain the boat's water tank, although the latter is more commonly positioned under the well-deck.

The design of the stern, like that of the bow, may vary considerably between different makes of boat, but in all cases will be formed with either a round or a square counter, with or without hull taper (by 'hull taper' is meant a progressive slight narrowing of the beam from a point several feet forward of the counter). The sides of the stern and counter, whatever their shape, show an unbroken surface with the sides of the main portion of the hull, but underwater the picture is somewhat different. Here the lower part of the hull tapers rapidly to a point just forward of the rudder, at the same time retaining a flat bottom profile. This tapering of the lower hull section is called the 'swim', the length and shape of which is of considerable importance in determining the performance and handling characteristics of individual craft as its purpose is to assist a smooth flow of water to the propeller, the shaft of which is carried through the after-end of the swim in a watertight stern gland. Immediately astern of the propeller, and directly in line with it, lies the rudder, a shaped steel plate

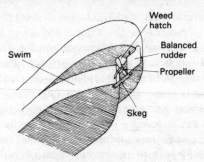

Fig. 10 Underwater profile of narrowboat stern

attached to a vertical steel bar (the rudder stock), the top section of which passes through the counter and is fixed just above deck level to the 'ram's head' – a Z-shaped tubular steel column – and at the bottom end pivots on a flat steel bar (the skeg) extending aft from the end of the swim. Into the horizontal top section of the ram's head is fitted the tiller, usually of tubular steel with a wooden handgrip, and secured to the ram's head by means of a removable pin, although it is not uncommon to find the whole tiller assembly formed from one continuous length of tube. Rudders are often of the 'balanced' type: a proportion of rudder area is positioned forward of the rudder stock to provide – as the term implies – a degree of balance and thus reduction in the effort required to move the tiller, especially when the boat is moving under anything approaching full power. The balancing effect is due to the fact that the propeller wash impinges on both parts of the rudder, and the pressure on that part forward of the pivot point partially balances the pressure on the main surface of the rudder, and so lessens the effort at the tiller. When the tiller is hard over it also has the effect – by virtue of increased rudder area – of utilizing more of the propeller wash, and thus increasing the effectiveness of the rudder (for an explanation of rudder action, see Appendix IV).

The stern-deck may be long or short and is often flush-decked or with merely a shallow well in order to provide space below sufficient to accommodate the motor and its ancillary fittings, including fuel tanks. On the relatively few hire craft with traditional short counters the engine is nearly always housed in a separate compartment within the cabin area. Where a stern-well is featured, side lockers – useful as seats – may be provided for the storage of batteries, gas cylinders and loose equipment, but in all cases the deck plates will be removable for access to the engine and other fittings. Included among the latter are two items of importance: the stern-gland greaser and the weed hatch. The stern-gland greaser usually consists of a capped metal tube filled with grease and connected via a small bore pipe to the stern gland. Rotation of a finger grip attached to the threaded cap forces grease through the pipe and into the stern-gland packing, thus maintaining a watertight seal at the point where the propeller shaft passes through the hull. The weed hatch is nowadays an indispensable feature of narrowboat construction – as anyone who has ever had an interior sprung mattress wrapped around the propeller will testify – and consists of a short length of vertical trunking, rectangular in section, situated immediately above the propeller. The bottom end of the duct thus formed is open to the water, while the top end protrudes above water level and is sealed by a hatch plate secured by wing nuts (or similar) to prevent propeller wash from entering the engine compartment. By first removing the appropriate deck plate and then the hatch plate, access is gained to the propeller and rudder for the removal of accumulated rubbish. A further item of importance is the bilge pump, the inlet of which is located in the bottom – or bilges – of the hull, usually within the engine compartment. The pump is usually operated by electric motor, or alternatively a diaphragm-type manual pump is sometimes provided.

The advent of longer stern-decks to accommodate more crew members has resulted, for the steerer, in the loss of two notable advantages of the traditional short counter: the opportunity to make use of the degree of weather protection and warmth offered by the cabin hatchway, and the availability of the cabin roof alongside the hatch for use as a seat. So far as weather is concerned, the open steering position common to all narrowboats means that the only realistic solution to the problem of protection – particularly on a long stern-deck – is to wear appropriate clothing (see Chapter 5) which, if sensibly chosen, will also provide the necessary warmth. Seating for the steerer – sometimes in the form of a demountable stool slotting into the deck, or perhaps a plywood seat fixed to the stern-rail – is now featured on many hire craft, but where no seat is provided boats fitted with stern-rails permit a makeshift seat to be constructed simply by resting the gangplank across the top of the rails.

The British Waterways Board's *Standards for Construction and Equipping of Pleasure Boats on the Board's Waterways* states that:

Every boat shall have ready for immediate use proper fenders of suitable material including a bow fender affixed in a position to prevent damage on impact with other vessels or structures and, in the case of boats fitted with a rudder which extends longitudinally aft of the hull, a stern fender secured to prevent the rudder being trapped between the mitres of lock gates

In the case of narrowboats the bow and stern fenders are usually of woven rope, and some hire firms even provide their boats with side fenders, but in my opinion the latter are quite unnecessary in the case of steel-hulled craft, and one cannot help but feel that their purpose is to protect the hull paintwork – a pointless exercise as side fenders cannot be used in narrow locks, precisely where most scraping of hull sides is likely to occur. A curious, not to say hideous, modification to the appearance of hire narrowboats in more recent times has been the fitting of 'bridge-guards' – robust tubular steel members secured to the forward outer edges of the coachroof and curved down in line with the taper of the bow to a fixing on the fore-deck. Their main function is the protection of the leading edge of the cabin top and the forward bulkhead against damage from overhead and projecting structures – in particular, low-arched fixed bridges and lift bridges when in the raised position. That they largely succeed in this is not in doubt, but any advantage thus gained is, in my opinion, outweighed by the consequent difficulty and awkwardness, not to say danger, that bridge-guards can present to crew members working from the bow.

Deck fixtures for mooring lines usually consist of a single steel T-stud welded to the fore-deck just abaft the stem-head, and one T-stud or dolly on each gunwale at the counter. Mooring lines – commonly of laid hemp or Terylene and made up with an eye splice at one end to slip around the studs – are provided at bow and stern. They should be of reasonable thickness and length, in good condition and free from knots; length is very important, as lines may be used for purposes other than mooring, and in some circumstances there can be few things more aggravating than trying to work a boat with inadequate lengths of line. A heavy lump hammer and at least two steel mooring spikes are included in a boat's inventory, together with a minimum of two windlasses and a long length of hosepipe for filling the water tank. The *Standards for Construction and Equipping of Pleasure Boats on the Board's Waterways* requires hire craft that intend to navigate the rivers and commercial waterways concerned to carry an adequate anchor and cable, and in some instances these are permanently fitted to the boat, usually with the anchor on the fore-deck and the cable stowed below in the forepeak.

Engines

Almost all hire narrowboats are powered by diesel engine, either air- or water-cooled, and ranging in output from about ten to thirty-five horsepower. There is good reason for choosing the compression-ignition engine: it is sturdy, reliable, economical of fuel and safe in operation as diesel oil, unlike petrol, is not volatile. Moreover, because of its economy sufficient fuel to cover three or four weeks' cruising can easily be carried in a boat's tanks, thus relieving the hirer of any worry about refuelling. The two main disadvantages are noise and vibration, both of which are allied to such installation details as choice of mountings for the engine and the degree of soundproofing applied to the engine compartment. The problem of noise in particular has caused a certain amount of concern among hire operators, some of whom felt that the loud thudding note of the 'traditional' air-cooled diesel was becoming less acceptable to their hirers, and out of step with the growing sophistication of hire craft design. They conse-quently turned to the installation of the quieter (or so it is claimed) water-cooled engine, with the result that the latter has become much more common in recent years.

Whatever the merits of the water-cooled engine with regard to noise (and not all are convinced of its superiority) it has another sort of advantage over the air-cooled variety: the utilization of hot cooling water to heat both the boat and its hot water circuit (see p. 83), although by no means all hire firms operating with water-cooled diesels have adapted them for this purpose. Two methods of supplying cooling water to the engine are employed: in the first, water is taken directly from the surrounding canal or river, filtered and pumped round the cooling circuit before being ejected overside (sometimes through the exhaust pipe); and in the second method by a closed-circuit cooling system, in which the recirculating coolant is itself cooled by means of 'skin tanks' of which a section of the lower hull forms a part, thus reducing the coolant temperature by heat loss to the surrounding water. Both methods entail daily attention on the part of the hirer: in the first case he is required to check and clean the intake filter, and in the second to check the level of cooling-water in the circuit and top up as necessary to replace water lost by evaporation.

Air-cooled diesel engines are much simpler in their arrangement. Air is admitted to the engine compartment through a grille in the hull side just below gunwale level, or through a duct positioned immediately above deck level (in the case of engines mounted in a separate engine-room cooling air is circulated usually by leaving the side hatches open), and is extracted through ducts leading to a suitable point in the upper hull or the superstructure. Whatever the type of engine, daily maintenance checks are the responsibility of the hirer, but are simple even for the least mechanically minded. Apart from the checks associated with water-cooled engines mentioned above, the engine oil dipstick should be examined each morning before starting up to make sure that the level is correct; if an engine is in good condition the level should drop only slightly over a week's running, but this is not always so and some companies provide a can of engine oil for topping up. On the other hand, any appreciable rise in level is a serious matter, and the hire operator must be contacted at once, for this is an indication that the engine oil is being diluted by fuel oil, which ultimately will result in the engine seizing up. This daily check is all that is required by most hire companies, although some ask for a similar check to be kept on the level of oil in the gearbox. Under all circumstances hirers are forbidden to attempt adjustments and repairs to the engine, its controls and other fittings – unless specifically requested to do so by the company.

Transmission of engine output to the propeller shaft is normally effected through a hydraulically operated gearbox by which any one of three control positions may be selected: ahead and astern propulsion, and neutral. Some hire craft are fitted with an alternative form of transmission known as 'hydrostatic drive', which in essence consists of two drive units connected by flexible pipes and filled with hydraulic fluid. The engine drives one unit directly and this then pumps the hydraulic fluid through the second unit, which is connected to the propeller shaft; as the second unit turns over it causes rotation of the shaft, the speed being governed by the amount of fluid pressure in the circuit, which in turn is related to engine revolutions. The great advantage claimed for this type of transmission arises from the fact that the engine, not being connected directly to the combination of transmission and propeller shaft, may be located in any suitable position within the boat merely by extending the pipes of the hydraulic circuit. A secondary benefit is the lessened chance of damage arising from the propeller blades striking a solid object, as the sudden shock to the stern gear and transmission is cushioned by the fluid drive.

Two other types of power unit should also be mentioned, even though, at the time of writing, neither has progressed much beyond the experimental stage. Both have been adopted as solutions to the problems of noise, vibration, pollution and maintenance and running costs associated with the conventional diesel engine (problems that are an ever-present concern to hire operators), and both depart entirely from the use of the diesel engine traditionally associated with narrowboat propulsion.

The first type of power unit consists of a petrol engine adapted to run on liquid petroleum gas, the fuel for which is carried in pressure tanks built into the hull and replenished from bulk pressure vessels at the hire base. It is claimed that the engine is particularly smooth-running and quiet with virtually no vibration, and that the somewhat higher fuel consumption (as compared with diesel) is offset by bulk-buying and storage. Much thought has been given to any possible dangers arising from gas leakage, which it is claimed have been virtually eliminated by such measures as filling the under-floor bilge space with plastic foam and using a gas detector and an extractor fan in the engine compartment.

Experiments with the other type of power unit resulted from some fresh thinking being brought to bear on the whole question of boat propulsion, and the solution adopted – electric power – although hardly novel, has been largely successful. Power is obtained from banks of high-density batteries driving an electric motor positioned in the aft cabin, with direct transmission to the propeller shaft. The motor revolutions are controlled by rheostat operated by the steerer, and the whole arrangement is extremely simple both to understand and to work. At the steering position noise is reduced to a low and scarcely audible hum, while in the accommodation section it is entirely absent and there is no vibration at all. Power is more than adequate, so much so that the motor is 'governed' down by means of a relay in the electrical circuit which, for emergency use, will allow full revolutions over a predetermined length of time before automatic-ally switching back to normal cruising power; the device also prevents rapid discharge of the batteries caused by prolonged running at full power. Battery charging is done overnight while moored to a suitable charging point, and battery capacity is such that this may be necessary only at intervals of a few days, depending upon the amount of power used. Electrically powered boats clearly have many advantages, and perhaps their use will become more widespread, although this is crucially related to the form and extent of the network of charging points that will inevitably have to be established.

Engine controls

Engine controls should always be mounted within easy reach of the steerer, and may be positioned either on a small console post protruding from the deck, or on the aft bulkhead of the superstructure. Both positions are equally convenient, provided that in the latter case the length of the stern-deck is not excessive. Herein lies the advantage of a control console, which may be fixed at any suitable point – usually under the steerer's left hand. On those few narrowboats that employ wheel-steering the wheel is situated on the left-hand panel of the aft bulkhead, with the engine controls mounted alongside. The controls consist of a throttle and a gear selector, the latter having three positions: forward, neutral and reverse. The gears are normally operated hydraulically by movement of the selector lever acting through a cable connected to the gearbox, but on occasion are

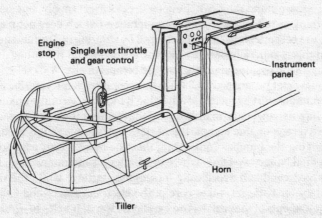

Fig. 11 The controls of a narrowboat

selected by means of a long lever attached directly to the gearbox and protruding up through the deck at a point just forward of the steering position.

The 'single lever' control, which combines the operation of throttle and gear selection in one lever, as the name implies, has become increasingly common over the past several years and is now fitted to the majority of hire craft. It is basically a very simple arrangement and therefore quicker and less confusing to operate – particularly for the beginner – than separate levers for throttle and gears. From a vertical position, which gives neutral, a forward movement of the lever immediately engages forward gear and thereafter any further forward movement increases throttle opening, while a backward movement of the lever causes a similar action, only in reverse. Just below the lever will be found a small cylindrical button which, when pulled out to its furthest extent, disconnects the lever from the cable control to the gearbox but leaves the throttle control in operation, thus allowing the use of partial throttle opening without gear engagement when starting the engine. Once the lever has been returned to the vertical, or neutral, position, giving 'tick-over' revolutions of the engine, the button is pushed in and the lever thus reconnected to the gearbox.

All inboard motors fitted to hire craft, whether fuelled by petrol or diesel, are provided with electric start, using either an ignition switch system similar to those fitted in vehicles where the final travel of the key against a spring return makes the electrical contact, or by a combination of ignition key and starter button. Petrol engines, of course, are stopped by switching off the electrical supply, but diesels, working as they do by compression-ignition (which does not require the use of spark plugs) must be stopped by shutting off the fuel supply, and this is generally done by moving a small metal rod situated in a convenient position near the engine compartment. A diesel engine should *never* be stopped by lifting the decompression levers. Facilities for manual start by means of a starting handle are virtually unknown on hire narrowboats, mainly due to the fact that the limited space in the average engine compartment does not allow enough room for swinging the handle. Considering this, the more recent adoption of the dual battery system – where one battery is maintained in a fully charged condition specifically for engine starting, while the other battery (or batteries) takes care of the electrical power and lighting requirements of the craft – is an excellent idea, as it helps to eliminate the possibility of breakdown due to a battery charge insufficient to start the engine.

Instrumentation is mostly kept to a minimum, and at best may be represented by an ammeter (or ammeters if a dual electrical system is fitted), oil pressure gauge, and – if the engine is water-cooled – a temperature gauge; or, alternatively, by the equivalent warning lights. Whatever form the instrumentation takes, it is often grouped with the ignition control and other switches, such as those used to operate the horn and headlight, on a panel which should be within easy reach and sight of the steerer, although unfortunately this is not always the case.

Accommodation, fittings and equipment

The whole of the space between bow and stern sections is given over to accommodation and is enclosed by the superstructure of the boat; it is in effect a long cabin subdivided into various compartments as required by the design. The superstructure itself is usually constructed of ply, fibreglass or steel, lined internally with a variety of materials including melamine board, veneered ply and natural timbers, and almost invariably incorporates some form of insulation to reduce internal condensation and heat loss. The cabin sides are pierced at intervals by windows to each compartment, and sometimes the upper parts of the forward bulkhead and door are also glazed to provide a clear view ahead – an excellent feature that has become increasingly popular. Access to the accommodation is gained through doors opening on to the fore-well and stern-deck respectively, and (although rarely) by side hatches positioned above gunwale level. Opening portions of windows are of various types: bottom-hinged inward opening ('hopper' windows), horizontal sliding, top-hinged opening out, or adjustable louvre. External doors are of ply, and at least one is lockable from the outside; those opening at gunwale or stern-deck level are provided with steps, and where these are internal a sliding hatch is fitted in the coachroof to allow sufficient headroom for access.

The sides of the superstructure slope inwards towards the roof – a feature known as 'tumblehome' – to reduce the chance of damage, and often have elegantly curved ends which improve the appearance

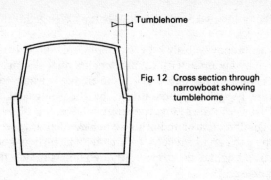

Tumblehome

Fig. 12 Cross section through narrowboat showing tumblehome

of the boat by softening what might otherwise be rather angular lines. The coachroof is cambered for increased strength and to throw off rainwater, and is provided throughout its full length with grabrails for the use of crew members clambering along the gunwales. These grabrails are fitted towards the edges of the roof and serve a secondary but very useful function as barriers that prevent any loose equipment on the coachroof from sliding overboard. Equipment that is often carried in this manner includes such items as the gangplank, water hose, mop, deck scrub, lifebuoys and boat shafts, but there is an increasing tendency to provide special roof racks for the gangplank and shafts and to stow away all other items in cupboards and lockers – with the exception of lifebuoys, which at all times should be kept above deck close to the steering position in readiness for emergencies.

The position of internal accommodation relative to the form of the narrowboat hull ensures that maximum width (about six feet) is maintained in all compartments together with full headroom throughout – a situation that is conducive to good layout and general comfort. As a rule the amount of accommodation provided is a function of the overall length of enclosed cabin space, which in turn is loosely related to the hull length – loosely, because of course the respective lengths of bow and stern sections vary between different designs of craft. It is a mistake, in my opinion, to cram too much into too little space, however brilliantly this may be achieved, as it will almost certainly result in eventual loss of comfort and convenience to the detriment of good relations among the crew. Internal layouts are surprisingly varied in different makes of narrowboat, and it is thus impossible to give more than an impression of certain main features that are fairly common to most.

Cooking, dining and sitting arrangements often share a common area on the open-plan principle, a type of layout in which versatility is combined with spaciousness to good effect. Dining tables may be either of the 'fold-down' variety, to be stowed away when not required, or of the 'drop-down' type which, when lowered, forms part of a double bed base in conjunction with the fixed seating. The latter is upholstered with foam-filled loose cushions that serve as mattresses at night. Drop-down tables are mostly used in combination with face-to-face fixed seating to form a 'dinette' – an excellent arrangement, especially when raised up on a shallow plinth so as to permit an eye-level view through the window. Because space is at a premium it is unusual for separate lounge or saloon seating to be provided in addition to that required for dining, although extra stools or stacking chairs may be furnished to supplement the fixed seats where necessary. Cooking equipment on modern narrowboats is nothing short of first-class: the majority of hire firms offer such items as a full-size four-burner cooker complete with oven and grill, a gas or electric refrigerator of reasonable size, a stainless steel sink and drainer unit and ample shelf and cupboard space for both kitchen utensils and food storage, not forgetting a bin or plastic sack for kitchen waste. A complete range of culinary equipment is supplied together with all cutlery, crockery, glassware and other similar items sufficient for the number of crew. As in domestic kitchens, all working surfaces are finished in melamine for ease of cleaning, and the layout of the fittings is generally to a reasonable standard, given the space limitations.

Due to the restricted beam of narrowboats, double berths other than those provided by conversion of the saloon seating are rarely featured; single berths are normal, either in 'Pullman' form (that is, double-tiered) or as a single bunk. Sleeping cabins may contain two single or two Pullman berths placed one on each side of a central gangway, or just one Pullman berth; the latter is a convenient arrangement in that it leaves space on the opposite side of the cabin for a fitted vanitory unit, drawers and a wardrobe, all of which would otherwise have to be sited elsewhere. Berths are usually constructed as fixtures in timber framing with a substantial ply or blockboard bottom; mattresses are of vinyl-covered plastic or rubber foam and are of sufficient thickness to ensure a comfortable night's sleep. It is perhaps worth pointing out that, other things being equal, a lower berth will always be effectively wider than an upper due to the tumblehome of the cabin sides combined with the reduced width of the boat above gunwale level. Upper berths invariably feature a raised side for the greater comfort and security of the occupant – a welcome detail in view of the narrowness of most of them. Berths are designed to accommodate a normal-sized adult and should be at least six feet in length; any exceptions to this general rule will usually be mentioned in the descriptive brochure. Folding or removable berths of the 'pipe-cot' type may sometimes be fitted in addition to the fixed berths, but in my opinion this is not a satisfactory arrangement as it indicates either poor planning of the internal layout, or over-use of the space available. Blankets and pillows are always provided; pillowcases, sheets, sleeping bags and liners may be included as part of the inventory, or may be supplied at an extra charge. Fitted vanitory units consisting of a washbasin built into a melamine-topped drawer unit are now featured in most hire craft, and may be combined with a full-height wardrobe; storage space additional to this is usually available under bottom berths. Fluorescent strip lights are the most common form of lighting employed in hire craft (although tungsten filament lamps are also used) and are positioned to give an even distribution of light throughout the boat; sometimes bed-head lights and other similar fittings are added to give an extra touch of convenience and luxury.

Toilets

Over the past few years a considerable transformation in the design of boat toilets has occurred, starting in 1970 when, following the publication of the *Jeger Report*, it became clear that both Government and the river authorities were no longer prepared to tolerate a source of inland waterway pollution that was obviously avoidable. The *Jeger Report* recommended that:

> ... discharge of sewage from boats into fresh water used for recreation should be prohibited ... Local authorities and boat hiring firms together with associations of private boat owners should work out a plan for the sanitary facilities needed on a waterway.

Consequently the various river authorities drew up the necessary by-laws, and these came into effect area by area, the first (with the exception of the Thames Conservancy area, which had been governed by by-laws prohibiting all waste discharge from boats for a number of years) being the authority responsible for an area that included the Norfolk Broads, the by-laws for which came into effect in January 1973. The total result of these actions was a comprehensive ban on all sewage discharge, leaving waste discharge to continue on practical grounds.

Before the ban, marine toilets had been in use virtually everywhere except the Thames, but the rapidly expanding number of boats made it obvious that measures would have to be taken if pollution was not to increase beyond desirable limits. Marine toilets, which discharge directly through the boat hull into the surrounding water, were replaced at first by chemical toilets of the open bucket variety consisting of a plastic container with hinged seat and lid into which fits a removable plastic bucket with loose lid. Before use the bucket is charged with diluted formaldehyde disinfectant and when full is emptied and cleaned at one of the many sewage disposal stations positioned all over the inland waterways system. Not surprisingly this somewhat crude arrangement proved unsatisfactory to many hirers, and the 'bucket-and-chuck-it', as it came to be called, was partly superseded by plastic proprietary toilets with a flushing rim working on either the recirculatory principle or using a fresh-water flush. In this type of toilet the contents of the bowl are discharged into a lower tank by operating a slide valve; when full the holding tank is disconnected from the bowl, emptied at the disposal station in the usual way, and recharged with chemical disinfectant. Although less offensive and more hygienic in use than the simple open bucket, this type of toilet is more difficult to empty and clean due to the moving parts involved in the design – and, of course, its introduction in no way eliminated the unpleasant duty of periodic disposal.

While the do-it-yourself method of sewage disposal may suit the private boat-owner (the great majority of whom use their boats only intermittently), hirers on the whole tend to expect on-board facilities of a nature similar to those they have at home, an attitude which, when allied to the intensive usage that hire craft receive, leads to an obvious solution: the pump-out toilet. Following a trial in 1972, the first operational network of pump-out stations was established on the Broads for the season of 1973 when the new by-laws came into force. During the same year the Association of Pleasure Craft Operators decided to set up their own system of pump-out stations to cover the main inland waterways, a decision which was implemented and in working order for the 1974 season. There can be no doubt that the arrangement works well and is much appreciated by the hiring public, in spite of the fact that hirers mostly have to pay an extra charge for the service.

One type of pump-out toilet is made of plastic, with the bowl, complete with hinged seat and lid, positioned over an integral storage tank which is isolated by a flap valve. The bowl is manually or electrically flushed with either fresh or recirculated water, and the accumulated waste is treated with a chemical solution in the usual way. Another type features a separate holding tank, usually of large capacity, and this combination permits a choice of toilet bowl, including a ceramic model much resembling the household WC. Some installations even have an auxiliary holding tank situated elsewhere in the boat, into which the contents of the toilet tank may be pumped at the discretion of the hirer, a facility that allows for increased flexibility in the use of the system. When it becomes necessary for the tank to be emptied, the boat is simply moored at the next pump-out station on the route and connected to a vacuum pump by means of a fitting in the gunwale. The contents of the holding tank are then pumped into a bowser on the wharf and the tank washed out and recharged with chemical solution, the whole operation taking just a few minutes, and relieving at least one crew member of an onerous duty!

In line with the general demand for all the comforts of home, modern hire craft feature amenities that for the most part were unheard of just a few years ago. Showers, for instance, are a standard fitting in all but the smallest boats, and the increased use of water that they entail is of little consequence since tanks – holding in most cases between 100 and 150 gallons – may be frequently filled at the now numerous sanitary station and boatyard water taps. Domestic-type units are usual, with provision for separate control of water volume and temperature, and waste water is collected in a sealed tray to be pumped overside by electric pump. A more recent development is the plastic hip bath with shower fitting – a very convenient combination, particularly for the bathing of young children. Toilet and shower facilities often share the same compartment, an arrangement that is not only economical of space but may provide a rather larger bathroom area than might otherwise have been possible. Electric shaver points are now installed in almost all hire craft, and consist of a compact bulkhead fitting containing a transformer which converts the boat's twelve-volt supply to standard domestic voltage, and a two-pin outlet.

These domestic comforts are rounded out by many hire firms by the provision of either black and white or colour portable television sets (usually subject to an extra charge), for which at least one twelve-volt socket outlet is fitted, often at a suitable point in the saloon.

Heating and hot water supply

Variability of the summer climate in Britain, together with a tendency for the cruising season to be extended in spring and autumn, has made necessary some form of space heating in hire craft if certain minimal standards of comfort are to be maintained. Today all hire boats are at least adequately heated, and some to a degree that provides very comfortable conditions even in severe winter weather. Heaters are either oil- or gas-fired (as might be expected with only a twelve-volt electrical supply available) and range from the simple radiant and convector types to full-blown circulating hot water systems with radiators and a central heating boiler. The convector and radiant heaters are the least efficient in terms of output, and have the added disadvantage of producing a great deal of water vapour which, through condensation, does nothing to enhance conditions within the boat. Much better, in my opinion, is the radiant catalytic heater, which gives off a considerable amount of heat for its size and is safer as it will not ignite inflammable materials. This seemingly miraculous state of affairs arises from the fact that no actual flame is involved in the operation of the heater: heat is given off directly from oxidation of gas on a catalytic bed.

Ducted warm air heaters are used with some success on boats, particularly where the internal layout lends itself to the easy routing and concealment of air ducts. In this type of heater air from within the boat is taken through a gas- or oil-fired heat exchanger and then circulated to the various outlets by convection, or is blown by electric fan. The installation is suitable for heating airing cupboards, and does not increase condensation as the products of combustion are taken out by flue and discharged above roof level. Circulating hot water heating has a great deal to commend it: flexibility in the positioning of radiators, safety, totally dry heat and – in conjunction with water-cooled engines – the use of a calorifier to provide 'free' heat for space heating and for domestic hot water, with a corresponding reduction in gas consumption. Of course, with the engine stopped no heat is available to the calorifier, and for this reason the latter is fitted with a gas-fired burner, which takes over at times when the boat is moored. This system, too, is ideal for use with airing cupboards, and the pipes and radiators provide an extra facility for the drying of clothes. Given all these advantages it is hardly surprising that this form of heating has enjoyed increasing popularity among hire operators.

Where no central heating boiler is fitted, hot water to the sink, shower and washbasins is supplied by a bulkhead-mounted instantaneous water heater similar in operation and appearance to the domestic patterns. Water pressure is maintained in both the hot and cold water systems by electric pump; opening a tap causes a drop in pressure which automatically switches on the pump and at the same time fires up (from a pilot light) the gas burner in the water heater or boiler. Pressurized water systems of this type are usually very efficient, but unfortunately can be rather noisy in operation due to the intermittent whine of the pump.

Headlights and horns

In accordance with the British Waterways Board *General Canal By-laws* (see Appendix II) all craft must carry a white light for use in tunnels exceeding 440 yards in length, and this requirement is met in the case of hire narrowboats by the provision of a powerful head-lamp fixed to the upper part of the forward bulkhead. Car-type head-lamps are sometimes used as they make excellent tunnel lights, especially when mounted upside down so that when dipped the beam is directed towards the tunnel roof (a necessary precaution to avoid blinding the steerers of oncoming craft), or, to achieve the same effect, the headlight may be mounted on a swivel fitting.

All craft must carry an appliance capable of producing the correct sound signals as used on inland waterways. Although the by-laws refer to this as a 'whistle', in practice hire craft are generally fitted with a car-type horn mounted in a convenient position at the fore-end of the boat. Both headlight and horn are operated by switches situated on the aft control panel or console.

Typical inventory of a four-berth narrowboat

BOAT'S GEAR AND NAVIGATION EQUIPMENT

2 windlasses (double-headed)
2 mooring spikes
1 lump hammer
2 mooring lines
1 ignition key ⎱
1 boat door key ⎰ on ring attached to float
1 BWB sanitary station key ⎰
1 water hose
1 water filler-cap key
1 long shaft
1 short shaft (with boat hook)
1 gangplank
1 lifebuoy
3 fire extinguishers
1 fire blanket
1 boat's instruction manual
2 navigation guides
1 set of steerer's waterproofs
1 door mat

GALLEY EQUIPMENT

1 carving set
1 carving dish
2 kitchen knives
1 bread knife
1 bread board
1 bread bin
1 butter dish
1 kettle
1 frying pan
1 large pan
1 medium pan
2 small pans
1 roasting tin
1 baking tin

1 flameproof casserole
2 heatproof basins
1 heatproof measuring jug
1 colander
1 wooden spoon
1 spatula
1 potato peeler
1 water jug
1 tea pot
1 coffee pot
1 milk jug
1 sugar basin
1 strainer
1 can opener/bottle opener/corkscrew
1 whisk
1 ladle
1 cheese grater
1 kitchen utensil set
1 toast rack
1 cruet set
1 washing-up bowl
1 washing-up brush
1 dish drainer
1 sink tidy
1 waste bin (with plastic liners)
1 pair of kitchen scissors
1 pair oven gloves
2 tea towels
2 ash trays

CROCKERY AND CUTLERY

6 dinner knives
6 dinner forks
6 dessert knives
6 dessert spoons
6 soup spoons
6 teaspoons
2 tablespoons
6 dinner plates

6 medium plates
6 small plates
6 pudding dishes
6 soup bowls
6 cups and saucers
6 mugs
6 egg cups
6 tumblers
6 wine glasses

CLEANING EQUIPMENT

1 sweeping brush
1 floor mop
1 deck mop
1 dustpan and brush
1 toilet brush
1 toilet bin
1 bucket
1 floor cloth
1 scrubbing brush
1 duster

BEDDING

4 pillows
4 pillow cases
4 sleeping bags
4 sleeping bag liners
8 blankets

It should be stressed that the above list is meant to convey some idea of what equipment may be typically included in the hire charge for a four-berth boat; some firms may provide a more exhaustive inventory, others less.

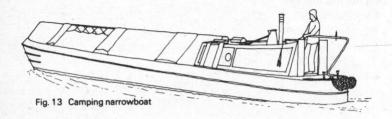

Fig. 13 Camping narrowboat

For those with a slightly more adventurous turn of mind, perhaps combined with a shallower pocket, the camping boat has a lot to offer. 'Campers', as they are called, will accommodate parties of up to twelve people (this is the maximum number permitted on inland waterways passenger-carrying vessels without a Department of Trade and Industry Certificate), and are particularly suitable for groups of young people, such as schoolchildren, scouts and sea cadets, as they are comparatively cheap to hire, and consequently the cost per head is very low.

The majority of campers are simply full-length working narrowboats adapted for passenger-carrying by the installation of pipe-cots, sink and drainer, food cupboards, gas cooker and tables and benches in the cargo hold, which is sheeted over with side- and top-cloths (into which flexible plastic panels have been inserted to give more light) for weather protection; otherwise the boat is left in more or less standard working trim. Sanitary arrangements are confined to the provision of a portable chemical toilet. The inventory on campers is fairly basic: no bedding, crockery or cutlery is normally supplied, and only the bare essentials of galley equipment are provided.

Although it will be obvious that the standard of accommodation and amenity, as compared with the ordinary hire narrowboat, is relatively spartan, the camper does offer other compensations, not the least of these being the opportunity to navigate a 'real' working boat – an experience otherwise denied to the vast majority of waterway enthusiasts, whether hirers or boat owners. Self-steer craft are hired out singly, but where the services of a boatman are obligatory (as they are with some companies), pairs of boats may be hired in the form of motor and butty (the latter is an unpowered full-length boat towed by the motor boat), thus increasing the possible number of passengers to twenty-four.

MOTOR CRUISERS

Strictly speaking, all craft whose beam does not exceed six feet ten inches are narrowboats, but for the sake of clarity it is preferable to restrict this term to include only steel boats with hull shapes based on the design of the traditional canal working boat; other distinguishing features being a continuous slab-sided cabin shell extending over most of the hull, and tiller-steering. All other craft are motor cruisers (we are not concerned here with sailing cruisers, a number of which are for hire on inland waters, notably the Norfolk Broads) of either narrow beam – similar to that of the narrowboat – or wide beam, which includes those craft having a maximum width greater than six feet ten inches.

The vast majority of hire motor cruisers are wide-beam, with overall lengths ranging from about twenty-five feet to about fifty feet and a maximum beam of about fourteen feet. Their designs and layouts are astonishingly varied – much more so than those of the narrowboat – because of the lack of constraints imposed by a narrow beam combined with, in particular, the almost unlimited possibilities presented by GRP construction. Although by no means all craft are built of this material, it has to a great extent replaced wood planking and marine plywood on account of the ease with which it lends itself to the methods and economies of mass production, its lightness combined with strength, and its lower maintenance costs in use. A few cruisers are built of steel, but although it has great strength, steel is heavy and is not so easily and economically worked into the shapes required of the smaller hull form, and therefore its use for this purpose has never been widespread.

Because of the wide variation in the design of motor cruisers it is impossible to give more than a general description of the main features common to the majority. Broadly speaking, there are two distinct types of wide-beam hire cruiser: one having the traditional 'launch' hull shape, and the other being based on what may be called a 'pontoon' hull. Nearly everyone is familiar with the shape of the launch hull with its raked stem, flared bow and a beam that reaches its maximum about one-third of the length abaft the bow, thereafter diminishing slightly to a square or gently curved transom. Gunwales often have a gradual sheer for the sake of appearance, but this is rarely pronounced, and the main deck is usually continuous from stem to stern, with reasonably wide side-decks made possible by the increased beam. On some boats a guard-rail, or 'pulpit', is fitted to the bow section to provide greater safety for crew members working from the fore-end. The great majority of this type of craft are steered from a centre cockpit, that is, a well-deck situated about amidships and raised above the main floor level to give sufficient visibility for the helmsman and, in many cases, to provide space below for the engine and tanks. The cockpit is roofed over by either a sliding canopy or a collapsible 'wheelhouse' structure, the latter being an essential feature of many Broads craft on account of the low bridges to be encountered on those waterways. Aft cockpit steering positions with collapsible canopies are usually confined to the smaller cruisers, but in a more recent development the steering position is raised up in the aft section of the boat and has a fixed structure glazed all round – the so-called 'sedan' style of cruiser.

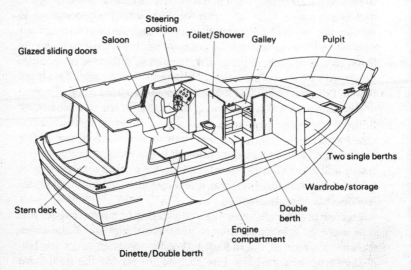

Fig. 14 Wide-beam sedan cruiser

In both centre cockpit and sedan cruisers the steering deck is almost invariably also the main saloon and dining area, furnished with a table and settee converting into a double bed. Centre cockpit boats naturally have their other accommodation positioned forward and aft of the well, and usually entered by steps down from the well to keep the height of the main superstructure as low as possible; even so, in many cases full standing headroom is not available except in principal cabins and saloons. Virtually all launch-type cruisers have one feature in common: the use of the forepeak as a sleeping cabin, with a single berth angled along each side of the bow and even double beds in the case of larger craft. Further sleeping cabins are situated in the aft section of the accommodation, and are furnished with either double beds or single berths, again depending on the size of craft, but sedan cruisers generally have all their accommodation forward of the main saloon, leaving a smallish stern-deck for use as a sitting-out area. Some of the larger boats have a sundeck positioned on top of the superstructure in the after part of the boat, and occasionally this is combined with an open 'flying bridge' containing a second steering position. Most large craft are fitted out with galleys in no way inferior to those found in narrowboats – that is, properly laid out with a full-size gas cooker, stainless steel sink and drainer, refrigerator and sufficient worktop space, drawers, and cupboards, although some leave much to be desired in this respect, particularly the smaller boats, which may have cramped galleys with inadequate cooking and storage facilities. Toilets and heating units generally are similar to those provided on narrowboats; the majority of cruisers are fitted with showers, electric razor points and pump-out toilets, and with pressurized hot and cold water systems. All craft have some form of heating, ranging from individual cabin heaters to full central heating throughout the boat.

Cruisers are wheel-steered from a helmsman's seat placed on the left-hand side of the cockpit (the nautical terms 'port' and 'starboard', applying respectively to the left-hand and right-hand sides of the boat when facing forward, are, for some strange reason, not used generally on inland waters), and by far the greater number are powered by a water-cooled diesel engine driving a single screw, although a few are fitted with twin screws, each with its own engine and single lever control.

Narrow-beam motor cruisers are now comparatively rare as hire craft, and are mostly to be found on canals. Because of the limitations imposed upon layouts by the small beam together with lack of full headroom in many cases, the interior tends to be decidedly cramped when compared with other types of hire craft; not all are fitted with showers or refrigerators (perishable foods being stored in a 'cool-box' instead), and galleys are often minuscule, with tiny cookers and a minimum of storage space. Propulsion may be by diesel engine, inboard petrol engine or outboard motor, but petrol engines, especially the outboard type, tend to be expensive on fuel, and in my opinion their safety in the hands of novice hirers can be questionable on account of the dangers associated with petrol fumes. Taking all of these factors into consideration it is really no wonder that hire firms prefer to equip their fleets with wide-beam cruisers whenever operating conditions permit. Nevertheless, the narrow-beam cruiser does have certain points in its favour: it is generally cheaper to hire, and its small size can be an advantage on some waterways.

'Pontoon'-type motor cruisers

These rather strange-looking craft were introduced some years ago and are now to be found in considerable numbers on sheltered inland waters, particularly the Norfolk Broads, the Thames and the Severn, and have proved to be popular with family parties. In the main built of GRP (a few are constructed of steel), their principal characteristics are a wide, parallel-sided hull that is often blunt-bowed, and a long, continuous superstructure of uniform height enclosing most of the hull area, sometimes with a sliding sunroof. Overall sizes range from about twenty-seven to forty-five feet in length, and many have a beam of twelve feet, resulting in a layout that is very spacious, with the added convenience of a floor that runs at one level throughout the boat. Both double- and single-berth cabins are provided together with all the amenities to be found on launch-type cruisers: galleys are invariably excellent, with full-size cookers, refrigerators, stainless steel sink units and ample worktop space and storage. The forward section of the accommodation is always taken up by the saloon, which contains a convertible settee and a helmsman's seat positioned in front of a steering console on which the wheel and instruments are mounted – the so-called 'forward control' steering position. The

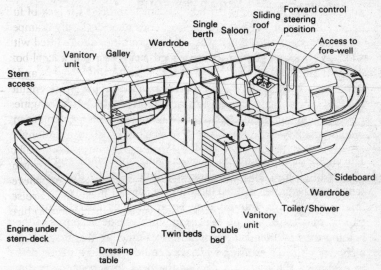

Fig. 15 Wide-beam pontoon-type cruiser

water-cooled diesel engine is housed under the small stern-deck, a position which tends to keep noise levels down when under way. At the bow there is usually a semi-circular well with moulded seats for sitting out, and wide side-decks allow easy access along both sides of the superstructure.

CHAPTER FOUR

CHOOSING THE CRUISING AREA AND THE BOAT

The choice of hire company, boat, cruising area, route and the time of year to go may all be considerably influenced by the manner in which the beginner is introduced to the idea of holiday-making on inland waterways. Interest may be aroused by advertisements in papers, magazines and on television; enthusiastic accounts of their boating trips by friends or acquaintances may fire the imagination; a chance visit to a cruising waterway could result in a strong desire to exchange the seat of a car for the deck of a boat; or perhaps experience in other types of craft on other waters might lead to a wish to extend that experience to rivers and canals; and so on. But whatever the way in which the beginner is prompted to take the first steps towards booking a waterways holiday, he will have to make at the outset several difficult judgements on a basis of no practical knowledge whatsoever. Of course, if an experienced friend is on hand to offer sound advice then the problem is largely solved, but for many people the only alternative is to study the relevant brochures, guides and maps, come to a decision – and simply hope for the best. Fortunately for the hirer, this approach mostly works in practice, not least because the majority of hire companies maintain a high standard, both in the service given and the quality of their boats.

THE CRUISING AREA

The first question that usually arises in planning any type of holiday is 'Where shall we go?' and an inland waterways holiday is no exception, but before an answer is arrived at the hirer should be clear as to what *type* of boating holiday he wants. It is not uncommon for someone with no experience of cruising to assume that boating is just boating, with nothing more to be said. The reality, however, is rather different, for not only is there a great deal of dissimilarity between certain kinds of boat, as will have become apparent from the previous chapter, but the cruising waterways are themselves extremely varied in character. Any final choice will normally have to take into account the preferences of family, friends or whoever it is that will make up the crew, not forgetting the important consideration concerning the amount and types of boating *activities*, including those away from the boat, favoured by the hirer (to avoid unnecessary repetition the term 'hirer' should be understood to include the whole crew), although one should not overlook the fact that for most people a boating holiday means just what it implies: that most of the activity and interest will be centred on and around the boat. Occasionally views are expressed to the contrary: that the prime purpose of boating is to explore the country surrounding the waterways on foot, and so the greater part of a holiday should be devoted to just this. I find this attitude quite incomprehensible, however; surely, to hire a boat at considerable expense and then regard it merely as a means of transport is completely illogical; one may explore places of interest much more conveniently by car if sight-seeing is the main intention. (There are exceptions: some navigations are so restricted in scope as to necessitate a lot of time being spent 'ashore' if the same ground is not to be crossed and recrossed *ad nauseam* – Windermere in the Lake District and the Brecon and Abergavenny Canal being good examples.) Boats, it seems to me, are for boating, that is – in the present context – making an inland journey by water, which as an experience can be of absorbing interest in itself: the exercising of skills in route-planning, boat-handling and navigation, and in general acquiring by slow degrees a competence that brings its own pleasurable reward. That is my personal view, but not necessarily, of course, the only possible one: it is up to the hirer to decide what type of boating holiday is likely to be most suitable, bearing in mind individual circumstances. Will the crew, for instance, include small children, elderly or infirm people, or pets, and will there be enough active people to manage the boat properly and safely? The hirer, after taking into account considerations such as these, will have to consider carefully how the final choice of cruising area might affect the enjoyment of any member of the crew, for the dissatisfaction of even one could well ruin the holiday for all the others.

As the reader will already have gathered, the amount of physical activity associated with a cruising holiday in any particular area is largely to do with the number of crew-operated locks encountered as opposed either to no lockage at all, or to powered locks operated by professional keepers (there are also a few keeper-operated manual locks, where assistance from boat crews is usually welcomed), alternatives which are fortunately more or less coincident with the various cruising areas.

As it happens, most of the physical effort associated with waterways cruising is centred on the canal system, and some of it is hard work indeed, for apart from the operation of locks, which may have stiff paddle gear and heavy gates, and in places occur in flights of up to thirty, the hirer on occasion will have to contend with lift and swing bridges demanding sometimes a fair degree of agility, weight and brute strength on the part of some member, or members, of the crew. In addition to this, mooring lines have to be got on to the bank, even though this may mean jumping for it if the water is too shallow for the boat to be brought in properly; considerable strength may also be required in shafting a boat off once it has run aground, and – sooner or later – someone will be faced with the wearisome task of clearing a badly fouled propeller while lying full length on the deck and working one-handed with an arm immersed in cold water almost up to the shoulder, perhaps for an hour or so. In these situations (apart from the last one) someone else will have to steer the boat – or at least, in the case of shafting-off, be able to operate the engine controls. All too frequently one sees the man at the tiller while his wife or girl-friend struggles with the heavy work: some women cannot, or will not, learn how to steer a boat, but equally some men will simply not give them the opportunity to do so. The rights and wrongs of this do not concern us here: what must be made clear is that first, someone should be available *at all times* to take over the steering with reasonable competence, and second, at least one other person should be ready and able to do the really hard work and, preferably, be able to steer as well. On a boat crewed by two people, both of whom are capable of stepping into the captain's shoes at a moment's notice, few problems are likely to arise, but otherwise situations can – and very probably will – occur in which bad temper and harsh words prevail, which hardly contribute to an enjoyable holiday!

It is difficult to offer comprehensive advice to a couple wishing to take a baby or a young child on a boating holiday because of the wide differences in family circumstances and relationships; some babies make few extra demands upon the parents, but others need constant care and attention both day and night, which, when combined with the degree of stress brought about by an unfamiliar activity (for most people there is inevitably a certain amount of anxiety associated with managing a boat for the first time), may even ruin the whole holiday. To reduce the chance of this happening it would be advisable to choose a cruising area involving the least amount of work on the part of a boat crew, so that one parent is always available to look after the child: this means that stretches of waterways with crew-operated locks or movable bridges are best avoided. The same advice applies in the case of young children, who may well have to be supervised much of the time and who may very easily become bored if the cruising periods between moorings are too long, denying them the opportunity to play on the bank and along the edges of the water. Of course, as soon as the children are strong enough to help with the working of the boat and thus feel that they are doing something useful, the situation becomes radically different as it now provides enjoyment for the whole family, and this enjoyment is likely to be the greater in proportion to a child's participation in the physical activities of a cruising holiday.

Elderly and infirm persons may find boating to be particularly relaxing and agreeable, always provided that there is a sufficient number of crew both to look after their needs and work the boat without fuss. The elderly cannot, in the normal course of events, be expected to do any of the hard work, but they can make useful contributions to the holiday tasks by cooking meals and perhaps keeping an eye on the children from time to time, although generally speaking it would be wise to regard them as passengers and not overload them with work and responsibility. Infirm persons almost certainly will have the greatest difficulty in getting on and off the boat, and even in moving about inside it if this involves climbing steps, which tends to indicate that the 'pontoon' hull type of craft with its single floor level, or a narrowboat with a comfortable forward saloon and good viewing windows, would be more suitable for them. For those who are unsteady on their feet one should select a boat that is stable and not noticeably subject to rocking as the crew's weight is shifted around; most of the larger wide-beam cruisers and most narrowboats meet this requirement, but all narrow-beam cruisers and some of the smaller wide-beam cruisers do not, and may have the added disadvantages of cramped space and lack of headroom. A boat's tendency to rock about is exaggerated by adverse weather conditions, and for this reason it may be advisable not to take the elderly and infirm on other than sheltered waters (to a certain extent this also applies to young children), which means avoiding those navigations that include large lakes.

In recent years there has developed a more enlightened attitude to the problems of the physically handicapped, extending to the provision of amenities for suitable physical activities, including boating. It is now possible for the physically handicapped and their families to enjoy a cruising holiday on narrowboats specially fitted out with hydraulic lifts for wheelchairs, correspondingly wider doors and beds, assistance bars and grips, modified toilets and washbasins – in short, all the features required to ensure that for the handicapped life aboard a boat is as comfortable as it can be made; even, in some cases, extending to the provision of wheel-steering so that the wheelchair-bound may lend a hand in navigating the boat.

Almost all companies allow hirers to take along their pets – usually dogs and cats – subject to certain conditions (see p. 114). Dogs in particular seem to enjoy waterways travel providing they are not confined too much to the boat and are allowed enough exercise on the bank – for more reasons than one! Like young children, dogs should be supervised at all times, and kept under close control at locks and while negotiating tunnels and aqueducts; even the best-disciplined dog may take it into its head suddenly to jump overboard, with perhaps disastrous consequences, and may even place the crew at risk in trying to rescue it (for a fuller discussion of safety aboard, see Chapter 9). Nor should one overlook the fact that a dog is capable of doing considerable damage to a boat's interior if it is confined below without supervision while the boat is being worked through locks or during the crew's absence in search of liquid refreshment, and such damage will have to be paid for by the hirer.

Depending upon his own circumstances the hirer will have therefore to take into account a number of factors bearing on the final choice of cruising area and boat, but in choosing the former there is a further point to be considered: distance from home and means of getting there, both of which could involve the hirer in considerable extra expense, plus the inconvenience of long travelling times and maybe the cost of hotel accommodation. For the first-time hirer, then, it would seem reasonable to choose a cruising area not too far from home, but one that ideally offers the right choice of hire company and boat to suit his requirements, which is in fact what most beginners do.

The following are the principal inland cruising areas of Great Britain and the Irish Republic, with a brief note on their respective characteristics and the types of hire craft available (a more detailed account of individual waterways is given in Chapter 10).

ENGLAND AND WALES

The canal and river system

This comprises a vast interconnected network of waterways over 2,000 miles in total length, covering a great deal of England and a tiny part of Wales. Most of these waterways are administered by the British Waterways Board, and the remainder by independent bodies; the Thames, although part of the interconnected system, is described separately here because of its special status. With the exception of certain tideways – which are definitely *not* for beginners – these are all sheltered waters, the canals in particular being eminently suitable for the first-time hirer, although the choice of craft type is virtually limited to the narrowboat. Two great advantages among others of a canal holiday lie in the almost unrestricted choice of mooring places along towpaths and the sheer length of cruising waterways available; the frequency and the number of crew-operated locks are extremely varied, some canals being noted for their heavy lockage and others being lock-free. Locks on the Rivers Severn, Trent, and Weaver, and on the Yorkshire commercial waterways (Aire and Calder, Calder and Hebble, New Junction Canal, and the Sheffield and South Yorkshire Navigation) are mostly mechanized and operated by keepers, and some other waterways have manually operated locks attended by keepers in some cases (Warwickshire Avon, River Wey, the Fens).

Wide-beam hire craft are available on the navigations connecting with the main canal system. On the Rivers Severn and Avon there are wide-beam cruisers of both the 'launch' and 'pontoon' types, a few narrow-beam cruisers and great numbers of narrowboats; the York-shire waterways support wide- and narrow-beam cruisers plus a majority of narrowboats; in the Lincolnshire area wide-beam cruisers of both the 'launch' and 'pontoon' types, together with narrow-beam cruisers and narrowboats, are to be found on the River Trent and the Fossdyke and Witham Navigation, and the same variety of craft make up the hire fleets of the Fens. On the River Medway there are wide-beam cruisers and narrowboats, and the two canals detached from the main system also feature a choice of craft: on the Lancaster Canal wide-beam cruisers of the 'launch' type together with narrowboats and narrow-beam cruisers, and on the Brecon and Abergavenny Canal narrow-beam cruisers and narrowboats.

The River Thames

As might be expected of a river with such a long history of pleasure-boating, there is distributed along the length of the non-tidal section a great number of hire companies which between them offer an astonishing selection of craft. Wide-beam 'launch'-type cruisers predominate, but there are also many wide-beam 'pontoon'-type cruisers and some narrowboats. More narrowboats and one or two wide-beam 'pontoon'-type cruisers are based on the neighbouring River Wey, which connects with the Thames at Weybridge. The principal access from the Thames into the canal system is at Oxford, where there are two junctions with the Oxford Canal; the latter, being a narrow-gauge canal, is not navigable by wide-beam craft. The other access to the canal system is at Brentford, where the Grand Union Canal joins with the tideway. Although the Grand Union is a broad-gauge waterway, it is not accessible to wide-beam hire cruisers from the non-tidal Thames as hire craft from that area are generally forbidden to enter tidal waters. Locks on the river are mechanized and operated by keepers, but may be worked manually by boat crews outside working hours. Some sections of the river are liable to become very congested with traffic during the peak holiday season.

The Norfolk Broads

As has already been noted, this is an extremely popular cruising area, entirely detached from the main river and canal system. For the most part these are sheltered waters, although some larger broads may become a little rough in very windy conditions, and there are no locks to negotiate. There is a very wide choice of hire bases distributed throughout the area and offering a selection of wide-beam cruisers of both the 'launch' and 'pontoon' types. On account of the widespread appeal of the Broads there tends to be a lot of traffic over much of the season, and at peak holiday times certain areas are likely to become very crowded indeed.

Windermere

Of the ten major lakes in the Lake District, Windermere is the one selected some time ago as the principal water-based recreation area (powered craft being banned entirely from most of the others) as a result of which it supports a great deal of traffic during the summer holiday season. Being open water, the lake can become very rough at times, but this is not a serious matter as sheltered moorings are never far away on account of its relatively small size. Because of the limited cruising area, holidays on the lake are usually combined with visits 'ashore' to sample the many and varied attractions of Lakeland and its magnificent scenery. The few hire craft available are 'launch'-type wide-beam cruisers.

SCOTLAND

The Caledonian Canal

The term 'canal' as applied to this waterway is something of a misnomer, as artificial cut makes up no more than about one-third of its total length, the rest consisting of lochs, including the famous

Loch Ness. The navigation traverses the entire course of the Great Glen with its truly spectacular mountain scenery, providing through passage for small ships from coast to coast. All locks are powered and operated by keepers; the normal limit of navigation for hire craft at the western end is the head of Banavie locks, but hirers with sufficient experience may be permitted to enter the tidal waters of Loch Linnhe below the flight. No hire craft are allowed to proceed beyond the top of the locks at the eastern end of the canal. Being open waters, the lochs can get very rough in wild weather, but all the hire cruisers available from the several bases in the area are sea-going-type wide-beam cruisers and will safely cope with these conditions.

Loch Lomond

Situated in a superb mountain landscape, Loch Lomond, with its area of about twenty-seven square miles, is the second largest freshwater lake in the United Kingdom (for comparison, the largest is Lough Neagh in Northern Ireland, covering about 150 square miles). Towards the southern end of the loch are numerous islands, making navigation by chart sometimes necessary. The loch can be very rough at times, but there are sufficient sheltered moorings in case of bad weather. All hire craft are 'launch'-type wide-beam cruisers.

NORTHERN IRELAND

Lough Erne

This navigation consists of two lakes – the Upper and the Lower loughs – joined together by the River Erne. The waterway is vast and mostly very complicated, and although the channels are well marked chart reading is necessary at times. Lower Lough Erne in particular presents a large stretch of open water, and can turn very rough in strong winds. The scenery is impressively beautiful, and there is no shortage of places to visit, exploration being the essence of a cruising holiday on these waters. Several hire companies offer a good selection of wide-beam 'launch'-type cruisers.

THE IRISH REPUBLIC

The River Shannon

The Shannon winds its way down the middle of Ireland through scenery that is always beautiful and in places wild and remote. It joins together a number of loughs of which the two largest, Lough Derg and Lough Ree, are almost like inland seas, requiring the use of navigation charts and binoculars to follow the navigation buoys and markers. The passage of these large open stretches of water can be extremely hazardous in high winds and in poor visibility, and should not be attempted by novices in these conditions. Otherwise, cruising is generally fairly straightforward; the few locks on the river are all operated by keepers, and there are many places of interest to visit and numerous excellent moorings. The hire craft are 'launch'-type wide-beam cruisers, of which there is a good selection based at boatyards distributed along the length of the navigation.

The Grand Canal and the Barrow Navigation

Long since deprived of any commercial role, the Grand Canal traverses the wild and remote peat bogs of central Ireland on its way from Dublin to Shannon Harbour, where it connects with the River Shannon. Locks are manually operated with keepers in attendance, and help from boat crews is generally welcomed. The one hire base on the canal is equipped with narrowboats, which may be taken down the Barrow Navigation, the length of the Grand Canal and also on to the Shannon in its middle section, but entry into Lough Derg and Lough Ree is not permitted.

The canalized River Barrow runs south from a junction with the Grand Canal near Robertstown, and although very beautiful it can be dangerous in flood conditions due to the unguarded weirs and strong currents. Conversely, after a dry spell water levels may drop considerably, making passage through the shallows hazardous and the use of a chart essential. Hire craft are not allowed to enter the tideway below St Mullins. Locks are manually operated by keepers, whose advice regarding navigation matters should always be taken. At the time of writing there are no hire bases on this river.

Detailed information concerning the amenities associated with the navigations described above is given in the guides and maps listed in Appendix I.

CHOOSING THE HIRE BASE AND THE BOAT

Once the question of the cruising area has been settled the hirer can then consider which base he would like to start from, and the choice of boat that would best suit his requirements. In fact the latter is likely to be the deciding factor, for the simple reason that any one base cannot possibly offer the full range of craft sizes and designs that are available in any particular area.

Some companies do not market their boats themselves but choose instead to use the services of a booking agency, which is then responsible for all advertising, brochure production and distribution, and bookings on behalf of the company; the agency itself is totally independent of all the firms it represents and does not own any bases or boats (contrary to the impression sometimes given), nor is it party to the contract between client and hire company. There can be little doubt that an agency can provide publicity and other services on a scale that many hire operators could not hope to match, but from the hirer's point of view there is a corresponding loss of quality in the information contained in agency brochures. Because of the sheer number of craft dealt with in some brochures (about 3,000 in one fairly recent case), illustrations and plan drawings are tiny, and descriptions of individual boats are sketchy to say the least, tending to call for reliance more on faith than judgement in coming to a decision. Of course, more detailed information regarding a chosen craft may be obtained directly from the hire company concerned (some even publish their own supplementary brochure), but as agencies do not advertise company addresses and telephone numbers the hirer will either have to obtain these from Directory Inquiries or by consulting the *Inland Waterways Guide* (see p. 304).

There are three specialist agencies dealing with boating holidays in Great Britain and Ireland:

Hoseasons Holidays Ltd, Sunway House, Lowestoft, Suffolk NR32 3LT. Telephone: Lowestoft (0502) 62181 (for Norfolk Broads); 62211 (for all other waterways)

Blakes Holidays, Wroxham, Norwich, Norfolk NR12 8DH. Telephone: Wroxham (06053) 2911 (for Norfolk Broads, 2/3 berth cruisers); 2913 (for Norfolk Broads, 4/5 berth cruisers); 2915 (for Norfolk Broads, 6–11 berth cruisers); 3221 (for the Canals, Severn and Avon, and the Fens); 3223 (for River Thames and Scotland); 3224 (for Northern Ireland and the Irish Republic)

Boat Enquiries Ltd, 43 Botley Road, Oxford OX2 0PT. Telephone: Oxford (0865) 727288 or 725333

The brochures produced by the 'independent' hire operators – that is, those companies that do not use the services of a booking agency – more often than not reach a much higher standard than do the agency brochures, and in some cases even provide details of possible cruising routes so that the hirer can see what is available before committing himself to a firm booking. Names, addresses and telephone numbers of the independent hire companies may be obtained from publications such as the *Inland Waterways Guide* or the *Waterway Users' Companion* (see p. 304), or from the advertisements carried by the monthly magazines *Canal and Riverboat* and *Waterways World*, both of which are obtainable from newsagents.

Once the relevant brochures have been acquired, select those boats that might be suitable and compare their relative costs. Boating holidays are not cheap, and some hire craft are very expensive indeed, but generally the hirer can expect a boat to be of a standard that bears some relation to the hire fee charged. Hire fees are not constant throughout the season, but vary according to the time of year: they are at their cheapest in the late winter and early spring, and again in the autumn; during the spring and early summer they rise gradually to the peak periods of July and August, with lesser peaks at Easter and Bank Holidays, before falling back to the winter rates, which commence about the beginning of November. If the hirer intends to take children of school age on the cruise he may be forced to book the holiday for the peak period during school vacation, but this time of year is best avoided if possible on account of cost and the crowded conditions on some waterways. Late summer and early autumn are perhaps the best periods in which to try out a boating holiday for the first time, for although the hire rates are not at their lowest, at least the hirer stands a better chance with the weather than in the early spring, when cold rain and wind, and even snowstorms, can make for unpleasant boating conditions.

Further savings on cost may be offered by the hire company in the form of discounts – an increasing tendency in recent years – although the two most common discounts, reduction of charges for a second, and any subsequent consecutive, week's holiday, and a reduction for previous clients of the company, are not likely to be of much use to the first-time hirer, who in any case does not qualify for the latter, and who on the whole will probably be inclined to restrict his first boating holiday to a period of one week.

As a general rule boats are priced according to both their size and the number of fixed berths available, including convertible settees and dinettes. Sometimes additional berths are on offer, usually in the form of temporary pipe cots, at an extra charge, but the wise hirer will avoid resorting to these as the extra numbers may lead to overcrowding. In fact, the very opposite course should be chosen, if the hirer can afford it, by selection of a boat that has one or two berths *more* than the number required by the party, thereby giving much more room and storage space for each person, with correspondingly increased comfort. One further point regarding cost: some larger boats are advertised as being suitable for two families and are laid out accordingly, with the added advantage that the cost per head is reduced considerably when the hire fee is split between eight to ten, and sometimes twelve, persons. This is not disputed, but the lower cost is paid for in much reduced space for each individual, and the respective families would have to be on the friendliest of terms to avoid all possibility of friction. The first-time hirer would be well advised to have nothing to do with this sort of situation, but limit the crew members to his own family or group of friends.

Once the choice of boat has been made, be as sure as possible that it is the right one, for it is unlikely that an alternative will be available later on. Any uncertainty in this direction can, of course, be removed by visiting the hire base and viewing the boat at first hand before making a firm booking, always providing that the base is within reasonable distance of the hirer's home. The visit could provide an enjoyable day's outing for the family, and whatever the decision reached, it will not have been a waste of time. The intending visitor should telephone the company beforehand to make mutually suitable arrangements as no hire operator is likely to be overjoyed at the prospect of someone appearing unannounced on his doorstep on a Saturday or Sunday morning during the season (these are the commonest 'turn-round' days for hire fleets, and on these days most boats are apt to be back at base) when all the staff are very busy with cleaning and servicing the boats in readiness for their new crews and have little time to spare for other matters. But there is no harm in trying to arrange for a visit at a weekend: you may be welcomed with open arms, especially if business happens to be slack. Just after the end of the cruising season is certainly a convenient time for inspecting boats, as all the fleet will be at base and still in cruising trim prior to the winter strip-down for maintenance and repair. A few companies even go to the trouble of arranging 'open days' sometime during the winter months, when selected craft are made available for viewing by the public; the dates on which open days occur may be mentioned in the firm's brochure, or perhaps advertised in the waterways press. Any hire company that refuses a reasonable request to inspect its boats should be regarded with the gravest suspicion, for one can only draw the conclusion that they have something to hide, and should be told by the prospective hirer that he is prepared to take his business elsewhere.

HIRE FEES AND CONDITIONS OF HIRE

Not all companies present information regarding the total cost of hire in a completely clear fashion, and therefore the hirer must be careful to decide which – if any – extras apply in his particular case and include them in computing the overall fee. This is especially important when comparing the relative costs of boats from different companies, for obvious reasons.

There are basically two ways in which hire fees are presented: the inclusive and the non-inclusive tariffs. The inclusive tariff covers the hire charge for the boat and its equipment, all bottled gas, fuel, complete bedding, pets and car parking at the base (charges are always calculated on a minimum of one week's hire, but depending upon the level of bookings some operators are prepared to let their craft for a lesser period at a reduced price). VAT at the current standard rate is almost always not included in the published prices, and must be added to the hire fee unless the company states that it is exempt. Any optional extras available, such as television sets, bicycles, dinghies, additional berths, cruising licences for other water-ways, transport to and from local railway stations, and so on, are charged for separately, although some companies provide some of these items free. Pump-out toilets almost invariably need to be emptied at some stage of a cruise, and the service has to be paid for on the spot by the hirer, but most companies will refund the cost (amounting to a few pounds) on production of a receipt.   In the case of the non-inclusive tariff the hire fee for the boat and its equipment is shown as a basic charge, to which must be added, as required by the hirer, the extra costs of those items covered by the inclusive tariff: namely, fuel, bedding, pets and car parking. The argument advanced in favour of this method of costing is that it allows the hirer to reduce the total fee by paying only for those items he actually needs; after all, why should one pay for pets, bedding or car parking when any or all of these may not be required? And why, if one intends to make a relatively short cruise, should one subsidize by paying an inclusive fee the fuel expenditure of those who travel long distances? These, to my mind, are specious arguments and are clearly weighted in favour of the hire company, for what matters most in the end is the total cost of hiring the boat, and how this is arrived at is irrelevant. Further-more, many people prefer to know in advance exactly what the total cost will be, and tend to regard any extras – particularly those whose cost is uncertain at the outset – with suspicion and annoyance.

Where fuel is subject to a separate charge the hirer pays for it by means of a substantial fuel deposit, from which is deducted the cost of the fuel actually used during the cruise, and the remainder refunded; or, if the cost of the fuel used exceeds the amount of the fuel deposit, the hirer must pay the extra, usually by deduction from the security deposit. From the hirer's point of view this is scarcely a satisfactory arrangement, for not only is he uncertain as to the probable size of the fuel bill, but in the end has no idea how much was actually used (hire craft are not, as a rule, fitted with fuel gauges), nor what it cost per gallon, which, on the part of some hire companies, can be excessively high. The situation is even worse with petrol engines which have a relatively high fuel consumption; scarcely any companies include the cost of petrol in the total hire fee, leaving the hirer responsible for the purchase of his own fuel and so adding considerably to holiday expenses.

To summarize: the hirer, having first obtained brochures and hire tariffs, should select those boats suited to his requirements and compare their relative sizes and costs, not forgetting to include any extras entailed by the non-inclusive tariffs, add VAT if applicable (note that VAT is not chargeable on fuel) and try to assess the relative *value-for-money* of the selected boats. If possible, he should visit the hire base to make sure that the final choice is a wise one, but in any case first read the brochure again thoroughly, including the Conditions of Hire, so that any queries may be cleared up before a firm booking is made.

CONDITIONS OF HIRE

The Conditions of Hire, which form the basis of the contract between the hirer and the hire company, vary to some extent from company to company, but all contain more or less standard clauses that differ only in detail, although the differences may sometimes be important: for instance, a few companies permit suitably experienced hirers to take their vessels on to tidal waters, and so any hirer wishing to do this must select a boat from one of those companies. The following is a brief explanation of the more common clauses:

Booking

All hire charges are payable in advance. Hire of the boat is secured only after the receipt by the company of a signed booking form and deposit, and a confirmation of booking issued by the company. The amount of deposit varies, depending on the company, from about one-fifth to about one-third of the hire fee, but hirers from overseas may be required to pay a larger deposit, even up to the full hire fee. The balance, including any VAT, becomes due from fourteen to fifty-six days before the start of the holiday, again depending upon the company. In the event of cancellation by the hirer he remains responsible for payment in full unless the company is successful in reletting the boat at the full hire fee, in which case the hirer will have his money returned, less a certain proportion to cover administrative costs. Should the company only be able to relet the boat at less than the full hire fee, the hirer will be obliged to pay the difference.

Cancellation schemes

Most hire companies will insure clients against their liabilities in the event of cancellation of the booking. The amount and nature of the cover varies among companies; the vast majority will allow refunds for only specific and limited reasons, such as illness, death, or accident involving any member of the party, jury service, and redundancy, and not all will refund the full hire fee; in some cases the insurance becomes invalid at a certain stated date prior to the start of the holiday. A few companies include cancellation insurance in the total hire fee, but most consider it an optional extra subject to an additional charge, although in the case of some companies the hirer is given no choice and must pay the cancellation fee. The last is an obligation that may not be welcomed by hirers in certain circumstances: for example, one or more persons dropping out from a group of friends is unlikely to cause the cancellation of a holiday in the same way that illness of a family member certainly would. In complete contrast, one or two companies offer cancellation schemes that are not only optional, but which provide for full refunds unconditionally.

Hiring restrictions

Most companies will not accept bookings from persons under eighteen, and sometimes twenty-one, years of age, and some will not hire out craft to youth groups and school parties on the grounds of increased risk of damage to boats and equipment. In some cases all-male and all-female parties are banned, or perhaps reluctantly accepted on payment of an increased security deposit. At the start of the holiday the company may, at its discretion, refuse to hand over a boat to any person who is deemed not fit to take charge, in which case the hire fee will be refunded in full.

Inventory

Normally the boat's inventory should be checked before departure so that any damaged or missing items may be replaced, as the hirer is liable for the cost of all such items at the end of the holiday.

Insurance by the company

All companies provide insurance cover for the boat and its equipment together with indemnity against third party claims up to a stated amount. This cover is included in the hire fee, but the hirer is responsible for an excess sum, commonly called the 'security deposit', from which small claims are deducted; this sum varies from about £25 up to about £100, depending upon circumstances. Should no claims or losses occur the security deposit is usually returned to the hirer within two weeks of the end of the holiday. Boat insurance does not cover injury to any member of the crew, nor loss of, and damage to, personal effects. Some companies will provide cover for these contingencies at an extra charge.

Hire period

Boats are usually made available during the afternoon of the first day of the hire period with the requirement that they are to be returned and vacated between 9 and 10 a.m. on the last day; some companies start their hire period in the late morning of the first day and end it in the late afternoon of the last. Return times must be strictly adhered to, for obvious reasons, and any serious delay caused by a late return may involve the hirer in claims for liquidated damages. Similar claims may be made for returning the boat in a dirty condition. In the event of the booked boat not being available and the company being unable to supply a suitable alternative, all money paid will be refunded, and the hirer debarred from further claim. Companies are usually strict about the number of persons aboard a boat, which must not exceed that agreed before the start of the cruise.

Delays

Any delays during the cruise, or non-completion of the proposed route due to breakdown, damage to the boat, floods, drought, obstruction of the navigation and the like, are deemed not to be the responsibility of the hire company, and therefore no claims in this respect will be allowed (in practice many companies are willing to make some refund if the cruise is seriously curtailed by persistent faults in the boat's engine or other equipment). Companies generally reserve the right to operate from an alternative base should they be forced to by circumstances beyond their control, such as navigation closures, flood, drought, engineering works and so on, in which case the hirer cannot expect any adjustment of the hire fee.

Accidents and loss of water

In the event of an accident the hirer is under an obligation to make an immediate and full report of the circumstances, including the names and addresses of any witnesses, to the hire company, and is specifically instructed never to admit liability. Failure to comply with either of these requirements may invalidate the insurance and leave the hirer responsible for any claims that may arise. The hirer will also be liable for any claims brought by water and navigation authorities for loss of water and damage to property caused by his own negligence. No repairs to the boat and its equipment are to be put in hand without the express permission of the hire company. Some companies reserve the right to repossess a boat following an accident if it appeared to have occurred because of the unsuitability of the hirer, or if there is a likelihood of further accident, in which case no refund will be made.

Boat instruction and the trial run

Upon take-over the company will provide detailed instruction and demonstration of the boat's equipment, engine and controls, and will take the hirer on a short trial run during which some boat-handling instruction will be given if necessary. Canal hire companies also give advice on lock-working, with an actual demonstration if a lock is conveniently close to hand. Once the hire company is satisfied that the hirer is reasonably competent, the boat will be handed over to him (but see under Hiring Restrictions, p. 111) and he will be solely responsible for its safe navigation from then on. It should be noted that no minor is allowed to control a hire craft without the immediate supervision of a competent adult.

Navigational restrictions

The hirer is required at all times to abide by the current by-laws of the water or navigation authority whose waterway he is cruising; ignorance of the relevant by-laws is held to be no excuse should infringement occur. Most hire firms prohibit their boats from cruising on tidal waters, and towing other craft, without the express consent of the company; navigation during the hours of darkness and in very restricted visibility is not permitted, nor may craft enter in races. It is common for companies to reserve the right to restrict cruising limits should unusual circumstances arise.

Fuel supplies

Bottled gas is always included in the hire fee, and the brochure will make clear whether the same applies to fuel. Should either of these items be in short supply for reasons beyond the control of the company, such supplies as exist will normally be shared out on an equitable basis, and the company will reimburse the hirer with the cost of fuel thus saved (this applies only to the inclusive tariff). Many companies will treat the hired craft as a stationary houseboat in the event of engine fuel becoming non-available, with a corresponding reduction in the hire fee of between one-third and one-half.

Hirer's property and pets

Companies generally disclaim any responsibility for loss of, and damage to, property belonging to the hirer, including vehicles and their contents parked at the base, unless due to negligence. Where pets are accepted on board craft they must be kept under control at all times, and not allowed to lie on bedding and seats. Any damage caused by pets must be paid for by the hirer. Many companies will not allow the hirer to take aboard the boat certain appliances, such as portable heaters, lighting equipment, TV sets, cooking stoves or electrical equipment (other than electric razors), without prior permission.

Brochure descriptions

With regard to brochure descriptions and other information supplied to the hirer there is usually a disclaimer to the effect that layout plans of craft are for general guidance and are not to scale, and may be subject to modification during construction or refitting.

The Conditions of Hire may generally appear to be heavily loaded in favour of the hire company, but in practice they are likely to pose few problems for the hirer who is prepared to exercise proper caution and common sense. The Conditions must obviously take into account the fact that at any one time a large proportion of hirers are complete novices, and that a not inconsiderable number are what might be termed 'improvers', and therefore the Conditions are framed in such a way as to offer them some guidance and protection, and at the same time make provision for the rights and interests of waterways authorities and waterways users in general.

CHAPTER FIVE

PLANNING AND PREPARATIONS FOR THE CRUISE

It cannot be stressed too often that the choice of cruising area and boat depends a great deal on what the hirer expects of a boating holiday. Navigation of the large lakes of Scotland and Ireland, particularly in rough conditions, has something of the flavour of off-shore cruising, in almost complete contrast with the more gentle atmosphere of the enclosed and still waters of the narrow canals, even though both come under the heading of inland cruising. And, as we have seen, the choice of cruising area determines almost entirely the types of hire craft available and the amount of physical effort to be put into the holiday; all of which, together with the length of the hire period, have some bearing on the degree of planning involved in a cruise.

The least amount of planning is associated with an 'out-and-back' cruise taken in short and easy daily stages over, say, a period of one week, and with no definite destination in mind. From the hirer's point of view this is certainly the most carefree and relaxing kind of boating holiday, and one in which decisions about what to do and how much further to cruise are taken purely on a daily basis without any obligation to maintain a certain rate of progress other than that required to get the boat back to base on time. But even this necessity is easily resolved, for the relatively short total distance the boat will have travelled by mid week leaves a decent safety margin for the return journey in case of unforeseen delay. Some thought needs to be given, of course, to matters such as buying provisions, taking on water, and in some cases, emptying the toilet, but even these tasks can be dealt with in a fairly leisurely fashion when visits ashore are likely to be frequent.

All the various cruising areas are suitable for this 'go-as-you-please' sort of holiday taken over a period of one week, but if the intention is to cruise for a longer duration and at a higher rate of progress then certain areas begin to have their limitations, and this happens in three ways. First, a longer holiday period creates the opportunity for much more distance to be covered; second, the relatively deep waters of these areas permit comparatively high boat speeds; and third, the areas concerned are simply not extensive enough to sustain this kind of cruising without much retracing of one's steps over the same ground. These cruising areas and their approximate total lengths are: Windermere (ten and a half miles); Loch Lomond (twenty-four miles); Lough Erne (fifty-three miles); Caledonian Canal (sixty miles); River Thames and the Norfolk Broads (each 125 miles). None of these navigations forms part of a waterway network (except for the Thames, but as already explained, most hire craft from the river are not permitted to enter the canal system), so therefore all cruising on them is of the 'out-and-back' variety, thus effectively doubling the total lengths given above, and all are best suited to the 'go-as-you-please' boating holiday planned on a day-to-day basis, perhaps within a fairly loose overall framework of interests and objectives. The topography of large island-studded lakes such as Lough Erne and Loch Lomond provides additional variety and excitement in the opportunities presented for cross-lake cruising and exploration, but in the case of Windermere the possibilities are very limited, as was made clear in the previous chapter.

The waterways of the Irish Republic are much more extensive, having a total length of no less that 280 miles, of which the River Shannon forms about 130, the Barrow Navigation about seventy, and the Grand Canal about eighty miles, providing between them over 560 miles of 'out-and-back' cruising. The greater part of these three waterways may be covered in about three weeks, but I think to indulge in this sort of hard going is to miss the whole point of holiday cruising in Ireland, which is surely to relax and enjoy the peaceful charm of the superb rivers and loughs, and to slip into the easy-going ways of the Irish country people themselves. The Shannon is, so to speak, made for 'go-as-you-please' cruising, and two weeks seem not long enough to explore the many attractions of its waterside settlements and remote harbours. Even if some little time is spent ashore, progress can be surprisingly rapid, for in its whole length there are few locks, and the deep waters of the river and loughs together with a thinly spread boat traffic mean that consistently high speeds can be maintained. Day-to-day planning is certainly to be recommended for this waterway (and for the Grand Canal and Barrow Navigation), not only for the reasons outlined above, but also because progress along its length is to some extent controlled by the weather conditions on the great expanses of Lough Ree and Lough Derg.

THE CANALS: PLANNING THE CRUISE

Boating on canals is utterly unlike river and lake cruising, and has over the years produced its own brand of enthusiast completely devoted to canals and their history, to the techniques of working the navigation, and above all to that symbol of canals, the narrowboat. During his first cruise the beginner could find himself caught up in this same enthusiasm; it is extremely addictive and may easily last for a lifetime. But perhaps all that lies in the future, and at the moment the hirer is wondering just what are the essential requirements in planning a canal cruise and how, given the necessity for a prompt arrival back at base, does one time a voyage lasting several days when the average speed of the boat is not likely to exceed a slow walking pace? And if much time has been lost for any reason, how can it be made up again when the boat's speed is so severely restricted and cruising during the hours of darkness prohibited? The mere fact that these questions can be asked at all indicates that canal cruising may not quite conform to that picture which undoubtedly exists in some people's minds of a totally carefree, slightly boring amble by boat along a series of somewhat uninteresting ditches during which there is nothing better to do than think of the timing of the next meal, or whether the pub ahead will be open! The reality, it turns out, is rather different.

The connected system of canals and rivers is about 2,250 miles long, of which canals comprise about three-fifths and join together various waterways in the form of a network, thus making possible many circular routes – or 'rings' – of differing lengths and combinations. As we have already seen, the 'go-as-you-please' type of cruise is always of the 'out-and-back' kind (unless the hirer has a great deal of time at his disposal, which would be unusual), but if the hirer sets himself a definite objective – as he certainly does on a circular trip, and may do on an 'out-and-back' cruise – then the need for advance planning becomes paramount.

In my opinion circular trips tend to be the more interesting as they do not entail retracing one's steps over the same ground, and somehow give a greater feeling of adventure in that one is always involved in traversing new country. Not that 'out-and-back' cruises are without their good points too: the surrounding countryside can look very different from the opposite direction, and the return trip does provide opportunities for visiting places of interest noted on the outward leg. In either case the temptation to cram in the greatest possible distance should be strongly resisted. For one thing, the first-time hirer does not have the experience to know what can be safely achieved in the time available, and the necessity to return the boat to base in an undamaged condition and within the stipulated time must take precedence over all else. To be certain of this the hirer should very carefully assess the halfway point of the planned cruise – and this applies to both circular and 'out-and-back' routes – so that in the event of an unforeseen and serious delay occurring before this point is reached he will know that an immediate turn-round must be made in the direction of base. The necessity for a premature return will be directly related to the amount of time allowed as a safety margin: the larger the safety margin the less the total length of the cruise and so the less chance of a serious delay affecting the planned itinerary – with the added bonus of a certain peace of mind springing from the knowledge that one has not bitten off more than one can chew.

The hirer who does not wish to be bothered with the details of route planning can always consult the hire company as to suitable cruises – indeed, some companies not only produce lists of routes that can be covered in a week or a fortnight together with total mileages and number of locks, but give detailed advice on moorings, lengths of daily stages, pubs, restaurants and so on. These recommended routes have in general been carefully selected as suitable for first-time hirers and some indication is given as to whether they are strenuous or easy, although the latter will depend to some extent on the number of active persons making up the boat's crew.

By following a published route the beginner certainly does relieve himself of any worries over what may be accomplished during the period of the holiday, but he also misses one of the pleasures associated with canal cruising: the crew's discussions about where and how far to go, the working out of the route and the distances to be covered in each daily stage, where to stop for shopping, watering-up and a pump-out, and making allowances for special visits to places of interest (buying porcelain in Worcester, going to the zoo at Chester, travelling on the Worth Valley steam railway at Keighley).

But before the route is planned in any detail a current list of stoppages should be obtained from the hire company or, failing that, the appropriate navigation authority. The very nature of canals and their associated engineering works means that, as compared with other navigations, much more maintenance work is required, and this sometimes results in complete closure of a section. The work is usually planned well in advance, and nearly all of it takes place during the months of late autumn, winter and early spring, but bad weather can prolong the stoppage programme into the cruising season, and unannounced or very short notice closures for urgent repairs may occur at any time. The latter, of course, cannot be taken into account when planning a cruise, and although sudden closure of a navigation may entail on-the-spot modification of the intended route, it would be a rare occurrence indeed if it resulted in abandonment of a cruise altogether. Sometimes hire bases are placed in a disadvantageous position by scheduled stoppages, in which case the boats are usually moved to a temporary base until the navigation is reopened, and inform their hirers accordingly.

Stoppages and restrictions are not always solely due to maintenance or engineering works, but may be caused by weather conditions. Unlike rivers, canals are not prone to flooding (at least, not in the same way), but they are vulnerable to drought, when locks may be worked only during certain hours each day, or closed altogether if water shortage becomes very severe. However, droughts by their nature are never sudden, and when approaching a critical stage are usually well publicized by the media; in any case, the hirer who is in doubt can always contact the hire base to find out what the local conditions are like, and if necessary amend his itinerary. River floods are a more serious matter, for not only are they liable to occur very quickly, but the rising speed and power of river currents can be extremely dangerous even for the experienced boater, and in these circumstances all pleasure-boat traffic is brought to a halt, sometimes for several days. There is no way that advance planning can allow for a contingency such as this, but the hirer should be aware of its possibility, and in the event be prepared if necessary to abandon the remainder of the intended route if a delay caused by floods is prolonged. Where a planned canal route includes a stretch of river cruising the risk of delay caused by floods may be avoided completely by allowing for an alternative continuation by canal, to be taken should weather conditions become severe enough to stop boat traffic on the river.

Having ascertained that the intended route is not subject to scheduled stoppages, the hirer may then proceed with the detailed planning.

On the canal system the rate at which ground is covered is slow indeed as compared with that possible on river navigations, as the shallowness and restricted cross-section of many canals simply prohibits any speed above a lively walking pace. For the beginner this leisurely progress will, if anything, be further impaired by his slowness in lock-working, running aground and being blown aground in windy weather, and suchlike delays due to inexperience, all of which may result in a lower average than anticipated. As experience grows, so the rate of progress might be expected to increase, of course, but for novice and experienced boater alike the only way to cover more distance is to put in the necessary time, which means long days on the move combined with a minimum of stops for shopping, watering-up, sight-seeing, and so on. How many hours are spent at the tiller is up to the individual; suffice it to say that very long days of almost continuous cruising can be extremely tiring, especially if combined with a great deal of lock-work, and doubly so if done in bad weather conditions. Carried to extremes this sort of cruising can lead to debilitating fatigue in all crew members after a few days, and morale will consequently suffer, with perhaps disastrous effects on the enjoyment of the holiday. Once this stage has been reached there may well be a temptation to throw all considerations of good manners and observance of the rules overboard – a situation to be avoided at all costs in the interests of other boaters and waterway users, besides being thoroughly bad boating practice. No one, I am sure, would wish to advertise his incompetence – for that is what it is – in this way. The competent boater is one who observes good manners on the waterways *all of the time*, who makes no fuss and travels quietly and smoothly over a cruising route carefully selected and matched to the time available for its completion and to his own expertise.

Time and distance – these are the primary factors to be considered when planning any route, and, as I have already stressed, this applies with particular force to canal cruising. With regard to time the hirer knows precisely how much he has at his disposal, right up to the minute when his holiday will end and he must vacate the boat, but distance is a different matter, and this is where cruising guides and maps enter the picture. The cruising guide is an invaluable aid to the navigator, including as it does virtually all the information likely to be needed on a trip: shopping places, location of drinking water and chemical toilet disposal points, pump-out stations, pubs, post offices, public telephones, places of interest and so on. The waterways themselves may be shown with their natural bends and twists, or as a straight line for convenience in layout, but in all cases the linear distances will be easy to compute as the maps are to scale or have mileages marked, or both, and all locks, fixed and movable bridges, tunnels and aqueducts are shown – in short, everything likely to be of assistance to the boater (for a list of maps and guides, see Appendix I).

From a study of this information the hirer is able to break down the total cruising distance into daily stages, but there still remains the problem of deciding how fast the ground may be covered. It is plain that we have two considerations here: first, the actual speed of the boat, and second, the amount of time spent in operating locks and movable bridges. The last two may be lumped together for convenience, so we are left with two apparently incompatible considerations which somehow have to be reconciled. If we think about the problem, however, we can see that both involve the element of *time*, and it is this common factor which allows us to regard boat speed and locking as in some way equivalent from the point of view of calculating time and distance. Here the beginner will meet one of those differences of opinion that seem to characterize inland cruising.

Some authorities maintain that, as regards time equivalent, one mile equals one lock: that is, during the time taken to work a boat through a lock it could have travelled a distance of one mile along the canal; but others say that in the time required to travel one mile, two locks may be worked. In the first case the number of locks in a given distance is added to the number of miles to give a total expressed in the unit known as a 'lock-mile', but in the second case the total number of locks is first halved and then added to the miles, again producing an equivalent number of lock-miles which, when divided by the time element, gives an average rate of progress measured in 'lock-miles per hour'. As it is obvious that the two methods give greatly differing results, which is the more accurate?

The answer mostly depends on the speed of the boat, and this must not exceed four miles per hour, which is the general speed limit over much of the canal network (speeds of this order are attainable, *without bank wash*, on only a few canals, excluding the major commercial navigations). When lock-miles are the straightforward sum of locks and miles, the higher the boat's speed the more realistic becomes the time allowance for lock-working, and vice versa. For instance, an average boat speed of three miles per hour equates with a time of twenty minutes to work each lock, which on the face of it might not seem unreasonable, but I incline to the view that a three miles per hour *average* speed is a little too high, and that two and a half miles per hour is more realistic, as I shall explain. To adopt this figure increases the locking time to twenty-four minutes per lock, which is – again on average – excessive, and although by equating one mile with two locks we halve the time allowed for locking, I think that this is overdoing things in the opposite direction.

A better solution, it seems to me, is to forget lock-miles altogether and simply add the results of two separate calculations: one for boat speed, and the other for lock-working. My reason for suggesting this is because conditions on the canal system have changed rapidly during the last few years, and congestion – particularly in the more popular areas and at peak holiday periods – has inevitably resulted in a general reduction in average boat speeds, notably on stretches where queuing for locks has become almost a daily occurrence. Consequently, the difference in the length of time to be allowed for a cruise in peak periods as against one taken in the relatively quiet spring and autumn months may be considerable, and this applies to both beginner and experienced boater alike. It is therefore more advisable to calculate cruising times according to the amount of traffic expected on the route than to adhere rigidly to the lock-mile concept, which takes no account of variations such as those just described. Peak holiday periods are also times when an above average amount of angling is probably taking place, and this is a factor which should figure in anyone's cruising calculations; boats should always slow right down when passing anglers, and obviously where there is a lot of fishing being done over considerable lengths of waterway this can result in a marked reduction in average speed.

Increased boating activity also implies that there is an added risk of collision at blind bends and bridge-holes, which the careful steerer will take into account, exercising special caution at such places accordingly.

It is for these reasons that I suggest an average boat speed of two and a half miles per hour as the figure to be used when calculating rates of progress on canals, with an allowance of fifteen minutes for working through each lock or movable bridge – these times applying in the first instance to peak holiday periods on heavily trafficked canals. On this basis the beginner could expect to cover a minimum distance of either twenty-five lock-free miles or, say, eighteen miles and twelve locks in the course of ten hours spent at the tiller. I stress that this is a *minimum* distance, because ample time has been allowed to accommodate the slowest conditions likely to be met, and it is a good principle to overestimate rather than underestimate time required. Moreover, the crew will almost certainly wish to moor up at intervals for shopping, visiting pubs or whatever, and it is always a wise course to top up water tanks each day. The daily itinerary should take these tasks into account using the information given in the cruising guides, with starting and finishing times planned accordingly: for instance, it is no use casting off at nine o'clock in the morning when the intention that day is to do some shopping in a town ten miles away and it happens to be half-day closing!

The guidelines for calculating times and distances that have been suggested are not to be regarded as infallible rules; they merely indicate to the beginner what he might reasonably make allowances for under certain conditions, and as his experience grows it will enable him to modify them. If the planned route includes a substantial section of cruising on rivers or major commercial canals the allowances for time should be altered considerably. On most of the larger rivers and the commercial canals a speed of six miles per hour is possible, and fifteen minutes should be allowed for the passage of each lock, although in the case of the Thames locking times may often be longer than this at peak holiday periods and weekends during the summer.

PERSONAL CLOTHING AND FOOTGEAR

When preparing for an active and unfamiliar type of holiday there is nearly always some uncertainty over how much to spend on the purchase of adequate gear and equipment. In the case of boating, there is occasionally no such uncertainty, as is obvious from the blissful oblivion of the few who from time to time arrive at their chosen hire base fully prepared for the rigours of a cruising holiday – the men clad in smart suits and the women impeccably dressed in flowered frocks and high heels. Fortunately such ignorance is rare, for most people these days are at least aware of the necessity to wear clothing suitable for outdoor activities, even if this sort of thing does not currently form part of their wardrobe.

What personal clothing and footgear to take depends broadly on two factors: the time of year and the type of boat. Bad weather is more likely during the early spring and the late autumn than during the middle months of the year, and so the proportion of warm clothing should be increased for these periods. Thermal underwear is excellent for boating in cold conditions, but for the first-time hirer is not an absolute necessity, as ordinary sweaters – preferably worn in several layers – will provide adequate warmth. Slacks or jeans will do for most boating, and the main clothing outfit is completed with the addition of a hip-length jacket or anorak. As much of a person's heat loss in cold weather goes from the head, it is advisable to wear some form of headgear such as a woolly hat, a cap or an anorak hood. In very cold conditions gloves become essential for most people, and these should preferably be both warm and windproof. Footgear should be chosen with some care and must have a type of sole least likely to slip (contrary to the impression given by some advertisements, there is no such thing as a *non*-slip sole), which means that smooth soles of any description are unsuitable, and steel-shod footwear must never be worn aboard boats because they damage walking surfaces. Training shoes and canvas boating shoes with a 'grip' sole are common favourites, but equally good are some types of lightweight boot with a patterned rubber sole, which have the added advantages of ankle protection and increased warmth. Some sort of rainproof outer clothing is necessary for wet weather, and this usually consists of a cagoule-type jacket and waterproof trousers; if these are worn with gumboots complete protection against the elements is assured, both on and off the boat.

The above advice applies to cruising in any type of boat, but particularly in the case of narrowboats, with their absence of weather protection for the steerer. All motor cruisers are fitted with an internal steering position, and whether this has a sliding roof, is in a collapsible wheelhouse, or is rigged with a removable canvas canopy, it can always be closed down in foul weather. Furthermore, the very nature of motor cruising, as we have seen, means that less time is spent on deck while working the boat, whereas for the narrowboat crew the opposite is often the case. The steerer of a narrowboat may have to spend long hours at the tiller in torrential rain and perhaps cold winds, and as he has to rely for warmth solely on the clothing he is wearing (unlike the helmsman of a motor cruiser, who in most cases is in a heated compartment), it is important that his outer garments are completely weatherproof. Makeshift gear will simply not do, nor will so-called 'showerproof' clothing, if the steerer is to remain reasonably comfortable. For maximum protection preferably he should wear a heavy duty PVC suit with hood, over anorak, sweaters and trousers, and in really cold conditions these will need to be augmented by some form of thermal underwear. The feet of anyone remaining virtually immobile, as the steerer does, are particularly susceptible to the effects of cold, and are probably best protected by wearing two pairs of thick woollen socks inside gumboots; if an insulating insole can be accommodated as well, so much the better. A steerer clad in this fashion can stand the worst of weather, but it must be stressed that extreme conditions of cold wind, continuous rain, and snow are rarely met with during the cruising season, although even for summer rain a good waterproof suit will be a great source of comfort. Some hire companies provide such suits as part of the boat's inventory, and if the hirer's company does not he would be well advised to borrow or buy one.

Summer cruising is generally a different matter altogether, and the choice of clothing correspondingly wider, although it is a good idea to include some warm clothing to cater for changes in the weather and for chilly evenings and mornings; the climate being what it is in this country, waterproofs for the whole crew should always be taken along. If the weather turns really hot, care should be exercised in leaving large areas of the body uncovered. Not only can this lead to heatstroke in some circumstances, but ultra-violet radiation is increased by reflection from the water and can cause severe sunburn. Other items of clothing, such as suits, dresses and so on for wear in pubs and restaurants are left to the discretion of the hirer; it is enough to say that the holiday wardrobe should be kept to reasonable proportions as closet and drawer space on boats is not unlimited. For this reason any suitcases in which clothes have been brought are best left in the car or stored at the base, and this applies also to boxes that have been used to transport food and may be required again when re-packing at the end of the holiday.

FOOD AND OTHER ITEMS

The initial stock of food taken aboard the boat should be at least enough to last until the first shopping trip of the cruise, which, if you start on a Saturday, will probably be two days later. Many hire companies will arrange for groceries to be delivered to the boat before the hirer gets there, and at some bases food may be bought at a grocery store on the site, perhaps with off-licence facilities as well.

For hirers with babies or small children some companies will provide a special cot-side that is fixed to the rail of a single berth to prevent accidents, and inquiries regarding the availability of these should be made at the time of booking.

Few companies include hand and bath towels on their inventories, and not all supply tea towels, washing-up liquid, soap and cleaning materials; if the inventory confirms this do not forget to take these items with you. A fairly powerful electric torch always comes in handy for boating and should be taken along together with your personal first-aid kit, even if these are provided on the boat. Aids for clearing obstructions from the propeller are not supplied (the hirer would be wise to forget those stories about using the bread knife from the galley), and some suggestions for a few suitable tools will be found on pp. 149–50; in connection with this and similar dirty tasks a small tin of chemical solvent, such as Swarfega, and some clean rags will be found very useful.

CHAPTER SIX

BOAT-HANDLING

On arrival at the base – preferably not more than half an hour before take-over time – the hirer should check in at the reception office, where he will be expected to pay any outstanding accounts and will be told whether the boat is ready for his party to board. When it is, all the food and gear can be taken below and stowed away, the inventory checked and cars driven off to the boatyard car park. A member of the company's staff will then demonstrate the working of the boat's equipment and fittings and what the hirer is expected to do in the way of daily maintenance – usually not much more than inspecting the levels of oil in the engine and gearbox, the level of engine cooling water, and giving the stern-gland greaser a couple of half-turns. Once all this has been explained to the hirer he is then shown how to start the engine and operate the controls, while the crew stands by ready to cast off.

For the first-time hirer unused to handling any type of craft the knowledge that he is about to be placed in sole charge of a large motor cruiser or a steel-hulled narrowboat displacing perhaps ten tons, can be nerve-racking. The boat-handling instruction given during the trial run will probably instil a little confidence in the hirer as he comes to realize that controlling a boat is not nearly so difficult as he had thought, and that the demonstrator's satisfaction with his performance indicates that he shows at least *some* aptitude, otherwise the chances are that he would not be allowed to take out the boat at all. The hire operator may refuse to hand over a boat to a completely inept crew, but such occasions are rare, as the great majority of hirers prove able to cope with the initial problems of steering a large and heavy craft, even if they do take some time to master the rudiments of manoeuvring in confined waters. Clearly, under the combined pressures of limited time and the understandable wish of the hirer to get away as soon as possible, only the bare bones of boat-handling can be imparted and probably most of that will shortly be forgotten in the general excitement of embarkation, leaving the hirer in a position where skill is largely acquired by trial and error. The only drawback is that error can be serious when one is dealing with a large boat, and the hirer would be well advised therefore not to rely solely on such last-minute instruction, but to study beforehand the principles of boat-handling so that he at least understands what it is he has to do, and why.

Simple though inland navigation may at first appear, as the novice gains experience he will discover that there is far more to be learned about it than meets the eye, and that the acquisition of boating skills depends not only on actual practice but also on the theoretical knowledge which underpins that practice. In what follows I have tried to keep theory to a minimum and to present it, in the main text, as simply as possible without undermining its implications for the better understanding of boating techniques, reserving certain fairly technical aspects of performance theory for inclusion in Appendices III and IV. Descriptions of boating techniques and related aspects of inland cruising are dealt with mainly in this chapter, and further information is included in Chapters 7 and 8. If it appears that the techniques associated with canals have been given undue prominence, this is because I believe that the novice canal boater has of necessity to learn a great deal more – at least initially – than his counterpart on a river cruiser, and that mastery of the difficulties to be encountered in navigating shallow and narrow waterways provides a more fitting introduction to the wider aspects of inland cruising.

TILLER-STEERING

All too often it is said – sometimes in hire firms' brochures – that if a person can drive a car then he can also drive a boat, implying that an acquired skill may be transferred automatically to a different situation, presumably on the grounds that both vehicles and boats have to be steered! This claim is, to say the least, ill advised, as it may mislead the unwary into assuming they possess skills that in fact they do not have, perhaps with dire consequences. What is probably nearer the truth is that those who had an initial aptitude for car driving may find that they also have an aptitude for steering boats. Even if this is so, they are not absolved from the necessity of learning to steer from scratch, but they may progress fairly quickly and easily as compared with those possessing less aptitude. It is better in the end to forget all about comparisons between cars and boats and concentrate on the details of boat-handling on its own account.

The majority of hire craft are equipped with only two controls: a single lever, operating both gearbox and throttle, and a tiller or wheel, and all manoeuvres under power are accomplished through the use of these two controls acting together. As we have seen in Chapter 3, from a central (neutral) position the lever control may be moved forwards, engaging forward gear and progressively increasing the throttle opening, and backwards, engaging reverse gear and similarly opening the throttle. All movements of the lever should be done deliberately and without haste (except in emergency) so as not to damage the mechanism and place undue strain on the cable and linkages. The tiller is normally held by the right hand, as most control consoles are positioned on the left-hand side of the boat, the steerer standing – or sitting if a seat is provided – between the tiller and the controls. Most novices will probably wish to stand, at least until they gain some confidence, in order to obtain better visibility, in which case the seat may be dismounted, if it is of the removable type, and stowed away where it cannot be tripped over.

The initial problem facing the novice is this: he cannot anticipate how the boat will respond to any of his actions, nor at what speed it will respond. The situation is worsened, if anything, by the fact that a large, steel-hulled boat takes considerable power to make it move at all, and then accelerates slowly, but once it is moving an equal amount of power is required to stop it again due to the momentum it has acquired, and it is precisely the factor of the momentum of the boat that the beginner cannot judge. He realizes, of course, that as a boat has no brakes, movement in one direction can be stopped only by applying power in the opposite direction until the craft is brought to a standstill. Rather ironically, one feature of boat-handling that always worries the novice is lack of time in which to think, even though he may be trying to execute manoeuvres at a speed no greater than a slow walking pace, or even less. These uncertainties concerning the probable outcome of his actions can give rise to a state of panic in which wrong decisions are made and ineffective measures taken, leading, for instance, to excessive – or insufficient – power being applied in an attempt to correct mistakes. Too much power, often applied for too long, is a common fault in the boat-handling of many novices as they try to overcome the inherent sluggishness of a boat's response. No amount of theoretical instruction can provide the novice with a sense of how the boat is likely to behave (except in the most general terms), and he can only acquire it through practical experience, by the 'feel' of the boat's movements, judgements of time and distance, and a sense of the amount of power being produced by the propeller – all of which require a long apprenticeship at the tiller, a willingness to learn by one's mistakes, careful observation of all that is happening, and a great deal of patience. If this sounds onerous, I can merely say that it is, in my opinion, the only way for the serious boater to acquire a reasonable degree of expertise on which to build in future years.

Narrowboats are almost always tiller-steered, and for good reasons. Not only is tiller-steering mechanically simple, it also gives an excellent 'feel' of the boat's movements as the water pressure on the rudder is transmitted directly through the rudder stock, ram's head and tiller to the steerer's hand and arm. This 'feel' is a very important factor in the control of a boat, particularly on canals, where navigation often requires steering of an accuracy not called for in most situations on open waters, and the experienced steerer achieves this by steering through the soles of his feet, so to speak, not by watching the banks and the movements of the tiller. However, the novice may be forced to think hard about the position of the tiller, remembering, for instance, that if it is moved to the left the boat's bow will swing to the right, and vice versa, and the harder over the tiller is pushed, the more pronounced the swing. To complicate matters further, the amount of power applied – that is, the higher the boat's speed – will also affect the rudder action and thereby increase the swing even more. An excellent rule is *always to use just enough power to accomplish what is necessary, and no more.* Applying this to steering, it is obvious that if one wishes to change direction quickly, and is using only half-throttle or less, there is not only a considerable amount of power in hand for the manoeuvre, but the boat feels more readily under control.

The wise beginner will therefore err on the side of caution by cruising at a lower, rather than a higher, speed, for not only will he then have a reserve of power in hand, but will also find that the tiller is lighter and more easily handled due to lessened pressure from propeller wash and torque, and there will be less tendency to 'snake' down the canal in an ever-increasing swing from side to side, caused by lack of anticipation and over-correction of the steering. To avoid this, watch the fore-end of the boat (that is, the fore-end of the superstructure, as on virtually all narrowboats the bow is hidden below the level of the coach roof as seen from the stern) and its position relative to the channel width, and make only the most gentle corrections to the steering, endeavouring always to 'feel' the position of the tiller corresponding to the boat's intended heading. Keep generally in the deeper water towards the middle of the canal, but if the bow feels to be swinging over slightly, let it do so; the channel often meanders to some extent and the boat will try to follow it, regardless of the steerer's intentions (the reason for this is given in Appendix III). Do not make the mistake of moving *too* slowly, as a boat needs 'steerage way' before it will respond to the tiller at all, 'steerage way' being the minimum speed through the water sufficient to cause a turning effect at the rudder, although in the case of powered craft the result of propeller wash acting upon the rudder is by far the most significant factor in causing initial change of direction, as we shall see.

So far I have dealt with a relatively simple situation, that of steering a course over a straight stretch of canal in which the novice has plenty of room to allow for errors, but sooner or later the boat will have to be navigated through a bridge-hole, and this will call for much more careful steering. Naturally, the narrower the bridge-hole, the more difficult the problem, but whatever the width of the gap a good solution is to ask a crew member to give the clearance on one side of the boat while the steerer checks the other and makes sure that the cabin top is not about to strike the bridge arch, making corrections as necessary to keep the boat on course centrally through the bridge-hole. If in doubt, slow down before making the manoeuvre, and always try to line the boat up some distance from the bridge in order to avoid last-minute gyrations with the tiller. After several bridges have been negotiated successfully the steerer will have gained enough experience to be able to judge the width of the gap and the clearances required, and may then dispense with the assistance of the crew member.

STOPPING THE BOAT

A boat moving freely down the middle of a channel may be brought to a stop in only one way (short of striking a large floating obstruction – such as another boat!), that is, by applying power in reverse gear. However, propellers do not act with the same efficiency when going astern, with the result that the boat will not decelerate as quickly as it will accelerate, which is another reason for keeping to lower rather than higher speeds. Moreover, as the boat depends for its steering largely upon the effect of propeller wash on the rudder, putting the propeller into reverse will destroy that effect, and the ability to steer will be lost instantly. In a real emergency this may be of little or no importance when compared with the urgency of bringing the boat to a stop in the shortest possible distance, but in many situations loss of steerage – hence loss of control of the boat – may itself provoke a collision with other craft or the bank. Again, lower speeds generally lead to better control in tricky situations, and may even eliminate the necessity to go astern at all, consequently improving the chances of taking avoiding action by steering rather than being forced into a panic stop. Reversing hard while the boat is still moving ahead will not only cause loss of steerage, but will also result in the boat slewing to one side or the other, depending upon a combination of effects, and in extreme cases the boat may come to rest almost broadside across the canal. Additionally, the high revolutions cause loss of propeller efficiency – and thus braking power – thereby increasing the risk of collision when making an emergency stop. Lower speeds are therefore both safer and better boating practice, for if circumstances demand that the boat be brought to a standstill quickly the power required will be much less and more efficiently used, and if judiciously applied will tend to maintain the boat on its heading without any significant swinging of the stern.

We now need to consider the effects of wind, for at least part of the time during any holiday cruise there is certain to be some wind in evidence, varying from the lightest of breezes up to maybe a full gale. Light winds have little effect upon a heavy steel-hulled narrowboat, but as the wind strengthens it will make itself increasingly felt, particularly if it is on the beam – that is, blowing more or less at right-angles to the boat's heading. Lighter craft built of GRP or marine ply will be more affected by windy conditions, and above a certain wind strength will be difficult, if not impossible, to steer. The complexities of boat-handling are always increased proportionately to wind strength, and may be beyond the competence of novices in what could be considered only moderate conditions; indeed, some hire companies advise their clients to moor up in such circumstances and wait until the wind drops sufficiently for them to go on. However, circumstances may dictate that the boat be navigated in adverse weather – after all, strongish winds sometimes persist – and the novice should therefore have some idea of the techniques to be adopted when steering and manoeuvring in these conditions.

With the wind blowing from dead ahead or dead astern there will be little effect upon the performance of the boat other than slightly

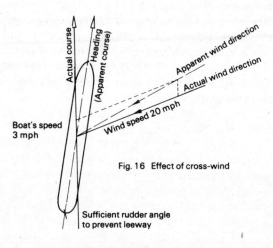

Fig. 16 Effect of cross-wind

to decrease or increase its speed. But even if the wind is at first favourable, there must eventually come a point where the waterway alters direction, and this will be accompanied by an apparent change of wind direction relative to the boat. With a wind on the beam the boat will tend to be blown sideways, and the stronger the wind and the larger the area of hull and superstructure offering resistance (this is known as 'windage'), the more pronounced this effect will be. If the wind is blowing from a point abaft the beam, the *less* will be its apparent strength, and conversely, with the wind blowing from a point forward of the beam, the *greater* will be its apparent strength. The wind also apparently undergoes a slight shift in direction due to the forward motion of the boat. It is therefore necessary to steer into a strong wind on the beam in order to counter the tendency for the boat to be blown steadily sideways down-wind (in nautical terms this down-wind drift is called 'leeway'), and the amount of counteracting rudder required to keep the boat on course is proportional to the wind strength. The forward motion of the boat in this situation is no longer directly along the fore-and-aft line but somewhat sideways – a condition known as 'crabbing'. If the wind is very strong a fair amount of power, and therefore speed, is needed to maintain the boat's attitude, and any reduction of power, or rudder angle, will result in a corresponding degree of leeway being made, until the boat eventually runs aground on the lee bank. So the maintenance of a certain minimum speed is esential in windy conditions, but what happens when that speed has to be reduced, as at locks, movable bridges, blind bends and so on?

When the boat has to come to a complete stop, as is probable at locks and movable bridges, the object must be to keep the bow up to windward until such time as the boat may proceed. A moment's thought will show why this is so: the steerer, by means of the rudder and propeller, may alter the position of the boat's stern at will, but he has no similar control over the fore-end, and this must always therefore be stationed with due regard to any future course of action the steerer may wish to take. If the towpath happens to be on the windward side of the boat (that is, the side from which the wind is blowing, the opposite being the down-wind, or 'leeward', side), well and good, and the boat may be run alongside and held there from the bank; or, if the water proves to be very shallow, the bow should be gently run aground at an angle and held in position against the wind by use of the engine. If, when ready to proceed, the boat is slowly reversed, the wind will start to swing the fore-end round as it comes free, when forward power should be applied at the appropriate moment to bring the boat into line with the bridge gap or lock mouth. Try at all costs to avoid being blown sideways against the bank in a strong wind unless you intend to remain there; in some cases it will entail a long and hard struggle to get off again, at the cost of frayed tempers and perhaps damaged paintwork.

Reducing speed for blind bends, and when passing oncoming boats, can be a very tricky business in strong winds. In the first instance, the very obstruction to the line of sight – perhaps a tree, a building or a bridge abutment – often provides some shelter from the wind, and even where it does not, the resulting backdraught from the obstruction will tend to counteract the worst of the wind's effects. If neither of these things happens, then good judgement will be called for in holding the boat's attitude right up to the moment when power is reduced, and in making the correct allowance for any falling away of the bow in order to position it accurately in the channel, taking care that the stern is not blown over and run aground.

Passing an oncoming boat presents much the same problem, but in this case a lot depends on the expertise of both steerers. If the other

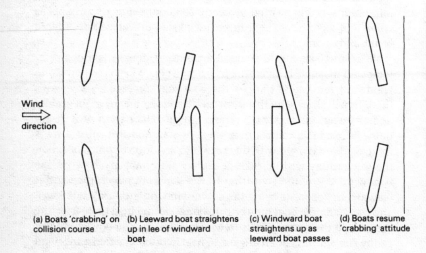

Wind direction

(a) Boats 'crabbing' on collision course

(b) Leeward boat straightens up in lee of windward boat

(c) Windward boat straightens up as leeward boat passes

(d) Boats resume 'crabbing' attitude

Fig. 17 Boats meeting and passing in strong cross-wind

boat is to windward you must anticipate the moment when your fore-end will enter the shelter of his, and reduce speed accordingly. Your boat will now straighten up on course but will be rapidly approaching his stern, which is slewed across the channel in a 'crabbing' attitude. It is then up to the other steerer to judge *your* approach and swing his stern aside at the right time to let your bow past, the normal effects of passing in a constricted channel then returning both craft to the centre line, when 'crabbing' can be resumed.

The problems of boat-handling in windy conditions are much increased in the case of light motor cruisers as their relatively large vertical surface area renders them particularly vulnerable to strong cross-winds, and this is mitigated only slightly by the provision of a small keel. To some extent the greater manoeuvrability of the smaller craft can make up for the disadvantage, but the difficulties of handling such craft in these conditions are apt to be beyond the competence of the novice, who would be wise to moor up until the wind drops.

STEERING ROUND BENDS

Steering round slight bends should present no problem to the novice who can confidently keep a straight course, but negotiating sharp bends, especially when they are accompanied by a narrow bridge-hole at the apex, can at first be somewhat intimidating, and if the manoeuvre is to be accomplished in good style it is necessary for the steerer to understand how a boat behaves in a turn.

When turning, all boats tend to rotate about their centre of gravity, which is usually situated at about the middle of the boat. Moving the tiller to the left puts the rudder to the right, causing the stern to swing to the left and the bow to swing to the right, the whole boat rotating around its mid-section. But as the boat is at the same time moving forward, the net result of these two movements is, at first, to cause a kind of skidding effect, although because the boat is partially immersed the skid is scarcely noticeable in the same way that, say, a skid on ice would be. Differential water pressures acting on the hull will then maintain the radius of turn according to the selected angle of rudder and the amount of propeller thrust (for a technical explana-

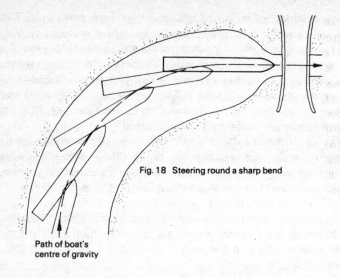

Fig. 18 Steering round a sharp bend

Path of boat's
centre of gravity

tion of these effects, see Appendix IV). It follows from this that reduced forward speed will result in greater control in a sharp turn as the swing of the stern under power will be more effective, and lower speed will enable short bursts of power to be applied should this be required for steering corrections. In any case, all blind bends and bridge-holes (and other situations where visibility is badly restricted) should be taken at slow speed to avoid risk of collision with oncoming craft. In turning into a bend no attempt should be made to cut across the corner; not only will this tend to reduce visibility still further, but will necessitate a sharp turn at the last moment in order to straighten up for the exit from the bend or for entry into a bridge-hole. Many bends also have the deeper water around the outside, leaving a shelf of silt on the inside of the bend, and even if the corner-cutting boat does not go aground on this, it may well lose steerage completely owing to the ineffectiveness of the rudder in very shallow water.

The correct way to approach a turn of this sort is to set the boat up on a course rather towards the outside of the bend (not too close to the bank as the stern requires room to swing), maintaining slow speed and constantly watching the position of the bow. This should appear to be underrunning the intended course during a turn – that is, on a right-hand bend the bow should be pointing somewhat to the right of the intended course, and vice versa on a left-hand bend. The reason for this is as follows: because the boat pivots around its centre of gravity it is this point which follows the true course during a turn; the bow, projecting forward of the centre of gravity, transcribes an arc inside the true turning radius while the stern does just the opposite – in other words, a boat 'crabs' through a turn (reference to fig. 18 should make this clear). Only as the boat straightens up again in coming out of the turn will the bow and the centre of gravity come into line once more. Always remember to sound one long blast on the horn (about four seconds) when visibility ahead is obscured. An oncoming boat should answer your signal with a similar one, but if the line of sight is very poor and you are in doubt, station a crew member at the fore-end to give you earlier warning.

TURNING AT JUNCTIONS AND WINDING THE BOAT

Turns through an abrupt angle – say at the junction of two canals – call for a rather different technique, particularly if the area of water available for the turn is restricted. The fact that many T-junctions (for the sake of clarity let us assume that the horizontal stroke of the 'T' is a main line canal and the upright a branch) feature a bridge carrying a towpath over the branch should make for added caution and emphasize the need to slow down in plenty of time, sounding a long blast on the horn before entering the junction at very slow speed.

A turn from the main line into the branch may be treated in exactly the same way as any bend, except that the approach and turn should be made very slowly, and care must be taken not to strike the underside of the bridge arch (if there is one) as the boat enters the branch at an angle. To carry out a successful turn in this way requires sufficient width of channel on the main line, and where this is not available then a standing turn must be made.

If proceeding from the branch canal into the main line, gently engage reverse as the stern approaches the junction and bring the boat to a halt, leaving just sufficient room for the stern to swing without striking the bank. Then put the tiller hard over and apply plenty of throttle in forward gear. Under the influence of rudder action the boat should pivot round without acquiring much forward way

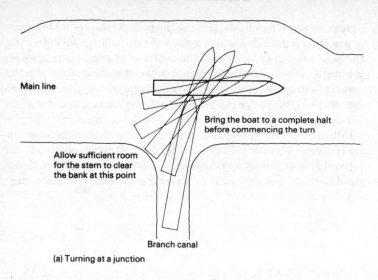

Main line

Bring the boat to a complete halt
before commencing the turn

Allow sufficient room
for the stern to clear
the bank at this point

Branch canal

(a) Turning at a junction

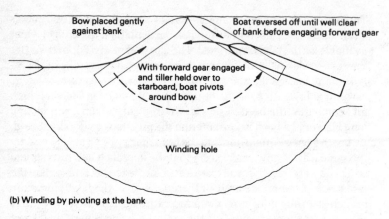

Bow placed gently
against bank

Boat reversed off until well clear
of bank before engaging forward gear

With forward gear engaged
and tiller held over to
starboard, boat pivots
around bow

Winding hole

(b) Winding by pivoting at the bank

Fig. 19 Turning the boat

and the turn be accomplished virtually within the boat's length. As
the bow nears the intended heading, throttle down and counter-steer
slightly to prevent any overswing.

The same technique may be used to turn a boat right round on to an opposite heading, always remembering that sufficient room must be available for the stern to clear any obstacles; remember too that all such manoeuvres should be accompanied by the appropriate sound signals if there are moving craft in the vicinity. Turning the boat right round is known as 'winding' (pronounced as in the wind that blows), hence the occurrence at intervals along a canal of 'winding holes', most of which were designed to allow the turning of full-length working boats. Other techniques for winding include the use of long shafts (where room is extremely restricted and the water shallow), hauling from the bank, and pivoting the boat around by the use of tiller and motor while the bow rests – or is held by the bow line – against the bank.

STEERING ASTERN

The majority of fixed-propeller boats steer badly or not at all when going astern, a characteristic likely to prove troublesome to the beginner, although common sense might indicate that if sufficient power is applied and the tiller reversed, the rudder would act to push the stern over in the required direction, just as it does when moving forward. Unfortunately, while apparently sound, this concept does not work either theoretically or in practice, for when going astern there is a basically unstable combination of water pressures acting on the boat's hull and forces generated at the rudder and propeller (the interested reader may work these out for himself by referring to fig. 60 on p. 337). This disadvantage may be overcome by lining the boat

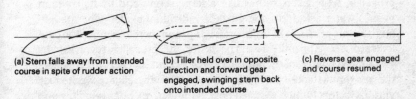

(a) Stern falls away from intended course in spite of rudder action

(b) Tiller held over in opposite direction and forward gear engaged, swinging stern back onto intended course

(c) Reverse gear engaged and course resumed

Fig. 20 Steering astern

up on the desired reverse heading and going astern gently; before long the stern will fall away from the heading, sometimes in the direction dictated by the displacement of axial thrust of the propeller (see Appendix IV), but not always. The way to correct this is to point the tiller *away* from the direction of swing and apply a brief burst of power in forward gear, which will push the stern back on course, and reverse gear may once more be engaged. This sequence can be applied as often as necessary to maintain the correct heading, remembering always to keep on sufficient stern way, otherwise progress will be very slow. Carry out changes of gear and throttle settings with deliberation, and never apply too much power unless it is definitely called for. With enough practice the boat may be steered astern quite accurately over considerable distances by this method.

THE CROSS-SECTIONAL RATIO

What the newcomer to boats and canals does not appreciate is the surprisingly complex behaviour of craft in constricted waterways, thinking instead that it is simply a question of applying power to move the boat forward in any manner desired by the steerer. This is just not so, for the shape, size and depth of the waterway all have a crucial influence on the boat's performance, and the reasons for such influence must be understood if the steerer is to be properly in control of the boat's movements. Probably the most important phenomenon is the 'cross-sectional ratio', as it affects all craft moving in water channels whose cross-sectional area is relatively small as compared with the cross-sectional area of the vessel (see Appendix III).

For the boat to move at all, power must be applied by means of the propeller, which acts rather like a large screw and by its rotation pushes water astern; in doing so the individual blades generate 'lift' on the same principle as an aircraft wing, and therefore move the boat forward (see Appendix IV). The faster the propeller revolves, the greater the boat's speed, but only up to a point; in deep, open waters the maximum speed at which a boat may travel is governed by various factors (which we need not examine here), but in shallow and constricted channels the boat will never approach this same speed, and to attempt to make it do so is futile. The main reason for this is that the propeller, in order to function at maximum efficiency, must draw enough water round the sides and bottom of the boat's hull proportionate to the amount pushed astern, and this it can do at lower revolutions without much trouble. But at higher revolutions the constrictions of the channel prevent sufficient water from flowing round the hull surfaces, and certain effects begin to appear. A pressure head at the bow is accompanied by a decrease of pressure along the hull, causing a drop in water level between bow and stern which forms a distinct slope, up which the boat appears to be perpetually ascending. As propeller revolutions increase still further, 'slope resistance' increases, resulting in loss of speed together with the formation of a breaking wave on each side of the hull abaft the stern and extending across the channel to both banks. At these higher revolutions a phenomenon known as 'cavitation' can occur, in which vapour is drawn out of the water by the propeller, thus lessening its effectiveness considerably, and the engine labours heavily, often throwing out dense black fumes of unburned fuel. This quite remarkable sight is to be seen on canals more often than one would wish, and invariably indicates that the boat is in the hands of an inexperienced steerer. Not only is the breaking wash destructive of banks and can cause damage to moored craft, but fuel is being wasted unnecessarily in the fond illusion that the boat is travelling at maximum speed, whereas in fact it is not; the steering in these circumstances will be heavy and, as previously mentioned, maintenance of this speed at blind bends and bridge-holes will increase the chance of collision with other boats, not to mention the greater likelihood of hitting the bank, running aground and picking up rubbish on the propeller.

The correct maximum – that is, optimum – speed is reached when the wave created by the boat does not break constantly at the bank; it may break occasionally, indicating that it is passing over a shallow area or that the boat is not at the moment correctly positioned in the deeper water, but this is not significant: what must always be avoided is the creation of a continuously breaking wave.

From this it is obvious that the optimum speed of a boat will alter from canal to canal as the cross-sectional ratio varies; indeed, on some canals it will be only about half of what it is on others, whereas on rivers the ratio may increase to the point at which a boat can travel at its true maximum speed. The novice should not consider that an optimum speed is also a *minimum* speed to be maintained regardless of circumstances, for apart from slowing down for reasons of safety the boat should be navigated slowly and with ample clearance if possible when passing moored craft (even if unoccupied), anglers, dredgers, bank piling and other maintenance craft, engineering works and the like.

PASSING ONCOMING CRAFT AND OVERTAKING

The condition of canals is very different now from what it was in the past. Many years of use by mechanically propelled craft has eroded banks and deposited the resultant silt in the main channels (many miles of which are sadly lacking the attentions of a dredger) to the point where cross-sections generally nowhere resemble those as originally built. If anything, the centre channel of most canals has been narrowed by silting, making it difficult for larger craft, especially those of deep draught, to pass without running aground ('stemming-up' is the traditional term). Pleasure-boats of standard draught, or thereabouts, tend to be less affected by this situation, although in many places some care is called for if running aground is to be avoided. As the deepest water is most often to be found in the middle of a canal, craft usually keep to the middle on straight stretches: the 'keep to the right' rule of the road does not mean that one should stay over on the right at all times, regardless of the fact that no other boat is in sight. Only when meeting another boat, or being overtaken by one, should it be necessary to move over. This should be done in reasonable time – not when half a mile distant, nor when the two craft are about to collide – with the aim of passing fairly close to the other boat, leaving a gap of three or four feet. When about thirty yards from the oncoming boat the throttle should be closed almost to tick-over, particularly if the canal is shallow, and the other boat will – hopefully – do the same. Failure to observe these points might result in one or both boats running aground, for the combined effect of the respective hull forms and propellers is to cause a temporary drop in water level around the two boats as they pass, and if either is too far into the shallower water at the bank the result will be to run aground.

Boats travelling under too much power and failing to shut off are very prone to this, and it is a common fault among novice steerers.

It is often much more difficult to overtake another boat, for not only does the manoeuvre take longer, but may prove impossible if the waterway is very shallow. For these reasons overtaking should be attempted only when a sufficiently clear, straight stretch of water lies ahead to enable overtaking to be completed safely. Good manners dictate that one should wait for a signal from the steerer of the other boat, who may well be in a better position to see whether the way ahead is clear; if in any doubt, wait until you can verify this yourself, then, when about to overtake, sound two short blasts on the horn and open up the throttle, steering to the left as you do so. At the same time the boat ahead should have moved over to the right and reduced speed to tick-over. Give the other boat as wide a berth as possible, but take care not to run aground yourself and do not use too much throttle: boats running side by side draw a lot of water down the channel and, as we have seen, too much power will only result in a worsening of the cross-sectional effect, and the boats will tend to be drawn together, making it almost impossible for your boat to make any progress in overtaking. Even if you are too far over to be drawn into the other boat, the use of excessive power will 'steal his water' and probably put him on the bottom; this would scarcely be the best way of returning the consideration he has shown you. Do not forget to thank the steerer of the other boat for his courtesy in assisting you to pass. It is the height of bad manners to hog the centre of the canal while moving slowly and so prevent other craft from overtaking, but unfortunately this seems to happen fairly frequently, whether from ignorance or malice it is impossible to tell.

RUNNING AGROUND

This is a fairly frequent occurrence on canals and is usually caused by failure to maintain a course in deeper water, often combined with a speed too high for the depth of water under the boat. Once a boat has gone aground, the ease with which it may be refloated depends very much upon its position. If the fore-end is aground, with the midships and stern still in deep water, then reversing off may be reasonably easy, because when a boat goes aground on a soft bottom the hull forces its way through the mud, leaving a kind of slot in which it sits. With the fore-end really hard aground any attempt to shift the hull sideways is likely to be unsuccessful, and the easiest way is to lighten the boat at the critical point by gathering the crew at the stern and reversing off as before: if this fails, then additional force will have to be applied by shafting-off from the stern. Should the stern be aground also, it is futile to use the engine as a means of retrieving the situation as this will merely tend to drop the stern and sit the boat even more firmly on the bottom.

Frequently a steerer will run in too close to a bank and succeed in grounding most (or perhaps all) of one side of the hull on the sloping bed of the canal, leaving the other side in deeper water. This situation is best dealt with by putting the engine in neutral and resorting to shafting the boat off – hence the necessity for canal craft to carry a long shaft. The crew should be asked to take up a position on the gunwale opposite to the side that is aground and towards the fore-end, while the person shafting off positions himself on the outer side of the stern and pushes on the bank or the canal bottom with the shaft. This action will result in the free-floating part of the hull being depressed, while the aground side will tend to rise, and with any luck the stern should float free. If this does not happen the crew should be asked to rock the boat from side to side in unison, which they are in position to do most effectively as they are already standing on the gunwale and holding on to the grab-rails – but beware of over-enthusiastic rocking as this can lead to the boat reaching alarming angles, with possible damage to unsecured fragile objects down below. The combination of rocking and shafting-off will invariably dislodge the stern, which should then be shafted clear of the bottom. From this point reverse power will usually pull the bow off, but if this fails then the shafting procedure will again have to be used, this time from the fore-end.

Running aground in deep silt is to be avoided at all costs, so do not attempt to navigate any areas of waterway off the main channel which you suspect may be shallow, such as 'wides' and disused basins. It is possible, indeed probable, that such stretches of water have not been dredged for years, and a boat venturing on to them will almost certainly become embedded in the silt – more so if travelling at speed. The suction which sets up between the flat bottom of the hull and the mud can be very fierce, and will probably resist any attempt to get the boat off again without outside assistance. The sheer depth of silt may in any case make shafting-off impossible, and trying to reverse off by using the engine will be useless. If the boat is well and truly embedded, even towing by another craft is likely to fail unless the towing boat is of deep draught and equipped with a suitable propeller – which is improbable. Towing from the bank by vehicle, preferably one with a four-wheel drive, may have to be resorted to, but do not arrange for a tow without first notifying the hire company, which will then issue instructions on what to do in the circumstances. Before this can be done, however, someone will have the highly unpleasant – and perhaps dangerous – task of reaching the bank to summon help if no one is within hailing distance.

CLEARING A FOULED PROPELLER

One of the unavoidable hazards of canal cruising is the debris of all kinds that lurks on and under the surface of the water, in the latter case mostly invisible due to the opacity caused by constant stirring of the silted bottom by the passage of boats. Plastic sheets and bags have become increasingly common rubbish over the years, but in fact all sorts of debris may be encountered, from fishing line to complete motor cars! Rubbish floating on the surface can usually be seen and avoided, but there is no way of detecting the submerged hazards of plastic bags, lengths of rope, wire, old clothing and so on, which may be picked up by the propeller and sometimes the rudder.

A badly fouled propeller will make its presence felt by a slowing down of revolutions, labouring of the engine – perhaps accompanied by black smoke from the exhaust – and vibration of the tiller, making the boat respond somewhat sluggishly and seem generally less lively. If this sort of thing happens, or if the presence of debris around the propeller is merely suspected, select neutral, let the revolutions drop, and then apply full throttle in reverse in a short burst. Select neutral again and repeat the process, then again twice more in forward gear, and watch the turbulence astern to see if anything has been thrown off the propeller.

This procedure will in many cases remove the obstruction, but if it does not, manoeuvre the boat up to the bank and hold it there. Switch off the engine and *remove the key from the ignition lock* in case the engine is unknowingly started up in gear. Next, take up the appropriate deck plate and remove the weed-hatch cover. Lying full length on the deck, reach down into the weed trunk and feel round the propeller boss and shaft to determine what the obstruction is. First try rotating the propeller by hand to see if you can unwind whatever is clogging it, and only use a cutting tool if necessary. Once the debris has been completely removed, replace the weed-hatch cover and gasket over the trunk, clamping or screwing the cover down tightly to prevent water thrown up by the propeller from entering the engine compartment, and replace the deck plate. *On no account must you run with the weed-hatch cover removed, as propeller wash will flood the engine compartment* and boats have been known to sink as a result of this. Do not throw any debris back into the canal, but carry it with you to the next rubbish disposal point.

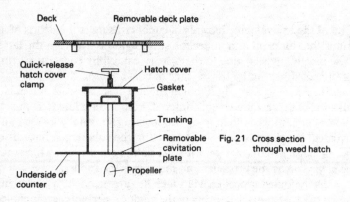

Fig. 21 Cross section through weed hatch

It is quite a good idea to check the propeller for obstructions at times when the boat is not moving, perhaps when about to descend a lock, or when moored. Stand on the lock side or the bank and feel around the propeller blades with the hooked end of the short shaft – in fact this is the only method available (short of actually getting into the water yourself) for removing rubbish from the propellers of those craft not provided with weed hatches. Obviously it is best not to pick up debris in the first place, so keep a lookout for it and put the engine into neutral when passing so as not to draw it into the propeller. The same applies to objects such as planks and tree branches, which may also become jammed under the bow and held there by water pressure. If this happens, send someone up to the fore-end with a shaft to poke the debris out, and if this fails stop the boat and reverse smartly, which will usually succeed in releasing it. Rarely should it be necessary to call for assistance from the hire company to free a propeller, but if the obstruction cannot be removed without the use of heavy cutting tackle, or if there is damage to the propeller or shaft, the base should be informed as soon as possible.

Removal of all other obstructions from the propeller is the responsibility of the hirer, although hire companies do not include any suitable tools on the boat's inventory. By taking along a few of your own you may save yourself a great deal of time and trouble in dealing with bad cases of fouling, and some of the tools suggested here could be useful in other situations as well.

Hand saw

A small hand saw of the cheapest kind, preferably with large teeth, is an excellent tool for ripping and tearing plastic sheet away from the propeller. It may just prove handy, too, in those infrequent situations involving a fallen tree blocking the canal, when sawing off a few strategic branches may make the difference between getting through or not.

Hacksaws

A large and a small hacksaw (with spare blades) may be essential when removing really tough wire or strip metal.

Pliers

A good pair of stout pliers equipped with cutting blades will deal with thinner wire.

Knife

A small sharp knife is useful for cutting cord, rope, and twisted plastic sheet.

Hammer

Although hire craft are provided with a hammer for driving in mooring spikes it does no harm to carry a spare.

Other useful items include an adjustable spanner, a mole wrench, a flat-bladed and a Philips screwdriver, a tin of Swarfega, some clean rags and a twenty-foot length of strong nylon cord (which can also be used as a washing line).

CASTING OFF AND GOING ALONGSIDE

These are apparently the simplest of manoeuvres, especially in deep water alongside a wharf or hard bank, but they can reveal incompetence to an astonishing degree. For instance, when the novice steerer is casting off it is not uncommon to see him put the engine into forward gear, shift the tiller over and expect the boat to move smartly away from the bank as though it were a car. What happens is that the boat moves ahead but *not* away from the bank, as this is impossible with the boat lying parallel to and close alongside it: as we have seen, the stern has to swing around the centre of gravity if the boat is to turn. Instead, the stern strikes the bank and grazes it, perhaps bouncing off as it hits a projection, and then returns to its former position against the bank as the rudder forces it over.

The boat must be moved bodily away from the bank *before* applying power so that the stern has room to swing. This may be done in more than one way: the fore-end may be pushed out first, either from the bank or by shafting from the boat, and the boat simply steered away towards the centre of the channel in a straight line; or the entire boat may be pushed away from the bank in such a manner that the fore-

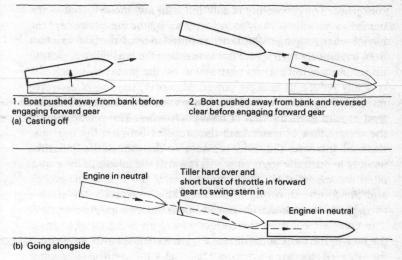

1. Boat pushed away from bank before engaging forward gear
(a) Casting off

2. Boat pushed away from bank and reversed clear before engaging forward gear

Engine in neutral

Tiller hard over and short burst of throttle in forward gear to swing stern in

Engine in neutral

(b) Going alongside

Fig. 22 Manoeuvring at the bank

end drifts out further than the stern; or the stern may be pushed out first and the boat then reversed under power until there is room in which to bring the bow round. The first method is only suitable when the water at the bank is deep enough to remove any risk of the propeller striking a submerged obstruction; the last two may be used when the boat is in fairly shallow water and perhaps even slightly aground. The drawback to the reversing method, so far as novices are concerned, is that they often do not reverse the boat out sufficiently far, with the result that the attempted turn in forward gear returns the boat to its original position close to the bank. It is essential that the stern be well over towards the other side of the channel before moving ahead and straightening up on the intended course, but care must be taken not to reverse too far and run aground stern first in the process.

Going alongside is another manoeuvre that seems to cause many novices a great deal of trouble, too high a speed usually being the reason for this. A sweeping turn under power followed by the application of full throttle astern may look and sound spectacular, at least in the imagination of the steerer, but more often than not it is a recipe for disaster so far as placing the boat neatly alongside the bank is concerned. The probability of collision with any moored craft in the immediate vicinity is likely to be increased by the inexperience of the novice when judging the distance required to bring the boat to a halt from a relatively high speed; not to mention the possibility of picking up (or already having) an obstruction on the propeller, which will critically reduce its braking power. Moreover, the use of excessive reverse power close to the bank has certain unforeseen effects that tend to ruin even the best of final approaches. The constriction of the reverse flow of water from the propeller between the boat and the bank increases the water pressure on that side of the hull, thus tending to push the stern outwards towards the middle of the canal, often accompanied by much shouting over the roar of the engine and the frantic throwing of mooring lines – scarcely the picture of competence originally envisaged by the unfortunate steerer!

In complete contrast, the correct way to go alongside is to angle the bow to the bank some distance – ten to fifteen yards, say – from the intended mooring position, put the engine into neutral after lining up the approach, and drift gently towards the bank. As the bow nears it, put the tiller over and use a very short burst of throttle in forward gear, with the tiller still over, to swing the stern into the bank, and select neutral again immediately. If the correct timing has been observed the boat will turn parallel with the bank and be almost at a standstill when the mooring is reached, and crew members will be able to step on to the bank with bow and stern lines, using them to check the momentum of the boat and to pull it up to the desired mooring place. Further use of the engine will usually not be required, and it should be stopped to avoid having to shout above its noise. The essence of this manoeuvre lies in the slowness of the approach under minimum power and, finally, no power at all, so that use of the engine and tiller is confined to any necessary steering corrections; if reverse power must be applied, then try to keep it to a minimum.

MOORING THE BOAT

One of the advantages of canals, as compared with rivers, is that the towpath, against which one has the right to moor, is constantly available. This is not the case on rivers, lakes and broads, as the great numbers of 'PRIVATE – KEEP OFF' signs testify. But just because this facility exists on canals it does not imply that one can moor anywhere one chooses: there are places where to do so would create an unreasonable or even dangerous obstruction to navigation, and indeed the British Waterways Board by-laws (see Appendix II) specifically prohibit the causing of such obstruction by moored craft. Obviously you should never moor inside of, or at the head or tail of, any lock, nor in tunnels, bridge-holes, aqueduct troughs nor any other place where a moored boat would block the channel. Nor should you moor on or adjacent to a bend, even though the temptation may be strong on account of the deeper water often found there, unless you wish to run the risk of being struck by craft rounding the bend – particularly larger craft, whose sterns are likely to be swinging fairly close to the bank. Mooring in the short pounds of lock flights is sometimes forbidden, but in any case it is most unwise because of the increased chance of the pound level dropping through severe gate leakage or a careless paddle operation.

Selecting a mooring is largely a matter of common sense, and if enough width of channel is left for others to pass by easily without having to resort to manoeuvring usually all will be well. Mooring on the offside of the canal – that is, the opposite side from the towpath – should be avoided, unless the landowner's permission has been obtained beforehand. Whenever possible try to find a deep-water mooring alongside a concrete bank with mooring rings or bollards, although it must be said at once that such sites are not frequent, and in many instances you will have to make do with what is available. Look for a suitably straight bank that is reasonably free of tree stumps, nettles and bushes, with enough depth of water for mooring, and when making the approach watch out for any obstructions (coping stones, rocks and so on) which may be lurking in the shallows. If the intended mooring place does not live up to its promise, do not dither about, but move on and find a better one.

Sometimes you may be forced – perhaps by gathering darkness – to moor up in water so shallow as to make it very difficult to get someone with a mooring line on to the towpath. Should the boat be unable to approach close to the bank there may be no alternative but to jump for it, but before anyone does this compare the length of your gangplank with the gap to be spanned: there is no point in going to a lot of trouble in mooring up only to find that the gangplank is not long enough. If you cannot go close alongside and particularly if the bank is very broken, it is inadvisable to attempt to leap the gap because of the risk of leg injury, although the problem may be solved in the case of smaller craft by reversing the boat diagonally across the channel, selecting forward gear and putting the bow firmly aground by steering into the bank. A crew member taking the bow line should be able to step easily from the bow on to the towpath, and the boat is then reversed off and brought round parallel to the bank so that the stern line can be thrown across. With the boat held in on the lines, the gangplank may be positioned, if possible from the stern deck, and another crew member sent off with the mooring spikes and hammer.

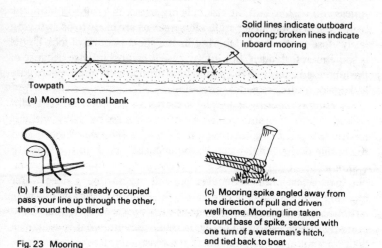

Solid lines indicate outboard mooring; broken lines indicate inboard mooring

45°

Towpath

(a) Mooring to canal bank

(b) If a bollard is already occupied pass your line up through the other, then round the bollard

(c) Mooring spike angled away from the direction of pull and driven well home. Mooring line taken around base of spike, secured with one turn of a waterman's hitch, and tied back to boat

Fig. 23 Mooring

Mooring spikes should be driven into firm ground to within a few inches of their tops, and angled away from the direction of pull placed upon them by the mooring lines. They should be positioned between the bank and the actual towpath (but not so close to the water's edge that there is a risk of their breaking away a portion of bank) so that neither they nor the attached lines constitute a danger to anyone walking the towpath, and arranged at an angle of about forty-five degrees to the side of the boat, either outboard or inboard – that is, either away from or towards the boat's centre. The mooring lines should not be secured too tightly, otherwise an overnight drop in the level of the pound, or perhaps the draw from passing craft, will result in the boat canting over. If the lines are very short they will have to be hitched directly to the spikes, but normally it is preferable to pass them around the spikes – at their bases, *not* their tops – and secure the ends to the boat's T-studs or dollies. A thoughtful gesture is to attach pieces of white rag or paper to the tops of the spikes so as to make them more visible to passers-by on the towpath. When mooring to bollards and rings use a similar procedure to that given above, although if a bollard is already occupied by someone else's line, pass your own mooring line up through the other before tying back to the boat, so that whoever leaves first does not have to disturb or untie the remaining line. Before finally retiring below, pull the gangplank aboard – not all boaters are considerate of moored craft, and the wash of a passing craft could easily dislodge the plank into the water.

STEERING MOTOR CRUISERS

The form, layout and steering of motor cruisers are all very different from the equivalent features of the narrowboat, and to some extent present the novice with a whole new set of problems in mastering the art of boat-handling. Foremost among these are the difficulties associated with wheel-steering, notably the loss of sensitivity due to its indirect action perhaps combined with a certain amount of slackness in the rudder controls, which together tend to make it less positive than a tiller; and the feeling of detachment brought on by steering in an enclosed wheelhouse or cockpit. By virtue of its position a tiller gives immediate indication of the rudder angle, but the physical separation of helm and rudder in motor cruisers renders this impossible, and some other means of judging rudder angle has to be used, always remembering that – unlike a tiller – a wheel must be moved in the *same* direction as the intended turn.

First it is essential to find the position of the helm with the rudder on the fore-and-aft line of the boat, and sometimes the wheel is marked to indicate this, but if it is not then a temporary mark may be made by sticking a piece of tape to the rim or spoke. Once the fore-and-aft position is known it is simply a matter of practice in learning how far the wheel must be turned in order to apply the desired angle of rudder, which, from the novice's point of view, is easier said than done. The tendency – usually even more marked than in the case of a tiller-steered boat – is to oversteer by not allowing sufficient time for the boat to respond to a given degree of helm; and then, because of its apparent sluggishness, to increase the helm so that when the boat responds in full the course correction is much greater than intended, leading to a panic reversal of helm and a repetition of the error in the opposite direction. The boat thus proceeds in a series of wild S-turns and in such circumstances is virtually out of control. As usual, the trouble arises from 'novice's disease' – too much, too soon. Wait for the boat to respond, then as the bow is swinging round to the desired heading, centre the wheel and apply a little opposite helm to stop the swing; if this is done carefully and firmly the bow should cease its swing just as it comes round on to the heading, when the wheel is held steady.

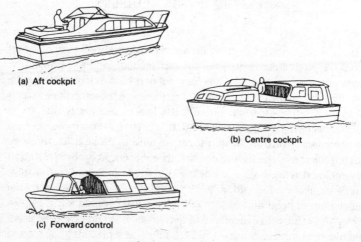

(a) Aft cockpit

(b) Centre cockpit

(c) Forward control

Fig. 24 Wheel steering positions

The advantage of a steering position at, or close to, the stern is that almost the whole length of the boat is both in full view of the steerer and in front of him, thus making the boat's movements in response to the helm much easier to judge, and so allowing any corrections to be made in good time. A centre-cockpit cruiser, with helm located amidships, presents a more difficult problem for the novice in that visibility aft may be restricted, depending on the design, and this will hamper the inexperienced helmsman when making turns and other manoeuvres in confined spaces. Any difficulties arise mainly from the inability of the helmsman to see the aft section of the boat and its movements under helm, and the resulting uncertainty may even hinder the keeping of a straight course at first. Worse still, in this respect, are craft with forward steering positions, as the helmsman is seated well up towards the bow and has extremely restricted visibility aft. The greater part of the boat is out of sight behind him, and while he has an excellent view forward and to the sides through large windows, there is little that can be used as a steering mark by which to judge the boat's movements. For this reason some novices find

Fig. 25 Use of steering marks: in this case strips of adhesive tape fixed to the windscreen and bow respectively, and lined up on the church steeple

forward-control craft very difficult to steer with any accuracy, and may find themselves over-correcting the helm even after several days' practice. This may be remedied to a certain extent by asking a crew member to stand on the fore-and-aft line and sight the bow for the helmsman, giving him the required course corrections as necessary; or the helmsman may do this himself by lining up a mark on the bow to relate with another mark or feature closer to the helmsman in such a way that an imaginary line joining the two is parallel with the fore-and-aft line of the boat. If the two marks are then lined up on a prominent feature (perhaps a tree or a waterside building) some distance ahead of the boat they will enable a reasonably straight course to be kept until such time as a fresh feature can be picked up. By this means the novice can adjust to the initial strangeness of this mode of steering, and when sufficiently confident he may dispense with the steering marks altogether. It is even more important for the helmsman of a forward-control cruiser to allow for the swing of the stern when turning, although should he feel nervous at the prospect a crew member can be stationed on deck to give the necessary directions, and in any case this precaution should always be taken when going astern.

STEERING MOTOR CRUISERS WITH OUTBOARDS AND OUTDRIVES

The hirer will rarely find himself in charge of a boat fitted with an outboard motor, although at one time these were much more common on hire cruisers, and are widely used by private boat owners. From a steering viewpoint their distinguishing feature is the extreme degree of manoeuvrability that they confer on a boat, both when going ahead and astern. This is due to the fact that the propeller axis is not fixed, as in most inboard-engined craft, but swivels with the whole engine unit, which is hung outboard of the boat's transom and connected by steering cables to the helm. Because the direction of propeller thrust is governed by the movement of the helm, no rudder (other than the small ones sometimes fitted to provide better control at low speeds) is required, and in fact the arrangement gives

The bow always swings away from the direction of thrust

Fig. 26 Outboard motor and outdrive steering

such sensitive control that with a little practice an outboard-powered boat may be steered almost as easily astern as forward. This rapid response to helm is likely to be disconcerting to the novice at first, and the remarks made above regarding over-steering apply with even more force in this case. An advantage of outboard motors in shallow waters is that they are designed to swing up should the driving leg strike a solid obstruction, and this facility also allows the leg to be raised out of the water for the removal of rubbish from the propeller. Unfortunately the leg cannot be moved in the opposite direction, and for this reason great care must be taken not to hit an underwater obstruction when going astern. The motor unit, too, is very vulnerable in its position outboard of the stern, and this must be borne in mind when manoeuvring in confined waters.

The outdrive (sometimes called a 'Z-drive' or 'inboard–outboard' unit) is a combination of inboard engine and outboard propeller unit fixed to the boat's transom like an outboard motor. In fact the design features the relative advantages of both fixed propeller and outboard-powered craft by placing the engine inboard, where it is not vulnerable to damage (and permits the use of a diesel unit), and by transmitting the drive to the propeller through the transom to a swivelling steering leg, thus providing the boat with manoeuvrability equal to that afforded by an outboard motor. The previous remarks concerning the outboard motor apply in full to the outdrive-propelled boat, the drive unit of which must be treated with the same degree of care.

CHAPTER SEVEN

WORKING THE NAVIGATION (I)

THE BASICS OF LOCK OPERATION

So far as the beginner is concerned there are two principal techniques to be learned before he will be able to cruise the inland waterways with reasonable competence. The first – boat-handling – is obviously unavoidable from the outset, but the second – lock operation – may be postponed if so desired either by selecting a lock-free stretch of waterway for the first holiday, or by cruising on river navigations with manned locks, such as the Thames or Severn, in which case it is merely a matter of following the lock-keeper's instructions. There is no reason why subsequent holidays should not repeat the same pattern, and indeed, those who return to the Norfolk Broads year after year never come into contact with a lock at all; nevertheless, for a great number of inland waterways devotees lock-working is an inseparable part of a boating holiday, and something to be enjoyed for its own sake once the necessary techniques have been acquired.

To the beginner the lock is an object of awe and appears to be impossibly complicated (this is particularly so with a staircase flight), although in fact it is fundamentally simple both in construction and operation. But as we know, unfamiliarity is capable of transforming the most simple object into something complex; in the case of the lock the fear of making a serious mistake and causing damage to the boat and structure, of wasting large quantities of water, and perhaps creating spectacular floods – all of these imagined possibilities tend to arouse nervousness at that inescapable moment when the beginner actually has to work his first lock unsupervised. We have already seen that if there is a lock within reasonable distance of the base a member of the company's staff will demonstrate the method of lock operation for the hirer, but not all firms have bases placed so conveniently, in which case verbal instruction is given instead. For some hirers this will be the first information that they get about operating locks, but the keen beginner will have read something about it beforehand. Don't worry too much about fine detail to begin with: learn the basic principles first and once these are clearly understood the refinements will follow as a matter of course. In what follows the reader is referred to Chapter 2 for the layout, structure and details of locks.

As the function of any lock is to enable craft to navigate successive pounds set at different levels, we may think of the lock chamber as a kind of lift shaft in which the boat is raised or lowered from one level to another, operations known as 'locking up' and 'locking down' respectively. The procedure may also be referred to as 'locking through', and this term is used here to help give a clearer understanding of the principles since it applies irrespective of whether the boat is moving uphill or downhill, whereas the earlier terms should be used in order to specify the direction of movement. If we visualize the actions implied by 'locking through', it becomes clear that the object is simply to pass successively through the gates at each end of the lock, but it is equally clear that this will only be possible once certain conditions have been met. The most obvious of these is that *water levels must be equal on both sides of the gate immediately ahead of the boat*, and this rule applies whether moving uphill or downhill and to all types of lock. Should water levels on both sides of the gate not be equal (or very nearly so) the gate will not open, and it is this basic fact which determines the next action to be taken: the equalizing of water levels by either filling or emptying the lock chamber as the case may be.

NARROW AND BROAD SINGLE-CHAMBER LOCKS

Before beginning to work any lock first check that *all gates are shut and all paddles are closed*, and this applies whether the chamber is full of water or empty. Laxity in observing this rule could result in considerable loss of water from the upper pound through paddles being left open (or partially open) at both ends of the lock, or by failure to close a gate. Always remember that only one set of paddles must

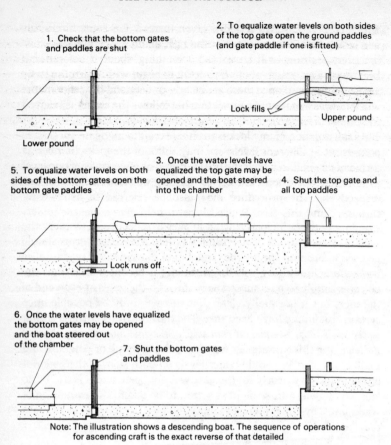

1. Check that the bottom gates and paddles are shut

2. To equalize water levels on both sides of the top gate open the ground paddles (and gate paddle if one is fitted)

Lock fills

Upper pound

Lower pound

5. To equalize water levels on both sides of the bottom gates open the bottom gate paddles

3. Once the water levels have equalized the top gate may be opened and the boat steered into the chamber

4. Shut the top gate and all top paddles

Lock runs off

6. Once the water levels have equalized the bottom gates may be opened and the boat steered out of the chamber

7. Shut the bottom gates and paddles

Note: The illustration shows a descending boat. The sequence of operations for ascending craft is the exact reverse of that detailed

Fig. 27 Operation of a single-chamber lock

be open at any time; either the top paddles *or* the bottom paddles, but *never both sets at once*. As with many rules there are exceptions to this one (see p. 169), but in operating a single-chamber lock the rule must be strictly observed. While making this check you will have noted whether the lock is set for you or against you – that is, whether the water levels on both sides of the gate immediately in front of the boat are equal or not; if they are (or nearly so), the lock is said to be set for you, and if not, it is against you. If the lock is in your favour open the gates(s), steer the boat into the chamber and close the gate(s) again; if it is against you do nothing further until you have checked whether a boat is approaching from the opposite direction, for if the lock is against you it is already set for the steerer of the other boat, and he therefore has priority in the interests of water conservation. A moment's thought will show you why this is so: to fill or empty a lock with no boat inside it is wasteful if that lockful of water could have been used to lock a boat through, and doing this in the face of an oncoming craft is absolutely inexcusable. Nor is it any defence to say that you did not see the other boat because your view of the pound was obscured by, say, a bridge parapet: you should have moved to a suitable viewpoint. Water conservation in these days of intense boating activity is of first importance, as anyone who cruised the canals during the drought years of the mid 1970s will confirm, and so it becomes the duty of all boaters to do their utmost in preventing unnecessary wastage of water. One further point: the steerer of an approaching boat seeing people around the lock might be uncertain as to whether the lock is being worked, and to set his mind at rest it would be a courteous gesture to open the gate(s) for him. Similarly, if when leaving a lock a boat is seen approaching, the gate(s) should be left open, *not* closed in its face. However, if no oncoming boat is in sight set the lock in your favour by either filling it (if you are travelling downhill) or emptying it (if you are travelling uphill), and to do this you will need to operate the paddle gear. (Incidentally, the terms 'empty' and 'full' as applied to a lock refer to the level of water in the chamber not to the absence or presence of boats in the lock.)

PADDLE GEAR OPERATION

The majority of paddles, whether ground or gate, are operated by means of the windlasses carried by boat crews. Windlasses are simple to use: just slide the square head of appropriate size on to the paddle spindle, after first making sure that the ratchet (if fitted) is engaged with the pawl, and wind the spindle round until it will go no further. This should be accompanied by a clicking sound from the pawl and ratchet unit, but if one is not fitted hold the windlass firmly in position at the end of its travel and lock the paddle gear by the means provided. Hydraulic gear has no provision for locking the spindle as the paddle is held in position by oil pressure, although should the gear be faulty there will possibly be a slight but continuous pressure loss, causing the paddle to fall slowly, and this may be prevented by holding the windlass in place on the spindle. As the spindle is turned there is usually a visual indication that the paddle is opening: in the case of most paddle gear the rack will rise above the paddle post, but if the gear is totally encased there will be some sort of moving marker provided to indicate whether the paddle is up or down (that is, open or shut, respectively); or there may be a moving collar as is used in the worm and collar gear employed on the Leeds and Liverpool Canal.

Once the water in the lock chamber has been adjusted to the correct level the gate(s) may be opened and the boat steered into the lock; the gate(s) should then be closed and the paddles firmly shut. All paddles must be wound down, *never* allowed to fall freely as this is likely to damage the paddle and its connecting bar, and perhaps put the lock out of action. *Windlasses should never be left on the spindles of raised paddle gear* in case the locking device slips, when the falling paddle will cause the spindle to rotate and whirl the windlass round at high speed before throwing it off with considerable force to the peril of those standing nearby. Never, if you can possibly avoid it, put a windlass down on a lockside or a balance beam in case it is accidentally kicked or knocked into the lock, or even left behind when the boat departs. Keep it in your hand all the time, or better still jam it behind your belt if you are wearing one.

LOCKING THROUGH: SINGLE-CHAMBER LOCKS

With the boat inside the chamber and all gates and paddles closed the lock is now ready for operation. Following the rule about equalizing water levels on both sides of the gate(s) immediately in front of the boat, you should now operate the paddle gear required to achieve this, emptying the lock if going downhill and filling it if going uphill. When water levels equalize open the gate(s) and steer out of the lock, closing the gate(s) behind the boat and ensuring that all paddles are firmly shut. Remember, all gates and paddles *behind* the boat (regardless of whether it is going uphill or downhill) *must be completely closed while it is in the lock chamber*. Observance of the procedure just outlined will ensure the correct operation of all ordinary single-chamber locks, and the same basic principles apply, moreover, to all other kinds of lock, although the actual details of operation differ according to the type.

Before finally leaving a lock always take a last look around to make certain that the gates are closed and all paddles *fully* shut.

NARROW AND BROAD SINGLE-CHAMBER LOCKS WITH SIDE PONDS

Fortunately for the beginner, who probably feels that he has enough to contend with in the operation of ordinary locks, single-chamber locks constructed with side ponds are relatively rare. However, if the beginner should happen to lack confidence in operating a side pond he may ignore it altogether as the lock will work perfectly well by using just the usual top and bottom paddles. This is not to be encouraged though, particularly in times of water shortage, and it really does not demand much greater mental effort to understand the working of a side-pond lock (see Chapter 2, pp. 48–9 for a detailed description). The only difference in fact between the operation of a single-chamber lock with side pond and one without lies in the discharge of water into, or from, the lock chamber itself. In the case of a side-pond lock the first movement of water always takes place between the lock chamber and the side pond (unless the side paddle has been operated wrongly by the crew of a descending boat, leaving the side pond completely drained), and only after the side-pond operation has finished should the ordinary ground and gate paddles be used to complete the lock operation. Assuming that the side pond is found to be in a normal state – that is, partially full of water – the side paddle should be opened first (after checking that all ground and gate paddles are fully closed), and this is done regardless of whether you are going uphill or downhill. The water levels in the lock chamber and the side pond will now equalize, following which the side paddle is shut and normal locking procedure thereafter followed. It should

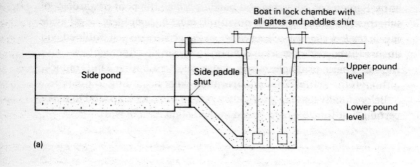

(a)

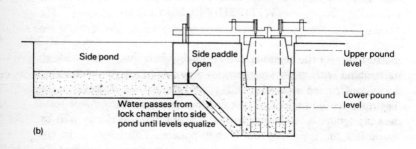

(b)

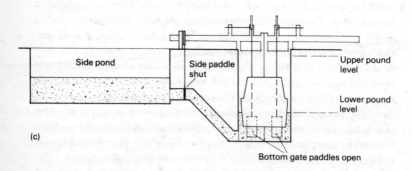

Note. The illustration shows a descending boat.
Ascending craft use the stored water in
the side pond first, and only after levels
in the side pond and the lock chamber
have equalized (and the side paddle has
been shut) are the top ground paddles opened

Fig. 28 Operation of a single-chamber lock with side pond

be noted that these instructions apply to a lock that is set for you, but should the lock be against you then the side paddle must be used twice: once while setting the lock, and again while operating it with the boat inside.

NARROW AND BROAD STAIRCASE LOCKS WITHOUT SIDE PONDS

This is the type of lock that confuses the novice probably more than any other on account of its rather daunting appearance combined with the apparent complications of its operation. There can be no doubt that under certain conditions staircase locks *are* fairly complicated to operate, but the key to understanding how they work is to be fully aware of the basic principles of *all* lock operation, which, when applied with careful thought, will guide the novice in working a staircase flight. There is a curious difference between certain staircase locks and flights of single-chamber locks: unlike the latter, the state of any staircase of more than two chambers is *always* favourable for a succession of boats travelling in the same direction, and craft moving in the opposite direction are faced with the laborious task of resetting the entire flight. The reason for this is that descending boats leave all chambers empty and ascending boats leave all chambers full, so that craft descending the staircase in succession have each in turn merely to refill the top chamber in order for the flight to be set for them. The lockful of water in which the boat floats is simply emptied into the chamber below until levels equalize, when the intermediate gates are opened and the boat transferred to the lower chamber. Once gates and paddles have been shut the process is repeated all the way down the staircase. Ascending boats follow a similar pattern: the bottom chamber is emptied, the boat enters, lower gates and paddles are shut and top paddles opened, allowing the upper chamber to empty into the lower until a common level is reached and the boat moves into the upper chamber, and the process is repeated until the staircase has been ascended.

Now consider the situation when it is desired to descend immediately after a boat has come up. The top chamber will be full, so

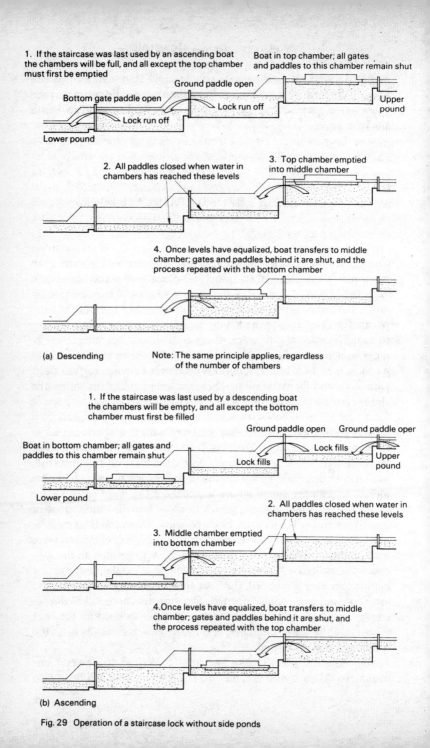

1. If the staircase was last used by an ascending boat the chambers will be full, and all except the top chamber must first be emptied

Boat in top chamber; all gates and paddles to this chamber remain shut

Ground paddle open

Upper pound

Bottom gate paddle open

Lock run off

Lock run off

Lower pound

2. All paddles closed when water in chambers has reached these levels

3. Top chamber emptied into middle chamber

4. Once levels have equalized, boat transfers to middle chamber; gates and paddles behind it are shut, and the process repeated with the bottom chamber

(a) Descending

Note: The same principle applies, regardless of the number of chambers

1. If the staircase was last used by a descending boat the chambers will be empty, and all except the bottom chamber must first be filled

Ground paddle open   Ground paddle oper

Boat in bottom chamber; all gates and paddles to this chamber remain shut

Lock fills

Upper pound

Lock fills

Lower pound

2. All paddles closed when water in chambers has reached these levels

3. Middle chamber emptied into bottom chamber

4. Once levels have equalized, boat transfers to middle chamber; gates and paddles behind it are shut, the process repeated with the top chamber

(b) Ascending

Fig. 29 Operation of a staircase lock without side ponds

that the boat, while able to enter it at once, is unable to proceed further as all the chambers below are also full, making it obvious that any attempt to run off the top chamber will result in fairly dramatic flooding. All the lower chambers must therefore first be emptied, starting at the bottom and working back up the flight, and this may be done either by draining one lock at a time – a long and tedious business – or by running off all chambers simultaneously. The latter is the usual – and quicker – method, but it does call for some care in controlling water levels. One ground paddle in each chamber should be opened (bottom gate paddle in the case of the lowest chamber) and the water allowed to run right through the entire flight and out into the lower pound while watching the level in each chamber carefully, particularly the top chamber containing the boat and the chamber immediately below it. The rate of fall in water levels in these two chambers should be adjusted until the levels are equal on both sides of the intermediate gate with the lower chamber full and the top chamber empty. All the remaining chambers should by now be almost empty – that is, they should contain just sufficient water to float a boat over the bottom sill – and at this point all paddles should be shut down. At the same time the boat is transferred to the next chamber below and the intermediate gates and paddles closed; as the whole staircase is now set, the boat is clear to descend.

Ascending a staircase in which all the chambers are empty – that is, set against you – is the reverse of the above procedure. Once the boat has been placed in the bottom chamber with the bottom gates and paddles shut, a ground paddle to each of the other chambers is opened all the way up the flight; when the levels in the bottom chamber and the one above it equalize, the paddle letting water into the upper chamber is shut and the boat taken into this chamber. Once all higher chambers have been filled all paddles are shut, and the boat worked up the flight in the normal way. From the mode of operation it will be appreciated that the wastage of water in using a staircase of this type can be very considerable.

STAIRCASE LOCKS WITH SIDE PONDS

This type of staircase lock works quite differently from the one just described because there are no paddles connecting the chambers, and instead of one lock chamber discharging directly into the next, all chambers except the lowest empty into large side ponds, from which

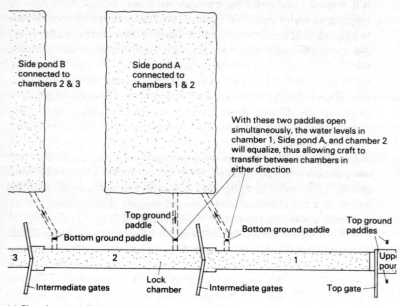

Side pond B connected to chambers 2 & 3

Side pond A connected to chambers 1 & 2

With these two paddles open simultaneously, the water levels in chamber 1, Side pond A, and chamber 2 will equalize, thus allowing craft to transfer between chambers in either direction

Top ground paddle

Bottom ground paddle

Bottom ground paddle

Top ground paddles

3

2

1

Upp pour

Intermediate gates

Lock chamber

Intermediate gates

Top gate

(a) Plan of part lock flight and side ponds

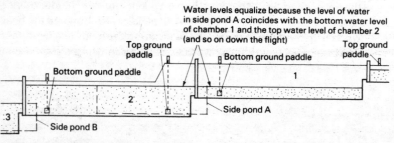

Water levels equalize because the level of water in side pond A coincides with the bottom water level of chamber 1 and the top water level of chamber 2 (and so on down the flight)

Top ground paddle

Bottom ground paddle

Bottom ground paddle

Top ground paddle

1

2

Side pond A

3

Side pond B

(b) Section through lock chambers

Fig. 30 Operation of a staircase lock with side ponds

all chambers except the topmost are also filled (see Chapter 2, pp. 49–51). Although apparently more complex, the method of operation is in fact much simpler than that of the ordinary staircase. Each chamber is provided with two paddles only: a top ground paddle to admit water from a side pond, and a bottom ground paddle to discharge water into a side pond (the topmost chamber in a flight of this type is fitted with the usual ground paddles connecting the chamber with the upper pound, and the lowest chamber has gate paddles). It must be stressed that, just as in the case of an ordinary lock, *both of the paddles serving any given chamber should never be open at the same time*. To equalize levels in any two adjoining chambers the ground paddle on each side of the intermediate gate must be opened: the bottom ground paddle of the upper chamber connects it with the side pond below, and the top ground paddle of the lower chamber connects that chamber with the same side pond. It is of no consequence which chamber is full and which is empty – the level of water in both chambers will equalize at the same level as the adjacent side pond, that is, at the filled level of the lower chamber, allowing a boat to pass from one chamber to the other in either direction. The method of operation is simplicity itself, and is only capable of misuse if one ignores or forgets the warning given above.

GUILLOTINE LOCKS

These are to be found mainly on the Rive Nene and in the Fens, and although the stop-lock at King's Norton on the northern section of the Stratford Canal is fitted with guillotine gates at both ends they are no longer in use, and remain permanently in the raised position. The Nene locks feature guillotine gates at the tail only, and have top gates (referred to locally as 'pointing doors') of the mitre type with ordinary paddle gear. Guillotine gates, which may be either vertically rising or radial, themselves act in lieu of paddles, as the initial movement of the gate allows water to escape beneath it. The gate should not be raised too much at first for fear of creating excessive turbulence in the lock chamber, as the top gates are designed to act as weirs at normal river levels and may have a considerable volume of water pouring over them. These large guillotine gates are tiring to work, not because any great strength is needed, but on account of the number of turns required to lift them through their complete range of movement – estimates seem to vary from about eighty to 120 turns. What is worse, they must be worked twice each time as the correct way to leave a lock on this navigation is with the guillotine raised so that the lock itself acts as a weir, when not in use, for the purposes of water control. A special key is needed to unlock the guillotine mechanism and this may be loaned from the river authority for a nominal sum.

LOCKING EMERGENCIES

While the boat is being worked through a lock a constant watch should be kept to ensure that nothing untoward is happening. Should the boat become jammed or hung up on gate or sidewall projections, or on the sill, all paddles must be closed *instantly* to prevent a worsening of the situation. If the incident is not serious, the boat can usually be freed by either slowly filling or emptying the chamber until matters are put right, but a boat that is firmly stuck must be treated with great caution, as hurried attempts at refloating may damage or sink it. If the boat is not in immediate danger and you are in doubt over what to do, telephone the hire company at once for instructions.

OPERATION OF SWING AND LIFT BRIDGES

These are always operated by boat crews except on the major commercial waterways of Yorkshire, the Gloucester and Sharpness Canal, the Caledonian Canal and in Ireland, where permanent bridge tenders are employed. The small swing bridges that are operated by crews are simple in design and use, and any difficulties experienced in working them will be due almost solely to poor maintenance in certain cases – usually those in which the turntable has become worn and partly misaligned, causing them to jam. Before operating any movable bridge, first make sure that no pedestrian or vehicle is about to use it, for although strictly speaking craft have priority, common sense and courtesy should be the rule, and to operate a bridge with a person or vehicle approaching and within reasonable distance is a breach of good manners. It is preferable for at least two people to be available for working movable bridges in case extra strength is required for their operation.

Swing bridges usually have a steel safety catch to keep them in alignment with the roadway; this should be lifted and the bridge pushed open using the projecting arm that forms an extension to the safety rail, and if the bridge is very stiff another person pushing at the opposite end will often be decisive in getting it to open. The bridge deck should always be swung to its fullest extent to provide maximum room for the boat to pass, and once this has been accomplished the bridge is swung back and locked in position by means of the safety catch, although it should be left open if an approaching boat is within 200 yards.

Lift bridges are of two types: the bascule design, of which there are a number of examples on the Llangollen Canal, and the less picturesque platform lift bridges to be found on the southern section of the Oxford Canal. The latter require merely a hefty downward pull on the balance beams to raise the deck, but bascule bridges are opened by either heaving on a length of chain or rope attached to the balance beams, or in some cases by a steel cable wound around a drum which is operated by a standard windlass. Occasionally the boater may find a bascule bridge devoid of its original dangling chain, and it will be necessary therefore to throw a line over the balance beam in order to operate it, so if in doubt take a mooring line with you together with a windlass.

All movable bridges should be *held* open so as to prevent them inadvertently closing, perhaps through wind pressure, while the boat is passing through; as this is your responsibility, never allow passers-by and children to operate them for you, even though the temptation may be strong at times. Sometimes movable bridges – usually of the accommodation type – are left permanently open for the convenience of boat traffic, so treat all bridges as you would farm gates: leave them as you find them. Swing bridges spanning lock chambers must always be opened before the lock is used, and although it is clear that a descending boat cannot enter the lock otherwise, ascending boats have been known to get into severe difficulties through omitting to do this.

BOAT-HANDLING AT LOCKS, MOVABLE BRIDGES AND THEIR APPROACHES

Where locks are crew-operated it is of course necessary first to put those who are to work the lock on the bank, and so far as the beginner is concerned the easiest way to do this is to bring the boat alongside the towpath and stop it as though mooring. The difficulty here may be lack of sufficient depth of water close to the bank, in which case the crew will have to jump for it unless the problem is solved by running the bow up to the bank at an angle as described in Chapter 6 pp. 153–4. The boat should be held back at least forty yards or so from the lock mouth in order to leave a large boat that may be about to emerge from the lock enough room to manoeuvre, but with greater confidence and a surer grasp of technique on the part of the steerer this distance may be reduced according to circumstances. If going downhill the boat may be taken right up to the head of the lock, providing there is no oncoming boat in the chamber, but when going uphill on no account should the bow be run up to the bottom gates, because there may be an oncoming boat in the lock that is about to emerge, or the lock may be full. Emptying a lock causes vicious turbulence at the lock tail with a strong undertow, and any boat close to the gates will be slammed into them with considerable force (and maybe some damage) and thrown about from side to side between the abutments: so keep well clear.

Once the bottom gates are open, steer into the lock. To the novice steerer a narrow lock chamber looks impossibly tight and he often has difficulty in entering it cleanly, not infrequently striking the abutments with some force and cannoning off the side walls until the boat finally comes to rest. This sort of thing is mostly caused by the same old problem of too much power, so enter the lock approaches *slowly*, lining up one side of the boat with the corresponding side wall so that there is apparently no gap between them, then check that the alignment of the boat with respect to the chamber is satisfactory, and use only small bursts of power in conjunction with the tiller to keep this alignment. When you are about halfway into the chamber put the engine into neutral, then gently reverse and bring the boat to a halt in the correct position relative to the length of the lock.

If going downhill, the boat should be held about midway in the chamber, and the important point to note here is that it must be sufficiently far forward to avoid grounding the stern on the projecting top sill as the water level drops – the steerer must watch for this constantly until the water has dropped below sill level. On the other hand, the boat should not be so far forward that the bow (or more likely the bow fender, if it is rigidly attached) is hung up on the bottom gates as the level drops. Gentle application of power, either forward or reverse as necessary, will keep the boat in the desired position as it tends to move backwards and forwards while the water surges out of the lock.

Rather more care is needed when ascending, as the force of water entering an empty lock can cause rather peculiar things to occur. Let us look at a narrow-gauge lock to begin with, and study what actually happens as the top ground paddles are opened. The force of water entering the chamber through the paddle culverts causes an area of violent turbulence about halfway or more down the length of the lock, thereafter flowing both forwards towards the bottom gates and backwards towards the top gates. These diverging flows form a slight water slope as they each run down to the ends of the chamber from the raised centred of the area of turbulence. Now in many cases the turbulence and its attendant water flows are insufficiently strong to affect the boat to any great extent, and the steerer is able to keep it in position by application of power in forward or reverse gear. But sometimes the turbulence is such that the boat is picked up by the backwards-running slope of water and thrown hard against the top sill, perhaps with some damage, if not to the boat itself then to loose and breakable items in the galley, not to mention the alarm and shock experienced by the steerer and anyone else who happens to be on the boat at the time. Such is the force of the water that full power in reverse has not the slightest effect in checking the onrush of the boat, and all that can be done is to shout a loud warning to those below. To avoid the possibility of this happening it is advisable first to move the boat right forward until the bow is resting against the top sill, hold it there on the engine, and only then open the top ground paddles, but not too quickly. After the inrush of water has lessened the engine

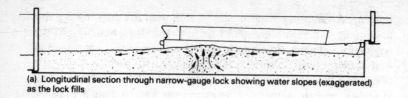

(a) Longitudinal section through narrow-gauge lock showing water slopes (exaggerated) as the lock fills

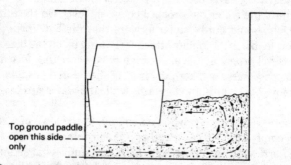

Top ground paddle open this side only

(b) Cross section through broad-gauge lock showing reversed water flow

Fig. 31 Water movement in locks

may be put into neutral as the boat is pressed against the sill by the water flow. When using this technique it is essential for the person operating the top paddles to check that the bow fender does not catch under any projections on the sill, and once the fender has cleared it and is resting against the rubbing plate (a steel plate fixed to the top gate to provide a smooth surface up which the bow rides as the lock fills) there should be little chance of anything going wrong. If the top gate is provided with a gate paddle this should be raised only after the bow has risen above the level of the paddle opening to prevent flooding of the boat by the descending plume of water from the aperture. For this reason gate paddles must never be opened first when the boat is hard up against the sill.

When ascending a broad lock different considerations apply. Opening a top ground paddle causes a strong flow of water from the culvert across the floor of the chamber to the opposite wall, where the flow is reversed and returns to the nearside at surface level. Opening a ground paddle on the same side of the chamber as the boat is stationed takes advantage of this, as the water flow from the culvert passes beneath the hull and the return flow of water at surface level presses the boat against the side wall and tends to hold it there. In spite of this, the boat should be secured in position by passing the bow and stern mooring lines around lock-side bollards and back to crew members on the boat who take up the slack as the boat rises; or, if there are no bollards, by standing on the lockside and holding the lines directly. Alternatively, the boat may be held on the forward line only and kept under control by going slowly ahead under power against the tension of the line. This precaution is strongly advised because when the other ground paddle is opened its water flow meets the first one, causing a confused swirl in which the boat may be swept across the chamber and dashed into a side wall or the sill if it is not secured. If the boat is held on the lines, and providing that it is far enough back from the top gates, gate paddles may safely be opened at the same time as ground paddles. When locking downhill the use of lines is generally unnecessary unless asked for by a lock-keeper, in which case they must never be made fast to bollards or any other fixture, otherwise the boat will be hung up. Once water levels have equalized, the gate immediately ahead of the boat is opened (with only one boat in the chamber there is no need to open both gates) and the boat steered out of the lock and stopped with its stern just clear of the gates ready for the crew to step aboard after all paddles and gates have been shut.

Manoeuvring at crew-operated movable bridges is similar to the technique used at locks. When putting the crew on the bank the boat should not be brought up too close, otherwise the final approach to the bridge gap will have to be done at an angle, making it more difficult for the inexperienced steerer to straighten up for the opening. In the case of lift bridges it is particularly inadvisable to make the approach at an angle as the swing of the bow may be misjudged and the cabin top seriously damaged on the underside of the inclined bridge deck – as the scarred undersides of many lift bridges testify. After passing through the bridge gap make certain that the stern is clear before moving the bridge back into position, but remain close enough to enable the crew to clamber aboard from either the abutments or the bridge deck itself.

BOAT-HANDLING AT MANNED LOCKS AND SWING BRIDGES

The completely different circumstances attending the passage of manned locks and swing bridges on rivers and commercial waterways place less of a burden on members of a boat crew other than the steerer, who must take careful note of all that is happening. Thames locks are provided with piled stagings set a short distance back from the head and tail of the lock and at the side of the navigation channel, and approaching craft should slow down and gently run up to these stagings, using them as temporary moorings until signalled by the lock-keeper to proceed; unless, of course, the gates are already open, in which case the boat may be taken straight into the lock and brought to a stop in the position indicated by the keeper. Craft must be held on bow and stern lines while in the chamber, and engines switched off (together with radios, cassette players and the like). On other waterways the boat should be brought reasonably close to the lock or swing bridge – taking care not to pass beyond any traffic lights showing red – and one prolonged blast sounded on the horn (craft going *downstream* on the River Weaver are required to sound one long blast followed by one short blast); then wait, holding the boat on station to one side of the navigation channel by use of the engine. When the keeper is ready for you to enter the lock he will signal, either manually or by switching the traffic lights to green. Proceed slowly into the chamber, watching for any hand signals from the keeper (which should always be acknowledged) indicating which side of the chamber you are to go. In some river locks there are vertical chains hanging down the side walls at intervals, and the boat must be positioned so that crew members in the bow and stern are able to hold on to these chains to steady the boat. Leave the engine on tick-over in neutral unless asked to do otherwise by the lock-keeper. Big locks can be a little frightening to the novice, mainly on account of their size, but the keepers are always very considerate when dealing with small pleasure-craft and operate the paddles in such a way as to cause a minimum of turbulence in the chamber, so do not forget to give the lock-keeper a wave and a word of thanks as you leave. Manned locks and swing bridges are subject to working hours, and you should remember to check beforehand the times when they will be closed. In manoeuvring at lock approaches when going downstream in a river take care to steer clear of weirs, and do not hold so far back from a lock that the boat is at or near the mouth of the weir channel, as you will be in considerable danger should the engine fail.

Manned swing bridges are approached in a similar manner to locks, taking care not to get too close to the bridge's radius of swing. Go ahead when signalled to do so, and thank the keeper as you pass by.

BOAT-HANDLING ON NON-TIDAL RIVERS

An important difference between boat-handling on rivers and on canals is that rivers are subject to currents, whereas canals are not (there is in fact a current on the Llangollen Canal which, although very slight, is sufficient to affect passage times). Moreover, rivers are prone to marked increases in current strength (and water depth) due to sudden flooding caused by excessive rainfall. As previously noted, all hire-boat traffic is stopped when flooding is severe, but even in normal conditions rivers should be treated with respect. Usually the strength of currents is not great, but it should be allowed for both when cruising and when manoeuvring close to the bank.

The current is always stronger towards the middle on straight reaches of a river and around the outside of bends, and this discrepancy may be used to advantage by navigating in the slacker water nearer the banks and the inside of bends when moving upstream. Craft going downstream must travel at a speed greater than that of the current in order to have 'steerage way', and at times this can entail speeds over the ground that seem frightening to the novice. Again, by using the shallower water closer to the banks the boat's speed may be reduced slightly, but the steerer must watch out for obstructions on the river bed and for raised 'bars' of silt. The latter are more likely to be present on or about the insides of bends, although they may occur at any place where the current is slowed and thus deposits silt. When a river is running strongly no attempt should be made to turn broadside on across the channel upstream of bridges, weirs, moored craft and so on because of the danger of being swept sideways on to them before the turn can be completed. An increase in current strength is usually accompanied by a rise in water level, and in these conditions the steerer must be alert to the consequences of reduced headroom at bridges, particularly if going downstream, when bringing the boat to a halt is much less certain because of the following current.

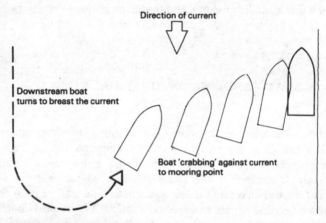

Direction of current

Downstream boat turns to breast the current

Boat 'crabbing' against current to mooring point

Fig. 32   Mooring on a river

Going alongside should always be done against the current, so that a boat moving downstream must make a sweeping turn of 180 degrees when coming abreast of the point at which it is intended to stop, and the boat's heading brought around until pointing upstream and at a slight angle to the bank. By a careful application of power in conjunction with rudder action the boat may then be balanced against the current and slowly 'crabbed' across to the mooring in a manner similar to that used when steering a straight stretch of still water with a strong wind on the beam. An upstream approach makes for much better control as the boat may be held at a standstill if necessary by opposing engine power to the force of the current, and altering position by means of the rudder. When stopping the boat from a downstream approach to a mooring, on the other hand, one has to rely upon the use of power in reverse, which not only may be insufficient due to the added effects of the following stream, but also cause loss of steerage, perhaps with expensive results if other craft are moored close by.

When mooring, the boat should be secured by the bow line first to prevent the bow from being swung out by the current, and mooring lines should be taken out at a wider angle than usual, leaving enough slack to accommodate an overnight rise or fall in river level. Do not forget to make sure also that the hull is floating clear of any obstructions and is not likely, for example, to jam up under a staging if the water level rises. The tendency for the bow to swing outwards on the current can be usefully exploited when casting off by pushing it out first to clear any obstruction, such as other moored craft, while at the same time holding the stern in by its line. As the bow comes round forward power is then gently applied, the stern line cast off and the boat steered away at an angle from the bank.

LARGE VESSELS AND OTHER HAZARDS

Large craft will almost certainly be encountered on rivers and commercial waterways and therefore a sharp look-out should be kept at all times as big vessels require a lot of room in which to manoeuvre, and invariably have to keep to the middle of the channel because of their deep draught. Pleasure-craft must steer well clear of them and be prepared to give way as circumstances demand, and so it is essential that all boaters who intend to navigate major waterways be familiar with the recognized sound signals (see Appendix II). Commercial vessels will signal their intentions clearly if they intend to depart from the usual 'rule of the road', or when about to manoeuvre, and the steerer of a pleasure-boat must know how to signal the appropriate response: he should not rely on the other helmsman having telepathic powers! For instance, should a vessel blow four short blasts on the horn, pause, two short blasts, the steerer must recognize instantly that this signal means 'I am about to turn, or to turn round, to port' (*his* left, *your* right). Furthermore, he should be aware that the larger craft will probably require most of the river width in order to do this, and should signal back with three short blasts indicating 'My engine is going astern', which will unmistakably indicate to the other helmsman that you are standing off, leaving him clear room to manoeuvre. Commercial vessels should always be given priority, even if you have to surrender your own 'rights' in the process, unless to do so would put either of you in danger, and you should never try to overtake without first having been given clearance by the other helmsman.

On rare occasions the steerer may have to navigate past a large river dredger, and for the inexperienced boatsman this can be alarming if the dredger is moored by cable to both banks, as sometimes happens. If you meet with this situation do *not* attempt to pass over a cable (which, under its own weight, will be sagging below the water surface) and run the risk of snagging it, but wait until you are given a clear signal to proceed after the cable has been winched out and dropped to the river bed. Dredgers at work indicate the side on which they are to be passed by displaying visual marks, usually a white spherical or cruciform shape, with a corresponding red shape on the other side.

The navigation channel should be followed at all times, and the temptation resisted to explore inviting creeks and backwaters, particularly when these are clearly marked 'unnavigable' on the guide or chart. Running aground can be a serious business, not to mention the danger of rocks and other underwater obstructions which may do considerable damage to, or even sink, GRP and timber craft.

Power-driven boats are not the only craft to be met with on rivers, and to find himself rapidly approaching a sailing or a sculling regatta can be rather disconcerting for the novice, who may be at a loss as to what to do when faced with a stretch of water apparently blocked by small boats. However, all sculling competitions set aside a marked channel for use by other craft, and this can be semi-permanent – as at Henley-on-Thames – or, more usually, a temporary course marked by buoys. Slow right down while passing the area of the competition and watch out for returning crews and small boats occupied by spectators. Sailing regattas present a somewhat different hazard: the dinghies, especially if tacking, may appear to be moving at random all over the river, effectively concealing from the steerer any obvious course to follow, so slow right down and keep as close to the bank as possible. In such circumstances the rule 'power gives way to sail' may be quite inappropriate as a sailing craft tacking towards your boat is far better placed to avoid you by going about, and any attempt to steer around it may simply result in confusion on both sides, with a much increased chance of collision. By maintaining a straight course at slow speed you show your intentions clearly enough, and sound signals are better dispensed with in this situation.

Canal tunnels may be classed under four headings: (a) narrow-gauge tunnels that may be entered at any time; (b) narrow-gauge tunnels that may be entered only at the times specified on notice boards fixed next to the tunnel entrances; (c) broad-gauge tunnels that may be entered at any time; (d) narrow-gauge tunnels, the traffic through which is regulated by tunnel-keepers during normal working hours. In the last case, which applies only to Harecastle Tunnel on the Trent and Mersey Canal, boats wishing to navigate the tunnel outside of working hours may only pass through at stated times as in (b) above.

When nearing a tunnel portal slow down until you have a clear view along the tunnel length and, if the entrance is fitted with a gauge, check that the boat will pass under it. Tunnel gauges indicate the height of the roof at its lowest point, and as this can be much less than the height at the entrance *on no account must a gauge be lifted to allow the boat to proceed*. If the tunnel takes only one-way traffic first look for a headlight to make sure that there is no oncoming boat inside it. The absence of daylight at the other end is no cause for alarm, as this may be due to diesel fumes or to a boat going through the tunnel away from you. In the case of a broad-gauge tunnel with two-way traffic you will always be clear to enter. Switch on the headlight and all the cabin lights to give the steerer maximum visibility and once in the tunnel keep to the centre at slow speed until you are confident that you can maintain a straight course (notices reading 'Keep to the right' at tunnel mouths are not to be taken literally, but merely serve to remind steerers that they must keep right when passing oncoming craft). Narrow-gauge tunnels with a towpath usually have a very constricted channel and it is virtually impossible to navigate them without touching the sides, but providing that you keep to a reasonable speed this does not matter. Do not apply too much power in any case as this will only make the boat harder to steer, and the increased exhaust fumes will not be particularly pleasant. Should you find that you are catching up with a boat in front reduce speed to match his and stay at least fifty yards behind; *never* attempt to overtake no matter how slow he is travelling. It is very bad manners to close right up to the stern of a boat under any circumstances but doubly so in a tunnel as the headlight of the boat behind distracts the steerer of the lead boat (who may himself be held up by a boat ahead), and collision will almost certainly follow if for any reason the lead boat has to stop suddenly.

In broad-gauge tunnels keep your attention fixed on any approaching headlight, and when you are within a few boat-lengths of it slow down and ease the boat over to the right-hand wall, keeping a foot or two away from it. By this time you should have dipped the headlight (if a dip-switch is fitted) or swivelled it upwards to shine if possible on the roof so as not to dazzle the oncoming steerer. Maintain a slow speed, and above all do not put the engine into neutral, or – worse still – use reverse, as you will lose steerage way and perhaps cause a collision. If there is another headlight a short distance behind the other boat continue to keep to the right – it may be a powered craft, but it could be a butty towed by the boat you have just passed, in which case make absolutely sure that you are as close to the tunnel wall as possible and on no account allow the bow to swing to the left as it may pass under the towline, leaving you to be caught broadside on by the bow of the butty, with highly unpleasant results. When all crafts are clear you may resume your course in the centre of the channel, switching the headlight on full, or readjusting its direction as you do so.

Throughout the tunnel length there may be much water dripping from the roof (particularly in very rainy weather), and fair quantities may be pouring from air shafts, so those who wish to remain on deck should wear wet weather gear. Do not allow any small children or pets on deck except under the closest supervision as it is fatally easy to lose someone overboard in the noise and darkness, especially from the stern, which is generally kept blacked-out by closing the aft bulkhead doors in order to preserve the steerer's 'night vision'. When about to emerge from a tunnel sound a long blast on the horn to warn any boats that may be about to enter, or which may be manoeuvring out of sight by the tunnel mouth, and finally, do not forget to switch off the headlight!

BREAKDOWNS AND BOW-HAULING

Breakdowns can be very annoying to the hirer, who naturally expects to make the most of a boating holiday and resents having to spend perhaps several hours immobilized, sometimes in less than agreeable surroundings. None the less, however well cared for the boat may be all things mechanical are prone to failure at one time or another, and unless there is unmistakable evidence of sloppy or careless maintenance the stranded hirer would do well to apply a little give-and-take, particularly if the hire company responds promptly to his call for assistance. The term 'promptly' can have a different meaning for different people, but I think that to interpret it strictly and without regard to circumstances is to be unreasonable. For instance, to call the hire company in the evening and expect them to send a fitter many miles that same night just to make a minor repair *would* be unreasonable, unless it concerned an indispensable part of the boat's equipment – the cooker, say, or the water pump. Anything that does not seriously impair living conditions aboard can wait until the next day, when a repair may be carried out the next morning, and probably more quickly, too, in full daylight. The length of time taken for the repair depends much upon the nature of the breakdown, but in all cases the boat must first be moved to a point near to a road so that the company's vehicle containing the tools and equipment can be brought up as close as possible. Very often the nearest access point for vehicles will be a road bridge over the canal, and when making the telephone call for assistance the number or name of this bridge should be given together with some idea, however vague, of the nature of the breakdown or fault. Once you have made this call do *not* move the boat on to another location, no matter how long the wait seems, but instead ring the company again to make sure that your directions have not been misinterpreted. If the fault does not prevent the boat from moving under its own power then taking it to the nearest road bridge will present no problem, but should this not be the case you will have to resort to bow-hauling.

'Bow-hauling' is the term used to describe the towing of a boat from the bank or towpath by manpower. It sounds hard work but in fact is surprisingly easy once the boat is moving – always provided that the towpath is in reasonable condition and there is little wind. Hauling is done using both bow and stern lines, the latter supplying most

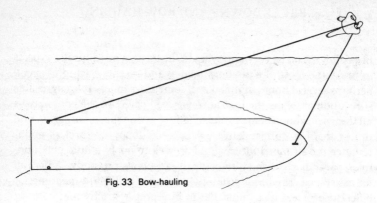

Fig. 33 Bow-hauling

of the motive effort while the former keeps the boat on course. The person on the stern line should haul from a position well ahead of the stern so as not to pull it into the bank and leave the 'steering' to the other person, who will be keeping station almost level with the bow. Alternatively, the boat may be hauled by one person pulling at a suitable point on a line joining bow and stern and formed by tying the respective lines together, but hire-craft mooring lines are rarely long enough for this method to be used effectively, unless the boat is fairly short. If, when cruising, you meet with a boat being bow-hauled you must, of course, pass it on the 'off-side' (the side away from the towpath) just as you would a horse-drawn craft, and slow right down to tick-over as you do so.

CHAPTER EIGHT

WORKING THE NAVIGATION (II)

FURTHER HINTS ON LOCK OPERATION

The novice is probably not unduly concerned about the efficiency of his lock operation, and at first is fairly content to work the boat through a lock without committing any serious blunders, but as confidence is gained he may at some stage begin to take pride in operating locks as efficiently as possible. Notice the use of the word 'efficiently', which is not necessarily to be equated with 'speedily', as may be judged from the number of lock crews who appear to go everywhere at nothing less than a gallop and still somehow contrive to hold up everyone else. Dashing about a lock is neither safe nor desirable, yet some people never seem to realize that a lock may be worked quickly and smoothly by a crew whose members never move faster than a walking pace. Knowing precisely what to do and when to do it is the secret, and to rest when nothing further can be done for the time being, particularly if there are another twenty locks in the flight ahead.

Members of an experienced crew can be recognized instantly: they walk up to the lock and separate to their respective tasks, one person continuing along the towpath to set the next lock, and all with scarcely a word spoken. Let us follow their actions in detail as they take a boat through a narrow lock in a flight, assuming that there are three persons involved, and that they have a 'hard road' – that is, the flight is set against them. The procedure is described first going uphill, then down.

As the person who is 'setting ahead' (see p. 190) walks on up the towpath, casting a quick glance in passing over the top paddle gear to be certain that all racks are fully down, the other two swiftly wind up the bottom gate paddles after first making sure that no descending boat can be seen in the next lock above, and then sit down on the balance beams while waiting for the lock to run off. When water levels are within a few inches of equalizing they each face 'uphill', place the small of their backs against the outer ends of their respective beams, and use the weight of the body to apply a little leverage on the gates. Just before the lock empties completely the gates give a slight jerk as they are relieved of water pressure, and after a moment or two the balance beams start to swing, assisted by the lock crew walking slowly backwards and pushing with their feet against the brick insets provided for that purpose, until the gates are fully open. By this time the boat is nearly at the lock tail and there is no delay before it enters the chamber, while at the same time the gate paddles are closed and the crewmen stand at the ends of the balance beams ready to swing the gates shut the instant the boat's stern clears them. The boat, with its engine running quietly in reverse gear, slowly moves up the chamber as the two crewmen walk along the lockside to their respective ground paddles, one of them looking down in passing to check that the sill is free from projections and that the boat – now in forward gear – is resting with its bow fender hard up against it. There is some leakage from the top gate and a narrow plume of water is falling on to the fore-deck and splashing into the well, but this is not serious as no water can flood the cabin (the forward bulkhead door having been closed and secured before the boat entered the lock), and what little there is in the well quickly drains out through the self-draining apertures in the hull. The top ground paddles are wound up slowly and water boils furiously under the boat, lifting the stern above the level of the bow as the fender heaves up the sill and on to the rubbing plate. Up goes the gate paddle and the lock fills quickly, the boat backing off the gate as the levels equalize to prevent the bow fender from catching under the gate handrail. As the gate starts to move the person at the offside ground paddle closes it, strides across the footboard as the gate is opening, closes the nearside ground paddle, and walks off towards the next lock. His partner closes the gate paddle while the boat gathers speed out of the lock, shuts the gate, takes a last look around to check that all paddle racks are right down, and sets off up the towpath. The boat is by now halfway up the pound and dead in line with the lock chamber ahead, the gates of which have already been opened by the person setting the flight.

When locking downhill the operation is carried out with the same economy of effort. This time the lock has been set by the crew member working ahead, and the other two arrive just as the boat enters the chamber. One person walks on to the bottom gates and stands ready with his windlass on the spindle of a gate paddle while the other shuts the top gate. As the breast post comes against the rebate the gate paddle is wound up quickly and the boat starts to drop at once (the practice of opening bottom gate paddles before the top gate is shut is to be deplored, on account of the wear and tear it causes to the heel post and its fastenings), whereupon the winder walks across the footboards and opens the other paddle, his partner joining him at the bottom gates while the boat slowly sinks down in the lock. Finally the levels equalize and the gates are swiftly opened, the steerer watching the lock crew for a signal to indicate whether they intend to 'walk or ride'. The next pound is a fairly long one, so they opt for a 'ride', closing the paddles as the boat emerges from the chamber and is halted with its stern close to the lock tail. The gates are shut the instant that the boat clears them; the lock crew take a last look around, walk down the steps and climb aboard just as the boat gathers way.

By describing the procedure of locking through in detail I have tried to give some idea of the way in which experienced crews save time and energy when 'working the navigation'. They possess no secret formula, nor do they resort to any of the sometimes dubious tricks used by the old commercial boatsmen. If there is a secret, it lies only in the fact that every action is meaningful and contributes directly to the saving of time, and is governed by a conscious effort never to do in sequence any operations that can be carried out simultaneously (a perfect example of this is the time-wasting of crews that close bottom gate paddles with the boat waiting in the lock, and only then open the gates). Simultaneous operation is well illustrated by the practice of 'setting ahead', in which one lock is being set while the boat is being worked through another.

SETTING AHEAD

This is a time-honoured practice dating back to commercial boating days when delays cost money and everything was subordinated to the necessity for 'getting on'. Eventually it became known as 'lock-wheeling', in which a crewman would cycle the towpath and 'turn round' any lock not in the boat's favour, thus cutting out avoidable hold-ups. Nowadays there is little reason for that kind of urgency, but occasionally a keen crew will use this technique, particularly if they are making a long trip and working to a tight schedule. Far more common is the practice of 'setting ahead' at lock flights, which is to be encouraged in the interests of reducing potentially long delays caused by a rapid build-up of traffic. The person setting should use discretion in judging how far ahead of the boat he may reasonably go, and must not (as sometimes happens) claim priority over on-coming craft by setting several locks in advance. Prudence should be the watchword here, for not only is it extremely discourteous to turn a lock round in someone's face, but a great deal of water is wasted at the same time. Certainly, if the flight is long and visibility up and down it good, then perhaps two or three locks may safely be set, providing no oncoming craft are in sight, but otherwise it is probably wiser to keep just one lock ahead of the boat. Doing this when the flight is set against you will also help to conserve water if the upper lock is not run off until the lock containing the boat has started to fill, for in this way lock will be emptied into lock, with little or no wastage of water over the bypass weir.

Setting ahead in a long flight with all or most of the locks against you can be an exhausting business, particularly if you are working single-handed, yet the task can become enjoyable and peculiarly satisfying if the locks are worked smoothly and efficiently. Extra care should be taken if you are alone and out of sight of the boat, for tiredness may be masked by enthusiasm and might easily lead to a serious accident – for instance, when stepping from one footboard across to the other during the process of opening bottom gates. This move should always be made with great care, particularly in wet or icy weather, but if it seems doubtful to you then walk right round the lock to open the other gate rather than risk a fall. To stride the gap in this way does, however, save a lot of time and effort when working single-handed uphill, and results in much quicker lock operation, as does the practice of opening the *first* paddle that you come to so as to start the lock filling up (or emptying) with the least delay. While a lock is filling, stand by the offside ground paddle and shut it the moment that the lock is full, then cross over and open the top gate *before* closing the remaining paddles in case leakage from the bottom gates runs the lock off slightly and prevents the gate from opening (and do the same with bottom gates, for a similar reason). Considered individually, these may seem minor points, but collectively they can make a big difference to the ease and smoothness with which a lock is worked.

CLEARING OBSTRUCTIONS FROM LOCKS

Some areas, usually in or around towns, are notable for the amount of flotsam of all kinds to be found in the canal. Through the movement of water and boats fairly considerable quantities of this rubbish can find its way into locks, or be thrown there by children, and sometimes enough accumulates to prevent the gates being fully opened. This is of little consequence in a broad lock (unless a breasted-up pair is about to enter), but a narrow lock gate that is not open completely will almost certainly prevent the entry of the boat, and because of the risk of jamming it would be unwise to try to force it in under power. It is a simple matter to clear away floating debris from behind a top gate as it is easily accessible from the lockside, but freeing bottom gates can be a much harder proposition if the chamber is very deep. The difficulty arises, of course, because you have to work from the lockside using the long shaft, which in some cases may have insufficient length to reach even water level. Assuming that it does, however, prod and push the rubbish out from behind the lock gates until they can be opened fully, then push the rubbish out of the tail of the lock and, if possible, to the side, where it can be lifted out of the canal and stacked under the towpath hedge. Do not leave any debris floating about the chamber in case it causes the boat to jam. Sometimes the gates cannot be opened fully and yet no rubbish is to be seen; this usually indicates that an obstruction is lying on the chamber bottom or the sill. Feel for it with the long shaft and try to determine not only its position but what sort of an object it is. If it is light in weight and suitably shaped – a bicycle frame, say – you may be able to hook it out fairly easily, but in the case of a large heavy block – perhaps a coping stone – this will not be possible and other measures will have to be adopted. Of course, you could always telephone the Section Inspector's office for assistance, but this is likely to be very time-consuming and in any case you may have to wait until the following morning before help arrives. Probably the best thing in most circumstances is to attempt to shift the obstruction yourself, which may prove less difficult than it appeared at first sight. Much depends on the equipment to hand: for instance, if a keb (a long-tined rake with a very long handle) is available there should be little trouble in removing almost anything, but this good fortune would be exceptional, and in most cases one has to improvise by using what items can be found on the boat. The two ways of shifting smooth and heavy objects from behind bottom gates as described here do actually work, and perhaps the ingenious reader will think of even more effective methods!

Having located the obstruction and obtained some idea of its nature by prodding with the long shaft, send someone to the boat for the bow and stern lines (and do not forget that the boat must be *held* into the bank once these have been removed). Attach one to the bottom of the long shaft about eighteen inches up from the butt using a round turn and two half hitches (see fig. 44 on p. 212). Station a crew member holding the end of the line on the opposite side of the lock, then drop the long shaft vertically downwards until the butt rests on the chamber bottom behind the obstruction (if the line proves too short, tie the second one to it using a fisherman's knot). While pressing down on the long shaft, direct the person holding the line to pull in the direction in which you wish the obstruction to move – usually towards the centre line of the chamber – keeping up a steady pressure as it is slid away from the gates. In this way it is possible to shift quite large and heavy objects with a minimum of effort. Once the obstruction is clear of the gates they may be opened and the lock worked, but without the proper equipment it will not be feasible to lift the object out of the chamber. Never attempt to flush out a heavy obstruction by raising the top paddles as the force will be insufficient to move it, and all you will succeed in doing is to waste water.

Another method of moving obstructions is to 'dredge' for them, and for this you will need both mooring lines and a windlass. Attach the

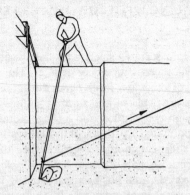

Fig. 34 Clearing bottom gates of an obstruction

lines to the windlass by passing their ends through the windlass socket and back through the respective spliced eyes, pull the loop taut and drop the windlass – which acts as a weight – behind the obstruction, taking a line to each side of the lock. The 'V' where the two lines meet should now contain the obstruction, which is moved by pulling on both lines as required.

Even if the gates are fully open there may be floating debris inside the chamber and this may jam between the hull and the lock side wall, bringing the boat to an abrupt halt. If this happens, do not attempt to force the boat forward by applying more power, but put the engine in full reverse and try to back off, at the same time moving the stern rapidly from side to side by pushing on each side wall alternately. Should this fail, try to dislodge the obstruction by means of the long shaft, and as a last resort open the top paddles to flush the boat clear while still applying the other measures, when, with perseverance, it should eventually come free. These methods are used when going uphill and should not be necessary in the case of a descending boat as any jammed debris will be immediately accessible from the lock side. If the boat is entirely within the chamber when it sticks, *never* attempt to float it free by closing the gates and operating the lock, otherwise you will probably end up by sinking it.

DEALING WITH LOW WATER LEVELS

This is a problem associated solely with canals, and one that most canal boaters will meet with sooner or later. The most serious and consistent cases of low water levels occur during periods of drought, when reservoirs are depleted and summit pounds subject to steady water loss through evaporation and lockage, sometimes in spite of constant back-pumping. In these circumstances little can be done until rainfall in sufficient quantities restores the situation, and before that happens a canal, or part of it, may have to be closed (the southern section of the Oxford Canal has been particularly vulnerable to this kind of water shortage in recent years). It is more common, however, to find individual pounds 'off weir'; that is, with a water level lower than the lip of the by-wash weir, sometimes to the point where the pound is almost dry. Not infrequently this is due to incorrect or careless operation of paddle gear, either by simultaneously opening paddles at both ends of a lock or perhaps by failing to ensure that all paddles are fully closed after the boat has been locked through. Whatever the reason for low water levels, the boater is presented with the problem of how best to deal with a more or less serious situation, and one that sometimes is compounded by inherent shallowness of the channel through lack of dredging.

When deciding what to do about low water levels the boater must use common sense, and deal with matters in the correct order of priority. If when going uphill you find that the next pound is well off weir, first check the lock to see whether any paddles have been left open, or partially open; any that are should be closed at once, and the situation then assessed. Unless the pound is almost dry there will usually be enough water depth to float the boat, providing that it has a standard hire boat draught of about two feet and manages to clear the top sill. Remember that entry into the pound will reduce its level by one lockful of water, and that although the effect of this will be greater in a short pound, the loss may be made good more easily by running water down from the pound above than it would be in the case of a long pound. However, do *not* run water until all else has failed. If the boat can be got into the low pound, keep going ahead at very slow speed, allowing the fore-end to seek out the channel while rocking the boat gently from side to side if it seems to be slowing down and grounding. Often this will be sufficient to keep the boat moving – no matter how slowly – until the next lock is reached, but if it goes solidly aground and is obviously in the middle of the channel other measures will have to be adopted. Hauling from the bank is one possibility (when negotiating very low pounds there must always be a lock crew on the bank to give assistance), although the mooring lines on most hire craft are rarely long enough, even when both are tied together, as the hauling line must be very long if the boat is not to be dragged out of the channel at an angle towards the bank. A boat tends to ground at the stern as this is the area of maximum draught, and so the stern should be relieved of as much weight as possible by sending all on board except the steerer right up into the bow, then rocking the boat while applying minimum power, and finally rocking and shafting without use of the engine. Should these measures fail, it is clear that the boat has no chance of moving further and will have to be floated off. Meanwhile, other craft should be prevented from locking up into the pound as this will only worsen matters.

What to do next depends on the severity of the problem, the length of the pound and the state of water levels in the pound – or pounds – above. Strictly speaking, someone should be sent off to contact the local lock-keeper, other canal employees in the neighbourhood (for example, piling gangs), or the Section Inspector's office. But sometimes none of these courses is possible, particularly out of working hours, and if in addition the nearest telephone lies in a village several miles away the boater is left with no sensible alternative but to deal with the situation himself. The greatest care must be exercised when running water down, especially if the pound concerned is already below weir. Top and bottom paddles must not be all opened fully, as the resulting rush of water may well bring down all kinds of rubbish, possibly jamming some of it behind the bottom gates (and on the sill if the bottom gates have been opened), and maybe in the paddle apertures as well. Probably the safest method is to operate the lock in the normal way, thus running one lockful at a time into the lower pound until the grounded boat just floats free; or, alternatively, to run water slowly through the lock using one half-open top paddle. Once the boat is able to move, shut down all paddles immediately to prevent unnecessary wastage of water from the upper pound (opening and closing of paddles may be signalled for on the boat's horn). Should the boat ground again, repeat the entire procedure (first rocking and shafting, then floating off) until the lock is reached. Hopefully, the boat will clear the sill, but if it does not then flush it into the chamber by raising a top paddle for a moment or two and apply power as the paddle is closed, when the temporary head of water in the chamber will float the boat in.

Craft working downhill through low pounds have the slight advantage of taking water down with them, but if water levels are very low this is of little consequence and the measures described above will almost certainly have to be used. Remember, though, to send someone on first to check that all paddles are closed on the lock ahead.

THE EXPERIENCED BOATER

The acquisition of boating skills is probably a long, slow process for most people, given that many spend no more than two or three weeks afloat each year, and taking into account the likelihood that a proportion of even those who return to the inland waterways regularly are fairly casual in their approach to boating. But in spite of the limited time at his disposal, the enthusiast tends to progress rapidly and within three or four years may have joined the swelling ranks of experienced boaters – a stage which for some holds its own dangers, for there is always a temptation to regard oneself as an 'expert', and in turn this can lead to over-confidence and sometimes a degree of recklessness. The true expert, on the other hand, although possessing a high degree of skill tempers his actions with caution, for in most situations he knows what can go wrong; and because of the wide range of techniques at his disposal he can simplify a problem – that is, if he has not already anticipated and avoided it in the first place. There can be no short cut to the acquisition of this level of expertise, which can only be gained through a long and wide experience of many different situations; indeed it is the sheer variety of this experience that sometimes leads to disagreement among experts, although usually only over details, not over the main facets of boating practice and knowledge, concerning which there exists a broad consensus of opinion.

The skills of the experienced narrowboat steerer are centred on two principal considerations: the position of the fore-end and the boat's speed. He knows full well that the fore-end must be correctly positioned at all times relative to the features of the canal such as bends, bridge-holes, the channel, other craft and so on, if the boat is to be steered accurately and is not to be run aground. And those same features demand increases and decreases of speed according to circumstances, balancing propeller thrust against rudder action, and both against wind and the effects of shallow water. All these things the experienced steerer senses rather than sees or calculates, feeling through the soles of his feet how the boat is swimming and thus how deep the channel is, ascertaining whether the engine is labouring or running freely with a smooth propeller wash, automatically correcting for the effects of cross-wind, noting the backdraught from the trees ahead, and observing without seeming effort many other small but vital factors likely to influence the boat's performance. Such a high degree of concentration, awareness and anticipation is unknown to the novice, but must be acquired if he is to progress to the ranks of experienced steerers.

For example, at this level of experience the steerer does not waste time by trying to manoeuvre the boat alongside the towpath at locks and movable bridges, preferring to drop the lock crew off at the preceding bridge-hole. If there is no bridge-hole he selects a suitable point and approaches the towpath at a shallow angle, putting the engine in neutral and swinging the stern slowly towards the bank, judging the swing relative to the observed depth of water so that the stern clears the towpath by the shortest possible distance yet does not go aground. In most situations the crew will now be able to step from the stern on to the towpath quite easily; at this point the boat is still moving, with its bow pointing towards the centreline of the canal, and when the stern is well clear of the bottom forward gear is engaged and the boat swung around until it is parallel with the bank and in the centre of the canal. Once the boat is lined up satisfactorily, neutral is selected again and the boat allowed to drift slowly to a halt facing the lock and about thirty or forty yards away (assuming an uphill direction of travel and a full lock). The experienced boater knows the state of a lock at a glance by noting the presence or absence of water leaking between or around the bottom gates; sometimes a lock can be seen to be empty by the daylight showing between the gates. The steerer then gauges his actions accordingly: if the lock is empty he continues forward in gear on tick-over, so judging the boat's speed that it is within a few yards of the lock mouth as the gates are opened. (Never carry out this sort of approach at high speed – an obstruction jammed behind a gate may mean that the boat is unable to enter the chamber, and it may be impossible to stop in sufficient time to avoid a bad collision with the gate or the abutment walls.) A full lock requires a few minutes to run off and therefore the approach demands more careful timing, and to complicate matters there may well be an oncoming boat out of the steerer's line of vision, in which case one of the lock crew makes an appropriate signal (shouting is generally useless on account of engine noise). Each crew may devise their own signalling system, but personally I use only two signals: an arm raised vertically with extended finger pointing upwards to indicate an oncoming boat travelling uphill (an 'up' boat), and an arm held out from the side with extended finger pointing downwards and pumped up and down twice to indicate a downhill boat (a 'down' boat). It is up to the steerer to watch his crew for signals at all times, and these should always be acknowledged.

If the boat is held up by an oncoming craft it is usually an advantage to be further away from the lock rather than closer to it, as there is more room to manoeuvre; that is, to hold the boat almost stationary with slight bursts in ahead gear to maintain the desired position in the channel, counteracting the effects of cross-wind as necessary. While the oncoming boat is locking through, the experienced steerer does not approach the lock too closely, but times it so that the emerging boat is several yards clear of the lock mouth before the two boats pass, thus leaving enough room to align the entering boat with the chamber. Knowing that any other boat may be under the control of the rawest beginner, he always allows plenty of room as a matter of courtesy and safety. A lock may be approached more closely if there is no oncoming boat in it; in fact accurate steering is helped by the slight current created by the lock's run-off, making it easier to maintain alignment with the chamber as the boat moves slowly forward on tick-over. How much water remains in the lock may be judged by the amount of turbulence at the lock tail, and when this indicates that the chamber is almost empty the boat's speed is increased so that it enters the lock mouth as the gates open.

A really strong cross-wind makes it very difficult to maintain an almost stationary position in the channel, and to avoid being blown against the bank it may be necessary to run the fore-end aground at as close an angle as possible to the wind, holding it there by putting the tiller over with forward gear engaged until the lock has been turned round. In a narrow channel this technique is not feasible and the boat may have to lie alongside the towpath if the wind is blowing from the offside, in which case some hefty pushing while holding off the bow with the long shaft will likely be required to get it into the lock. It is much easier with the wind blowing in the opposite direction as the boat may be held alongside the towpath using the boathook hooked over the grab-rail amidships; when ready to move off the boat is simply released, whereupon the wind blows it out into mid channel. In fact, with growing experience strong winds, rather than being regarded as a total menace, may be put to good use in all sorts of situations; for instance, with the wind on the beam a stationary or slowly moving craft will be blown sideways – a boon when attempting to moor in a gap between other moored boats.

In the case of a single boat it is sometimes more convenient, certainly with an under-strength lock crew, to operate broad locks from one side only, opening one gate at top and bottom and using the paddles on that same side. This 'single-sided' working eliminates the necessity for walking completely round a broad lock in order to close the gates and shut the paddles, and is not that much slower in total time taken. Moreover, when travelling uphill the use of the ground paddle nearest the boat not only creates less turbulence in the chamber but, as explained earlier, holds the boat against the lock wall. When negotiating flights of broad locks, which are heavy to work, the lock crew expends less energy, and if there are only two people available for locking then one is free to set ahead.

HANDLING FULL-LENGTH NARROWBOATS

At one time full-length narrowboats of any type were not available for hire to beginners, but nowadays this rule is applied with less stringency, although some companies refuse to bow to commercial pressures and still insist that the hirer be adequately experienced. There are good reasons for this caution. Full-length narrowboats are the largest hire craft on the canal system: the draught of a full-length boat may be as much as three feet when under way, making steering very difficult in the shallower canals, and the relatively large area of superstructure makes them exceptionally vulnerable to strong cross-winds. It is important to realize, too, that a full-length boat is something more than just a sixty-footer with another ten or twelve feet added, for that extra length puts it into the class of craft whose overall dimensions are determined by those of the narrow-gauge canals, which means that on those canals the boat is working at the very limits of the waterway configuration. For these reasons manoeuvring a full-length narrowboat in confined waters can be a tricky business, calling for good judgement and anticipation of the boat's movements; even on straight sections constant attention must be paid to the steering to ensure that the boat keeps to the deeper water, and on bends the channel (which these days does not always lie on the outer radius of the bend due to shallow draught craft cutting the corner) must be followed faithfully if the boat is not to run aground. Great care must be taken to position the bow correctly in the turn so that the stern does not swing out of the channel, but on very sharp bends it is sometimes difficult to avoid running the fore-end too close to the inside shoulder, with consequent loss of steering. The boat may be controlled more readily if speed is reduced before entering the bend so that power may be applied for steering corrections if necessary. *In the case of a full-length boat it is most essential that the correct sound signals be given and speed reduced when the view ahead is obscured.*

Camping boats are particularly vulnerable to strong cross-winds and sometimes 'crab' to such an extent that they block off the central channel completely. Passing oncoming craft in these circumstances calls for precise timing if neither boat is to collide or run aground; the steerer should only straighten up at the last minute to allow the other craft to pass, although if he loses his nerve or is too slow to react both boats may finish up on the mud. It can be very difficult to get a camper aground on a lee bank off again in a strong cross-wind. Pushing the fore-end out with a long shaft held from the bank is sometimes effective, but occasionally the wind is too strong even for this, in which case you should get a line (if necessary the mooring lines tied together) from the bow across to the other side of the canal and haul the fore-end off, at the same time pushing the stern out from the bank with the long shaft. Continue to hold the boat in the channel, moving along with it until the steerer has worked up enough way to proceed unaided. Ex-working boats form the majority of camping craft, and with their deep draught they can be very hard to steer in shallow water, especially if they are trimmed down by the stern. A stern trim shifts the centre of gravity further aft and this increases the effort required at the tiller, in which event it is wise to change over steerers at fairly frequent intervals. Weed hatches are not normally fitted to working boats, and so clearing a fouled propeller can be a more serious business; plastic, fabric and so on may be removed, using the hooked end of a shaft handled from the towpath in a bridge-hole (with the engine stopped and the ignition key removed, as always), but anything more complicated may necessitate someone getting into the water.

Particular care must be taken when locking through in any full-length boat as some locks have little end clearance and therefore the steerer must be constantly alert to the danger of being hooked up on the gates or grounding the stern on the top sill. Large craft are obviously more difficult to manoeuvre in confined spaces, and it is often much easier to use the long shaft in these circumstances: a manoeuvre done in this way may sometimes be executed in a fraction of the time spent in trying to achieve the same end solely by use of the engine.

TWO-BOAT WORKING

So far the hirer and his crew have been treated as though boating in splendid isolation, never taking other craft into their company nor sharing locks with them, but of course this is not always the case, particularly at peak holiday periods. Indeed, on the more popular waterways at these times one may rarely be out of sight of other craft throughout the entire holiday, and lock sharing becomes absolutely essential both to speed up traffic flow and to conserve water.

Sharing narrow locks is generally less easy for the narrowboat hirer on account of the length of his craft, which in many instances will exceed forty feet. Sometimes, however, it happens that two narrowboats are each small enough to share a narrow lock, and should find little difficulty in doing so providing that extra care is taken to prevent the boats jamming or being caught up on gates and sills. Consideration must be given to GRP cruisers sharing narrow locks with steel-hulled craft; in this case the latter should enter first and come to rest against the top sill (if ascending), or move as far forward as possible (if descending). The cruiser should then move up close to the stern of the other boat and be held there on its lines, making sure before anything further is done that both craft are clear of any obstructions such as gates or sills. If ascending, the lock should be filled rather slowly to begin with to ensure that no surge is likely to arise and damage the lighter craft, while movement of the steel-hulled boat is easily prevented by taking a turn of the bow line around the top gate strapping-post, or the handrail.

In broad-gauge locks much the same applies, but with the difference that now the boats lie alongside each other. Make sure that their respective bows are level to prevent water turbulence slewing the craft diagonally across the chamber and causing them to jam against the walls and gates; this applies whether going up- or downhill. Again, the heavier boat (or boats) should enter the chamber first, followed by any lighter craft. If in doubt use the mooring lines to hold the boats parallel to the lock walls.

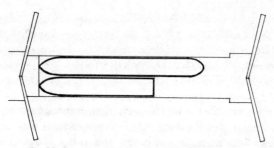

Fig. 35   Boats' bows levelled off in broad-gauge locks

Holidaying in company with friends on another boat can be very pleasant, and adds an extra dimension to waterway cruising through the interest created by the accompanying boat. On canals this arrangement means that a very adequate crew is likely to be available for lock working, and there are some positive advantages to be gained from two narrowboats handled in combination – although the latter can be realized only if the hire company does not prohibit towing.

I refer here to the practice of tying the two boats together (known traditionally as 'breasting up') when working through broad lock flights; a technique which, besides being enjoyable for its own sake (but only for the more experienced), releases another hand to swell

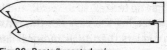

Fig. 36 Boats 'breasted up'

the lock crew. The boats are lashed together by first securing the sterns using a mooring line between the respective T-studs or dollies, then the bows, which are similarly held tightly together by a forward mooring line between the fore-deck T-studs. To prevent fore-and-aft movement of the boats diagonal straps should ideally be used, but on hire craft no provision is made for securing these, and the use of long diagonal straps is prevented by the boats' superstructures. However, in practice the bow and stern lines generally prove sufficient, and if pulled in really tight will reduce relative movement to a minimum. Both engines should be running, for although only one is used the other will be immediately available should an emergency arise. The boat with the more powerful engine should be used as the tug, and if it has a right-handed propeller should be the left-handed boat of the pair (and vice versa) so that axial displacement of thrust is counteracted, not augmented, by the drag of the 'butty'. Breasted-up boats steer very ponderously, and until they have gained enough momentum there is a tendency for the tug to swing around the butty. Conversely, when power is reduced the opposite happens, and these tendencies should be anticipated and corrected by use of the tiller. The approach to lock chambers requires very careful judgement if a clean entry is to be made, and this should be done at slow speed to avoid hard reversing, which has the effect of slewing the boats sideways – do not forget that the pair of boats may well exceed a combined weight of twenty tons! Steering a pair of breasted-up boats astern is much easier than a single boat as both engines may be used, thus effectively transforming the pair into a twin-screw craft. By use of the respective throttles and gears a remarkably accurate course can be followed over quite long distances.

Towing on a line calls for considerable skill, and is definitely not for novices (again assuming that it is not prohibited by the hire company). A broken-down craft may be towed to the nearest road bridge or wharf more quickly and conveniently than by bow-hauling, and if lying stationary in a tunnel a tow may be the safest way to remove it. The towed boat must have an experienced steerer, for without the use of an engine it has no brakes, so to speak, and the inadequate area of rudder will make steering less easy (for this reason working butties have much larger rudders than their motor boats). A mooring line, or even two tied together, will have to be used as a tow rope, and this should be attached to the fore-deck T-stud of the towed boat by means of a waterman's hitch (see fig. 44 on p. 212) so that it can be easily cast off in an emergency. The tug should commence the tow close up to the bow of the other boat, taking up the slack very slowly and then reducing further strain on the line by paying it out under control around a stern dolly or T-stud until the desired length is reached, securing the end with a waterman's hitch. In strong winds it is better to tow on a short line for safety's sake, and this can be arranged by taking two lines from the towed boat's fore-deck stud, crossing them over the stemhead and down to the stern studs on the tug. When handling tow lines great care must be taken to keep fingers clear as the tug takes up the strain, and the tug steerer must remember to keep an accurate course at bends and bridge-holes so as not to jeopardize the tow. If the boats have to be stopped – as at locks and movable bridges – the tug is first slowed down and the tow line taken in as the tow comes alongside to be brought to a halt by means of a quick turn of line around the respective stern studs. At the same time the tow line, having already been taken up to the fore-end of the tug, is used to breast the pair together.

Fig. 37 Towing on crossed lines (traditionally called 'cross-straps')

It is improbable that the hirer will be placed in the position of having to work a boat on his own, but nevertheless he should have some idea of how to set about it should he be forced by an emergency into single-handed working. First – and this is very important – he must take great care at all times, particularly in bad weather conditions. An accident may be a serious matter at any time, but in a situation where no crew members are immediately to hand and no other people around it could be absolutely disastrous, perhaps even fatal. Therefore do not take any chances, never rush, and remain patient, for progress is bound to be slow when one person has to do all the work normally done by two, three or more.

Both mooring lines are essential to single-handed working, and the longer they are, the better; the long shaft will occasionally be useful, but only if it has a hooked end. Rig the boat for breast line mooring by attaching one of the mooring lines (the shorter, if they are of different lengths) to a grab-rail about amidships, and secure the other end to a mooring spike using a round turn and two half hitches to prevent it being lost in the water. You are now ready to moor parallel

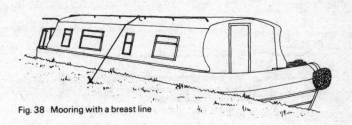

Fig. 38 Mooring with a breast line

to the bank when this is called for, and so that you may get off the boat quickly keep the mooring spike end of the line (and the lump hammer) close to hand on the cabin top. Lead the bow line as far aft as it will go and behind the grab-rail on the same side as the breast line – that is, the nearside. Do *not* lay lines along the gunwales, as they tend to roll underfoot if trodden upon. Experienced boaters who have worked single-handed all have their favourite techniques, and these include use of the engine at locks, climbing up gates, jumping down from high lock sides on to the cabin roof, operating the throttle remotely by means of a long length of string, using portable ladders and so on. In my opinion much of this sort of thing is unnecessary, and sometimes downright dangerous. Keep the procedure simple by treating the boat as though it were an unpowered butty, and little can go wrong, for any size of steel-hulled boat can be manhandled by one person, given a little patience.

As always, the two principal hindrances to progress are locks and movable bridges. Travelling downhill through narrow locks presents few problems: halt the boat right up in the lock mouth and get off at the bow – taking the bow line with you – fill the lock if necessary, then push the boat away from the lock mouth so that the gate may be

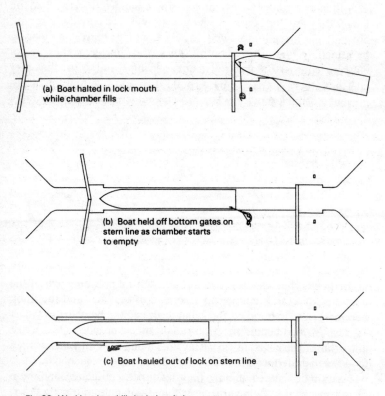

(a) Boat halted in lock mouth while chamber fills

(b) Boat held off bottom gates on stern line as chamber starts to empty

(c) Boat hauled out of lock on stern line

Fig. 39 Working downhill single-handed

opened, and haul the boat in. Shut the gate and paddles, transfer the bow line to the stern and open the bottom paddles, holding the bow off the bottom gates by means of the line until the fender is able to rest against the solid part of the gates. When levels have equalized pull the boat back from the gates and open them, then haul the boat hard out of the chamber on the stern line, taking a turn of the line around a balance beam or handrail to stop the boat as its stern clears the gates, which are then shut and the paddles closed. Take in the slack line as you descend the tail steps and climb aboard the boat. If there are no steps or other access at the lock tail use the breast line to control the boat, and haul it to the bank once it is clear of the lock.

Locking uphill may be more difficult, particularly if there is no access at the lock tail. Do not try to climb or leap from the fore-end on to the sloping top of the abutment walls, but instead moor the boat a little way back from the lock using the breast line and mooring spike, or tie up to a bollard if one is available. Set the lock, then haul the boat in on the bow line. Access at the lock tail makes things somewhat easier, as the boat can then be stopped with the bow in the lock mouth and the bow line taken up and held while the gates are opened. If the lock is full pull the boat right up to the gates so that the fender rests against them, take a couple of tight turns of the line around a balance beam, and run the lock off. The turbulence at the tail will hold the bow hard against the gates until the levels equalize. Open the gates and haul the boat up to the top sill, checking it on the line as it approaches. Make sure there are no projections on the sill or gate which might snag the fender, then take a couple of turns of the line around the balance beam or strapping post. Close the bottom gates and paddles and open the top ground paddles, taking in the slack line as the boat rises. Watch carefully to see that the fender does not catch on anything, and only open any gate paddle when it is safe to do so. When the lock is full transfer the bow line to the stern and drive the boat out, checking it on the engine as the stern clears the top gate. Take a turn of the line around a ground paddle post, close the gate and shut all paddles, then pull the stern back into the lock mouth and climb aboard. In the case of shallow locks where it is relatively easy to step from the cabin roof on to the lock side, the boat may be driven into the chamber if so desired, although in the end this may scarcely be quicker than hauling.

Broad locks should always be worked single-sided for obvious reasons, with a similar technique to that used for narrow locks. When

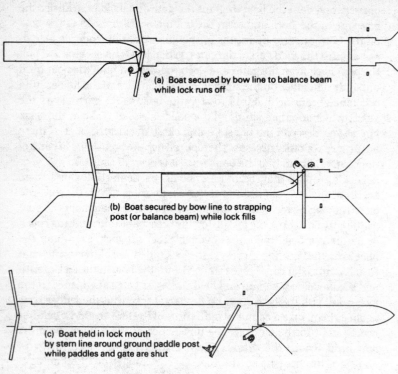

(a) Boat secured by bow line to balance beam while lock runs off

(b) Boat secured by bow line to strapping post (or balance beam) while lock fills

(c) Boat held in lock mouth by stern line around ground paddle post while paddles and gate are shut

Fig. 40 Working uphill single-handed

going uphill the boat will be held against the lock wall by pressure of water from the ground paddle; when descending, any tendency for the boat to drift about the chamber can be checked by using the breast line.

Movable bridges are among the most difficult obstacles that the single-handed boater will encounter. For one thing, they are generally operated from the offside, which means that the boat cannot sensibly be moored to the towpath, and for another they almost always need two people in attendance: one to work the bridge and the other to steer the boat. Swing bridges in good condition are an exception, as the boat may be brought up to them on the offside and held on a line while the bridge is swung open. The boat is then hauled (not easy) or driven through, and again held on a line until the bridge is closed. Unfortunately such an easy passage is most improbable, as we have seen, and most likely the single-handed boater will have to wait for reinforcements in the shape of another boat crew. Similar considerations apply to the platform lift bridges of the southern Oxford Canal, which require to be held open by a fairly hefty person. Bascule bridges, on the other hand, may be tied in the open position using a line to secure the bascule beam to the diagonal bracing strut that serves as a stop. Other frustrations may arise in the form of those bridges without towpaths that span some lock tails, and in this kind of situation my advice would be, do not take risks by trying fancy tricks, but wait for assistance from another boat crew. It is futile to attempt the negotiation of very low pounds on your own unless you do not mind ploughing through deep mud in order to reach the bank from a stranded boat; far better to stay put until another boat arrives and there are sufficient people to do something effective. The same applies in windy conditions, when the boat may become unmanageable by one person once it has been brought to a stop.

ROPE-HANDLING AND KNOTS

Good rope-handling technique is an essential part of boating expertise, yet, astoundingly, many boaters show not even the rudiments of the skill. Thrown lines which fall short in a tangle, lines coiled in such a way that kinks are wound into the rope, and poor knot-work are some of the more obvious faults, and usually arise from a total unconcern over the essentials of rope-handling.

The ropes provided on hire craft – bow and stern mooring lines and an anchor warp – may be manufactured in either natural or artificial fibres, and are generally of 'laid' construction – that is, made up of strands (usually three) twisted together diagonally. The ends are stopped by whipping or splicing, and often one end features a spliced eye for placing over studs and cleats. The fact that the strands are wound around each other means that a directional tension is built into a rope, thus predisposing it to perform more readily in some ways than others; the basis of good rope-handling lies in knowing the

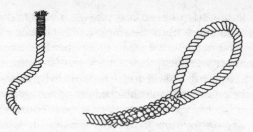

Fig. 41 Right-hand laid rope with whipped end and eye splice

correct methods of managing a rope so as to work with this bias and not against it.

For instance, when coiling a line the coil being formed must follow the lay of the rope (and this applies whether one is right- or left-handed), the rope being rotated slightly between the fingers each time a coil is formed. As most ropes used in boating are laid right-handed, or clockwise, coils should be made in a clockwise direction. Coiling against the lay, or without rotation, will increase the tension in the rope, resulting in kinks and 'figures-of-eight' as the rope tries to return to its natural degree of tension. For this reason it is better to coil a rope with the coils hanging free from one hand (or by flaking it down on

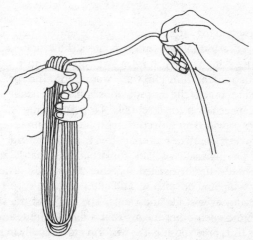

Fig. 42 Coiling a line (right-hand lay)

deck) rather than around hand and elbow, as this again tends to increase tension. A properly coiled rope should have all the coils of the same size and hang fairly limp in the coiled state, although this may be difficult to achieve in the case of a new or stiff rope. Coiling a rope with one of its ends fixed, which is the most common situation on boats, as the lines are usually attached to a stud or dolly by means of an eye splice, should always commence at the *fixed* end so that any added tension runs out at the loose end, otherwise the result will be a tangled mass. Lines should be neatly coiled to a manageable size and placed in a position where they are unlikely to be disturbed or trodden upon, and one end should remain secured to the deck fitting, except in the case of the traditional counter, where the small area of deck increases the risk of the line being tripped over or being kicked overboard into the propeller; to avoid this the coils should be placed on the cabin top within easy reach. Lines coiled in a flat spiral may look neat and decorative, but they should have no place on a boat, for in an emergency they will have to be recoiled for throwing. Never leave lines just lying around in a tangle, but get into the habit of coiling them immediately they have been used.

Throwing a line calls for careful judgement and timing. The line must be properly coiled to begin with, otherwise the attempt is unlikely to succeed, and some slack should be allowed at the fixed end if the line is not to be jerked back by its own weight. Use a sideways sweeping motion of the arm and release the coils cleanly, aiming not directly at the person who is receiving, but slightly to one side. If the rope is long or heavy then divide the coils evenly between each hand and release the coils in the holding hand a split second after throwing with the other. The catcher should wait until the rope is comfortably within reach before attempting to grasp it, and not make wild grabs while the rope is still in flight.

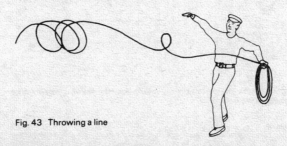

Fig. 43 Throwing a line

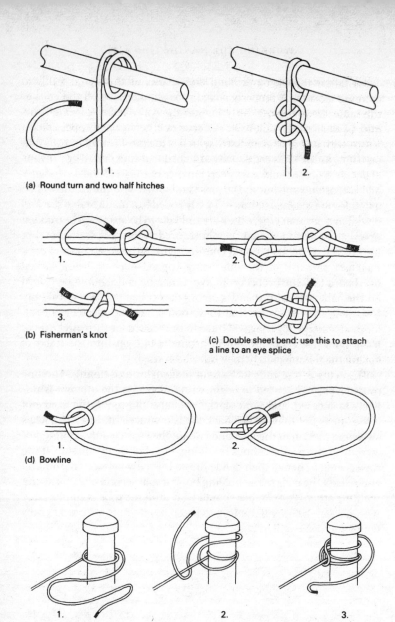

(a) Round turn and two half hitches

(b) Fisherman's knot

(c) Double sheet bend: use this to attach a line to an eye splice

(d) Bowline

(e) Waterman's hitch: the greater the expected strain, the more bights should be looped back over the bollard

Fig. 44 Knots

It is pointless to learn too many knots when just a few will suffice for most of the situations likely to be encountered on inland waterways. The *round turn and two half hitches* is a good knot to use if a line is to be securely fixed and will not be subject to heavy strain. The *fisherman's knot* is probably the best method of attaching two lines together, and will certainly not come undone, but is liable to jam under strain. The *double sheet bend* is almost as good as the *fisherman's knot* for joining two lines together, especially if one line ends in an eye splice. For making a fixed loop the *bowline* can scarcely be beaten and is relatively easy to untie, even after being subjected to a heavy load. In all instances where a line has to be secured to a fixed anchor point, such as a stud, dolly, cleat, bollard or mooring spike, the *waterman's hitch* should be used. It is suitable for both light and heavy line and will take continuous and intermittent strain with equal ease. Even under the heaviest loads it does not jam, and is very simple to form and undo.

As mentioned on p. 155, it is always advisable when mooring to secure the lines finally to the boat if they are long enough to permit this (thereby reducing the chance of interference by anyone on the bank). When tying up to bollards and mooring spikes it is sensible to take one turn of a waterman's hitch around them before returning the running end of the line to the boat and forming a second waterman's hitch around the stud or cleat; not only does this make it harder for anyone on the bank to undo the mooring, but in the case of a mooring spike will reduce the chance of it being lost in the water should a passing boat travelling at speed cause the spike to be dragged out of the ground.

TIDEWAYS

Only a few companies permit their boats to be taken on to tidal waters and then restrict this permission to experienced hirers only. In addition, they will usually specify which sections of tideway may be used – prohibiting, for example, entry into the lower Thames tideway below Limehouse, and passage of the tidal Trent and Yorkshire Ouse through Trent Falls between Keadby and Selby. These restrictions are sensible, bearing in mind the unsuitability of the majority of inland hire craft – particularly narrowboats – for the sometimes dangerous conditions and swift currents to be found in open tidal waters. *On no account should beginners attempt the passage of tideways*; an exception perhaps being the upper tideway of the Thames between Brentford and Teddington, which presents few hazards and may with care be navigated safely by the novice, providing he has the consent of the hire company.

HOW TIDES ARE FORMED

Tides are caused by the gravitational pull exerted on the earth's seas by the moon, and also – but to a much lesser extent – by the sun. Briefly, there are two conditions which define the range of influence of these bodies. In the first, when sun and moon are either in conjunction (new moon) or in opposition (full moon), their respective gravitational forces relative to the earth are in line with each other and so give rise to a greater height and range of tides, the so-called 'springs'. With sun and moon at right-angles to each other (first and last quarters) their combined gravitational pull is less, producing tides which have a higher low water than average and a lesser range: these are known as 'neaps'. Thus the tides follow roughly a half-monthly cycle, but are subject to a time lag in response to the tide-generating

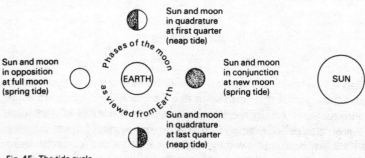

Fig. 45 The tide cycle

forces, springs occurring about two days after new and full moon, and neaps about two days after the moon's quarters. The predictability of the respective movements of the sun and moon permit the compilation of tide tables, which list the anticipated approximate times (in Greenwich Mean Time) and heights of all tides in a selected area for the coming year, although these may be influenced in the event by variations in barometric pressure, the direction and force of winds, and by storm surges.

On a tidal river the range of tides decreases in proportion to the up-river distance, as does the tidal velocity, although both can be influenced by the amount of land water coming down the river. The length of time over which a tide runs up-river (a 'flood' tide) also varies, diminishing as it runs further up-river, with a corresponding increase in the time taken to flow down again (an 'ebb' tide). For example, a spring tide at Trent Falls (junction of the Trent with the Humber) may flood for about three and a half hours to produce a rise to high water of about sixteen feet, whereas at Cromwell Lock (the upper limit of the tideway, fifty-three miles upstream of Trent Falls) the same tide may rise only about one foot over a period of one hour and ebb for the remainder of the tide cycle (about eleven hours). Tidal velocity may at times present difficulties for low-powered craft: spring tides sometimes reach a speed of about seven miles per hour on the Trent and the Yorkshire Ouse, where the hazard of strong currents is increased on occasion by the Aegir, or bore, a tidal wave which can exceed a height of five feet and which is liable to occur when spring tides are greater than twenty-six feet at Hull. The famous Severn bore is even more spectacular, but affects the river only below Gloucester and can thus be avoided by craft using the Gloucester and Sharpness Canal.

NAVIGATING TIDEWAYS

Moving water tends to flow faster around the outside of bends, and tideways are no exception to this rule. The relatively slack water on the inside of a bend causes a build-up of silt, forming in some cases large shoals that extend well into the river, and care must be taken to avoid these. An additional hazard is caused by high flood banks such as those on the Trent, which restrict the view at bends with the result that the unwary boater may suddenly find himself facing an oncoming large commercial vessel in the middle of the channel. In this event he must give way immediately, at the same time sounding the appropriate signal on the horn. On all tideways keep a constant lookout fore and aft.

Entry into tidal waters is always effected through a manned tidal lock and is usually restricted to a period of an hour or two either side of high water. Make sure to travel with the tide, never against it, as the boat's engine may not be powerful enough to 'punch' a swift-moving current; and even if it is, progress will be dismally slow, with a much increased chance of engine breakdown due to mechanical failure or overheating. Tideways can become extremely rough in bad weather, so never take chances but ask the lock-keeper for advice – and accept it, no matter what you had intended. Always plan a tidal passage in advance, using the current tide tables and the best chart available, and note carefully where overnight stops are sited so as to take best advantage of the tides. *Never anchor in a tideway except in emergency.*

You are in the hands of the hire company as regards the condition and equipping of the boat, but needless to say it would be foolish to venture on to a tideway in any hire craft provided by a company in which you had less than the greatest confidence. The boat must be fitted with an anchor of appropriate weight to which is shackled a good length of chain (not less than twelve feet) and a warp of length suitable for the river to be navigated (see below). At least one lifebuoy must be carried and should preferably be attached to a fifty-foot length of light throwing line with the other end fixed to the boat. All crew members should wear buoyancy aids and should not walk about the cabin roof nor the gunwales while the boat is under way, particularly in rough weather conditions; children and pets must be kept under strict control. As rough weather may occur it is advisable to secure all breakables lying on open shelves, and to place TV sets where they cannot fall over. Finally, and just before entering a tideway, check that the propeller is clear from fouling, that the weed hatch cover is securely locked in place, and that the bilge pump and horn are both in working order.

The actual boating techniques used on a tideway are no different from those employed on non-tidal rivers, as described on pp. 179–81, but remember that everything will probably be exaggerated: tidal currents run more strongly, making the passage of bridges more hazardous, and water levels rise and fall over a greater range more quickly, so that particular care must be taken when mooring to allow sufficient slack in the lines and to ensure that the boat is neither caught under nor hung up on obstructions. Watch out for driftwood, which can sometimes accumulate in quantity and may be of alarming size, notably in the Thames tideway. In a word: always be alert and aware of what is happening around you.

NAVIGATION MARKS

Navigation marks are to be found on both tideways and non-tidal sections of rivers, and also on the larger lakes. During recent years the new IALA (International Association of Lighthouse Authorities) system of buoyage has been introduced in the United Kingdom and Eire, and the boater should be familiar with at least the more common marks. The direction of buoyage in rivers and estuaries remains unchanged under the new system: that is, from seaward inwards, so that, for example, a port hand mark indicates the left side of the channel when proceeding up-river, and vice versa.

Lateral marks indicate the position of a navigation channel, and consist of:
Port hand:
Colour: red
Shape (buoys): can or spar
Topmark (if any): single red can

Starboard hand:
Colour: green
Shape (buoys): conical or spar
Topmark (if any): single green cone, point up
Note: In exceptional cases, black may be used instead of green.

Cardinal marks indicate that the deepest water is on the named side of the mark; indicate the safe side on which to pass a danger; draw attention to a feature such as a bend, junction, bifurcation, and the end of a shoal, and consist of;

North cardinal mark:
Colour: black above yellow
Shape: pillar or spar
Topmark: two black cones, one above the other, points upward

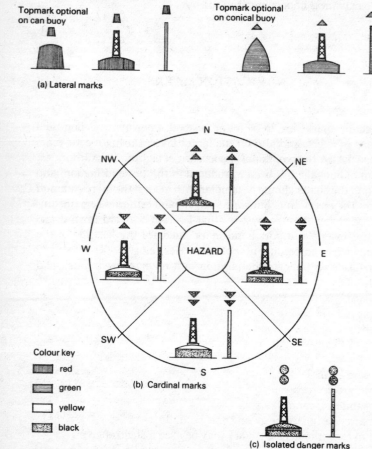

(a) Lateral marks

(b) Cardinal marks

(c) Isolated danger marks

Colour key
- red
- green
- yellow
- black

Fig. 46 IALA buoyage system

East cardinal mark:
Colour: black with a single broad horizontal yellow band
Shape: pillar or spar
Topmark: two black cones, one above the other, base to base

South cardinal mark:
Colour: yellow above black
Shape: pillar or spar
Topmark: two black cones, one above the other, points downward

West cardinal mark:
Colour: yellow with a single broad horizontal black band
Shape: pillar or spar
Topmark: two black cones, one above the other, point to point

Isolated danger mark indicates an isolated danger which has navigable water all around it, and consists of:
Colour: black with one or more broad horizontal red bands
Shape: pillar or spar
Topmark: two black spheres, one above the other

The above marks may also be fitted with flashing lights, but this is of little consequence to the hirer, who will be navigating only during daylight hours. Do not approach too close to any kind of buoy, including those used for mooring, otherwise you may foul their cables.

ANCHORING

Hire craft are often fitted with a Danforth pattern anchor, although a CQR, or plough, anchor would do just as well. Ideally, the whole of the anchor cable should consist of galvanized chain, but weight and cost considerations result in the common compromise of using chain for the first twelve feet or so and natural or artificial rope (called 'warp') for the remainder. A composite cable of this type should have a length of at least five times the anticipated greatest depth of water, and preferably more, but the hirer will find that he is stuck with whatever the hire company thinks is sufficient. If the free end of the warp is not already securely attached to the boat it should be fixed to the forward T-stud. Before entering rivers and tideways the anchor, cable and warp should be checked, the anchor placed on the fore-deck or in the fore-well, and the cable and warp flaked down on deck ready for instant use – which does *not* include mooring on rivers and tideways. Needless to say, an anchor must never be used on a canal as it might damage the clay puddling.

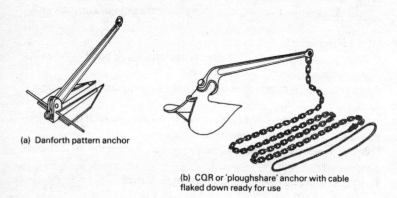

(a) Danforth pattern anchor

(b) CQR or 'ploughshare' anchor with cable flaked down ready for use

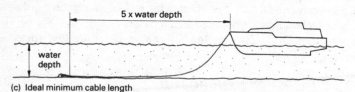

(c) Ideal minimum cable length

Fig. 47 Anchors and anchoring

The main purpose of an anchor on inland navigations is to act as a brake in emergencies, which will usually centre on loss of propulsion, leaving the craft at the mercy of the current. Although in normal circumstances the anchor is dropped only after the boat has been brought round head to stream (or wind), loss of power will make this impossible if going downstream, when at best only a part turn will be practicable on whatever way remains. Get to the fore-end immediately and drop the anchor carefully but quickly, taking care not to snag or snarl up the cable as it goes and keeping limbs and fingers clear of the running warp. Once all the warp is out, check that the anchor is not dragging by feeling for vibration in the warp, and by observing whether two landmarks in the line of sight change position relative to each other. If the anchor seems not to be holding at all you may have to heave it in and try again, although this might not be a practicable proposition against a strong current with no power available and perhaps a weir or a bridge pier immediately downstream! With power restored, the anchor is raised by going ahead slowly while taking in the warp until the 'up and down' position is reached, when the boat is held on the engine against the current (or wind) as the anchor is broken out and brought aboard.

When carrying an anchor make sure that at least one other person knows the proper procedure for its use and can be relied upon in an emergency. Do not entrust the responsibility to anyone whom you consider doubtful, and above all, *never* to a child.

CHAPTER NINE

SAFETY, ACCIDENTS, AND EMERGENCIES

Safety on board a boat is very largely an attitude of mind embracing a sense of responsibility towards not only oneself but all other members of the crew. Among most crews someone is probably acknowledged – usually by common consent – as 'skipper', but even if this person rarely has to exercise any kind of authority in the normal course of working the boat, he (or she) should consider it his duty to look after the welfare and safety of all on board. This applies whether the crew are all novices, including the skipper, or experienced 'old hands', although the latter, as might be expected, will be in a better position to take care of themselves. Accidents can happen to anyone and not even the most experienced and best prepared are exempt, but at least they will probably have taken all reasonable safety pre-cautions and will only rarely be caught out by an unthinking lack of awareness, or by outright carelessness.

Many aspects of safety have already been touched upon in previous chapters, but may be mentioned here for the sake of completeness.

UNDER WAY

In spite of all the warnings and advice, many people regard the wearing of buoyancy aids on inland waters with a certain amount of scepticism – except, of course, as it applies to children. There is some justification for this in the case of canals, which are mostly relatively shallow and only reach any significant depth within the confines of a filled lock chamber, but rivers and tideways are a different matter altogether, for not only are they deep, but contain swift currents and undertows, not to mention the more obvious dangers arising from weirs, bridge piers and other obstructions, and from waterway traffic. Lakes in particular can be extremely dangerous on account of their sheer size and depth, the very rough conditions which can sometimes arise and the cold currents that are present in many. These kinds of hazard have brought even good swimmers to grief, and of course the ability to swim is useless to an unconscious person, as it may be to someone heavily clad in foul weather gear. So make a practice of wearing a buoyancy aid in all potentially dangerous situations right from the outset, and this includes when using a dinghy to go aboard a cruiser anchored offshore in a lake: it is, in fact, more likely that someone will fall in at this time rather than when the cruiser is actually under way.

'Man overboard' can be a serious matter at any time – more so in open waters during rough and cold conditions – and no time should be lost in getting the unfortunate person back on board again. The immediate action to be taken will depend greatly upon circumstances, but in all cases that occur while the boat is under way the first priority must be the avoidance of injury (or worse) to the person by the propeller; therefore select neutral instantly, and do not re-engage gear until it is safe to do so. If the boat stops fairly quickly – as it may do against a current or a headwind – it should be possible to throw a lifebuoy with line attached to the person in the water and pull him towards the boat, but if he has been left well behind then throw a lifebuoy as far as you can in his direction (with any line detached) and turn the boat on a reciprocal course, approaching the person on his leeward side. Never come up to him from windward as the boat may be drifted on to him with some force. At the shout of 'man overboard' someone should be detailed to watch the person constantly so that he is not lost sight of, giving directions to the helmsman if required until the person is alongside. Once the boat is hove-to with the engine in neutral, rig a boarding ladder (if available) or drop a line with bowline loop to act as a foothold. Waterlogged clothing and the effects of cold and shock may make it impossible for the person to climb aboard unaided, and in this case a line attached to a lifebuoy, or a bowline in the end of a line placed around the chest under the armpits will enable the crew to haul him aboard. If there is much freeboard this may not be easy, in which case the two lines should be hauled in alternately, the person's weight being held on the footrope as slack is taken in on the chest line, and vice versa.

Falling overboard into a canal is rarely a serious matter except in the case of children, but in all instances the propeller must be stopped *immediately*. Most adults should be able to stand up in the water without difficulty, and it is probably easier for them to wade or swim to the bank rather than attempt to struggle back on to the boat, but children may well be in a state of panic. If this happens, go astern and then bring the boat to a halt with a burst of power in forward gear a few feet away from the child, who will be in no immediate danger *provided that he (or she) is wearing a buoyancy aid*. As the boat drifts slowly alongside the child may be lifted bodily from the water, but if this proves difficult it is no hardship for an adult to go overside and render assistance from below.

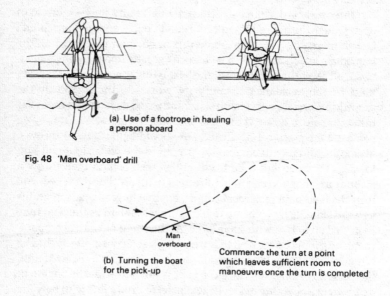

(a) Use of a footrope in hauling a person aboard

Fig. 48 'Man overboard' drill

Man overboard

(b) Turning the boat for the pick-up

Commence the turn at a point which leaves sufficient room to manoeuvre once the turn is completed

If the person recovered from the water is little the worse for his experience he may require nothing further than a warm bath or shower and a spell of rest tucked up in bed with a hot drink. More serious cases may need the services of a doctor, particularly if the person has been knocked unconscious in the fall, swallowed a lot of water (for artificial respiration, see below), or been immersed in badly polluted water.

Other types of incident which may occur while a boat is under way are mainly to do with the consequences of collision with either another boat or a fixed feature. The momentum of even slowly moving craft can be considerable, yet all too often one sees hands and feet being used to fend off, apparently without thought of the possibility of serious injury to those involved. Sometimes shafts, boathooks and deck mops are brought into play, their users unaware that these implements may actually *increase* the chance of material damage to the craft being caused, not to mention injury to themselves. If a collision of any kind seems imminent, do all that can be done to avoid it, but beyond a certain point stand clear and let it happen – far better a broken window than broken limbs or loss of fingers. For similar reasons always make sure that crew members understand that they must never sit with arms or legs dangling over the side, particularly when approaching stagings, wharves or lock chambers, or when negotiating tunnels and aqueducts. On wide waters with good separation between craft under way this is unlikely to lead to accidents, but on canals especially the possibility of collision, and of passing craft being drawn together, makes it imperative that this rule be strictly observed. Injury can also result from impact with overhead obstructions such as bridges and tree branches; anyone on the cabin roof is very much at risk from low-arched bridges, as are persons walking along the gunwale. Try to cultivate the habit of always glancing forward *before* emerging fully from a side hatch and when coming up on deck while facing aft, so that you are instantly aware of any approaching hazard.

AT LOCKS AND MOVABLE BRIDGES

Innocent as they may look, locks are potential death traps for the unknowing and the unwary. Children and dogs are the ones mostly at risk, and must be watched constantly. Keep young children who are on the boat away from the gunwale edges so that there is no danger of limbs being trapped, and restrain excitable dogs from leaping about the deck. Any youngsters on the lock side should be kept away from the edges of the chamber and the abutment walls in case they fall into the water and are drawn through the open paddle apertures or the culverts; should anyone fall into – or adjacent to – a lock, instantly close all paddles first, then rescue them after all water movement has been stopped. Never allow young children to assist with boat lines. Keep clear of gates and balance beams when a boat is entering the chamber, as a misjudgement on the part of the steerer could result in the gate being struck with some force, and anyone sitting on the balance beam could be thrown off, perhaps into the chamber. When opening gates make sure that no one is standing between the beam and the edge of the lock, and when pushing on beams with the small of the back look over your shoulder to make sure that you do not walk off the edge of the abutment wall – on occasion the end sections of balance beams project beyond the perimeter of the abutments at some point in their travel.

Treat all movable bridges as you would moving craft: keep limbs and fingers clear in case they should be trapped, and remember that swing bridges in movement possess a lot of momentum: above all, make sure that no one is pulling a swing bridge shut with their backs to any stop post, otherwise they run the risk of being crushed.

Fig. 49 Safety at locks

Lack of awareness can cause accidents: the person shown pushing on the balance beam is not only about to step backwards off the abutment wall, but could also sweep the child off the lock side

FIRE

All hire craft are required to be equipped with fire extinguishers of an approved model, usually of the dry powder type. Make sure that all on board know where they are positioned, and how to use them. In the event of fire, alert the crew and get those who are not involved in fire-fighting as far away from the blaze as possible, then reduce the draught through the boat by closing all doors, windows and hatches. On a river or canal, steer for the bank so that crew members may leave the boat and be sent for help if necessary. In the meantime detail a crewman to switch off the gas and electrical circuits at the master switches, and tackle the fire with the extinguishers provided. Direct short bursts at the base of the flames, working inwards towards the centre of the fire until it is extinguished. If you think that the extinguishers might be exhausted before the fire is properly out, ask someone to fill buckets and containers with water, but never use this on burning oil or fat as it will cause a miniature explosion, throwing the flaming liquid everywhere. Should there be any risk of the fire spreading to the engine compartment, switch off the engine and shut the main fuel valve. Once you are satisfied that all immediate danger is past, investigate the area affected by the fire to make sure that no smouldering embers remain, and to ascertain if possible the cause of the fire, and only then ventilate the boat to remove smoke and fumes. Inform the hire company of the circumstances of the incident immediately.

In the event of a fire getting completely out of control with consequent risk of gas and fuel explosion, do not persist in attempts to extinguish it but abandon ship at once. If you are on a wide river or a lake, make sure that everyone is wearing a buoyancy aid (those not already wearing one should have put one on at the first sign of fire), launch a dinghy (if provided), and make haste to get as far from the boat as you can, taking lifebuoys and other buoyant objects along with you, together with distress flares (if provided).

FIRST AID

First-aid kits are not provided on all hire craft, and those that are may not always be adequate, so it is advisable to take your own. The kit need not be elaborate, but should be sufficient to deal with the more common ailments and injuries, and as a minimum should contain the following items:

    a triangular bandage
    a 3-inch crêpe bandage
    a 1-inch roll of adhesive plaster
    a 2-inch roll of waterproof adhesive tape
    a pack of cotton wool
    10 gauze packs
    a pack of sterile non-adhesive dressings
    a pair of scissors (blunt-nosed)
    a box of assorted safety pins
    a clinical thermometer
Drugs:
    Paracetamol, aspirin (pain)
    antiseptic cream or liquid (infection)
    aluminium hydroxide (indigestion)
    Senokot (constipation)
    Lomotil (diarrhoea)
    Calamine lotion (sunburn)
    Anthisan cream (insect stings and bites)

Resuscitation

The cessation of the oxygen supply to the brain, either through respiratory failure or interruption of the blood flow, can result in death after two minutes, and at ten minutes will almost certainly prove fatal. If breathing stops, start artificial respiration immediately. In the case of drowning this is extremely urgent, and no time must be lost by loosening clothing, looking for a heart beat or removing false teeth (unless dentures have been partially swallowed into the airway).

Mouth-to-mouth artificial respiration

First lay the patient on his back on a firm surface with the head turned to one side and clear out the mouth with a finger, allowing any fluid to drain away. Return the head to the forward-facing position, support the nape of the neck and tilt the head backwards to straighten the airway, which is then freed from blockage by the back of the tongue by pushing the lower jaw forward through pressure at the angle just below the ears. Keep the patient's head extended, pinch the nostrils shut, take a deep breath, place your open mouth completely over the patient's so that no air can escape, and blow until his lungs are filled. Sit back and watch his chest fall as air is expelled. If breathing does not restart repeat the procedure every five or six seconds. When dealing with young children you may have to place your lips around both mouth and nose; adults with injury to the mouth and jaw area may have to be resuscitated through the nose.

If after ten inflations of the lungs the patient fails to resume natural breathing and his colour remains blue-grey, start external cardiac massage. Strike the chest sharply once on the lower breast-

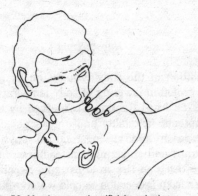

Fig. 50 Mouth-to-mouth artificial respiration

bone, then check for heartbeat by pressing gently with the fingertips on the carotid artery, just to the left of the windpipe. In the continued absence of a pulse repeatedly strike the chest about six times at intervals of three seconds. Should this fail, commence cardiac massage. First place the heel of the hand on the lower half of the breastbone (not the ribs), cover this hand with the other and, keeping your arms rigid, press vertically downwards and release once each second, using your whole weight. In an adult, deflection of the breastbone must not exceed one-and-a-half inches, otherwise ribs may be fractured; children should be given a quicker and lighter pressure using one hand. Continue mouth-to-mouth artificial respiration while cardiac massage is being given, in the ratio of five compressions to one lung inflation; if one person has to perform both functions the ratio should be two inflations to every fifteen compressions. Resuscitation should be kept up for at least an hour following the appearance of any signs of life – that is, change of colour back towards normal, carotid pulse, recommencement of breathing and contraction of pupils.

The cardiac massage may be stopped once the pulse is steady, and when unassisted breathing has been restored the patient may be stripped off and put to bed, massaging limbs under the covers to increase the circulation. When the patient is able to swallow, warm drinks may be administered, but not alcohol. Keep the patient quiet and under observation until medical help is available.

Hypothermia

This is a condition of the body brought on by exposure to cold, resulting in a profound lowering of body temperature which, if unchecked, leads to death. Its onset is marked by any or all of the following symptoms: irritability and unreasonable behaviour, difficulties with speech and vision, retarded physical and mental responses, cramps and shivering, unsteadiness. Boaters on inland waterways are rarely at risk from extreme hypothermia, but mild cases may arise from immersion in cold water, and from long spells at the helm in an exposed steering position during cold, wet and windy weather, particularly if alcohol has been drunk in quantity and the sufferer is not adequately clad for the conditions. Treat all cases as serious and get the patient into bed at once in a warm cabin. Keep him under observation and administer warm drinks. Do not give alcohol as this may prove lethal under certain circumstances. The object should be to restore body warmth *gradually* and without disturbing the body's balance of heat.

Shock

Shock is a condition brought on as a result of accident or illness and is the symptom of a sudden drop in blood pressure. The patient is often in a state of collapse, his skin is cold and clammy and his breathing rapid, while the pulse may be either very rapid or very slow. Treat all cases as serious. If the state of shock has been brought on as a result of an accident, treat cardiac and respiratory failures immediately, and control any bleeding. Providing his condition allows it, put the patient to bed but do not overheat; warm drinks may be given if he is able to take them and you are satisfied that there are no internal injuries. Do not give alcohol. Seek medical help at once, but in the meantime do everything possible to keep the patient quiet, calm and reassured (this advice applies to all instances of injury and illness in which the patient is conscious).

Fractures and sprains

A fracture is a broken or cracked bone, and may be: (a) *simple* – that is, without rupture of the skin; (b) *compound*, where the broken bone pierces the skin to form an open wound; or (c) *complicated*, where the bone has caused injury to internal organs, nerves or blood vessels, accompanied by internal bleeding. Symptoms include: pain, swelling, deformity, loss of power in the affected limb and abnormal movement of the limb. Get the patient to bed immediately unless the seriousness of his condition dictates otherwise, in which case make him as comfortable as possible, cover him up and protect him from the effects of weather. Find the seat of injury and listen to what the patient has to say if he is conscious. Treat cardiac and respiratory failures first and control any bleeding, but be careful not to impede circulation by tight bandaging. Loosen any tight clothing and place the injured limb in the position most comfortable to the patient, supporting it with cushions, rolled blankets and so on. Unless the patient is unconscious and restless do not bother with splinting or binding to immobilize the fracture, but wait for medical assistance.

Fractures of the skull are extremely serious, particularly when accompanied by brain damage. The patient will require medical assistance with least possible delay, but in the meantime stop any external bleeding and treat cardiac and respiratory failures. If possible, place the patient in the coma position (see fig. 51) and note any discharge from the nose or ears, and the state of the pupils, for the information of the doctor.

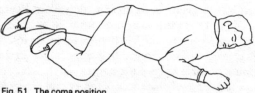

Fig. 51 The coma position

Spinal injuries can also be very serious, as damage to the vertebrae may cause paralysis. If this affects the breathing then start mouth-to-mouth resuscitation at once, and control any bleeding. *Do not move the patient* as this may cause further damage and even death, but cover him up and provide protection from the weather. Injury to the spine should be suspected and treated as such if there are signs of paralysis, loss of feeling, tingling sensations, severe pain in the back and neck or inability to control the bodily functions. Medical assistance will be required without delay.

Sprains of the ankle, wrist or knee are usually caused by twisting of the joint and consequent damage to the ligaments. Apply firm support to the injury by wrapping the joint and the area of limb immediately above and below with crêpe bandage over a layer of cotton wool. Keep the patient quiet and immobilized until the swelling subsides. If you are in doubt as to the nature of the injury always treat it as a fracture.

Bleeding

Excessive blood loss will cause the rapid onset of shock, and this should be treated as detailed above. Get the patient to bed if possible. Most bleeding can be stopped within a few minutes by applying a sterile dressing padded out with a folded triangular bandage and pressed directly over the wound. Release the pressure every five minutes or so to examine the state of the wound, if bleeding is undiminished, increase the pressure and elevate the bleeding area. Once bleeding has stopped do not disturb the blood clot, but bandage firmly over a sterile dressing. Check at intervals to see that bleeding has not started again. The use of a tourniquet is now generally considered unnecessary, as the risk of tissue damage outweighs any benefit, and bleeding in any case can be efficiently controlled by the pressure method.

Nose bleeds are rarely serious and may be stopped fairly quickly by sitting the patient down with head slightly forward so that the blood drips into a receptacle held in the lap; ask him to breathe through the mouth, and gently pinch the soft part of his nose for five to ten minutes, after which all bleeding should have ceased.

Burns and scalds

Major burns – those involving more than 15 per cent of the body's surface – are very serious, although any burn which causes shock symptoms should be treated as major. Deal with any cardiac and respiratory failures first, and treat for shock if necessary. Do not try to remove charred clothing stuck to the skin, but immerse the affected part immediately in clean, cold water for fifteen minutes to reduce the temperature of the burned area. Clean the burn *gently* with cold water and cover with a sterile dressing, adding further padding as required to absorb the plasma soaking through the dressing. If the patient is able to take them, give warm drinks at intervals to counteract shock and the effects of dehydration. Seek medical assistance at once if you judge the burn to be serious.

Heart attack

This is signalled by intense chest pains extending sometimes to the shoulders and upper arms, accompanied by difficulty in breathing and perhaps a bluish hue around the mouth. To the patient the onset of an attack may resemble very severe indigestion. If the attack causes unconsciousness, check that a pulse is present and that the patient is breathing; treat for cardiac and respiratory failures as required, and for shock if present. Get the patient to bed, prop him up with pillows into a comfortable position and give a large dose of painkillers if he is conscious. Drinks may be administered in small sips, but *not* alcohol. Send for medical assistance at once.

Fits and seizures

A person having a fit may well injure himself through the violence and uncontrolled nature of the accompanying muscular spasms, so the first priority must be to restrain the patient, but without undue force. Lay the patient down, if possible on a bed or settee, and loosen any tight clothing. If he is choking this will usually be due to obstruction of the airway by the tongue, and should be dealt with as described on p. 229, although in this case treatment will not be easy, as the mouth will probably be tightly shut and the teeth clenched. Force them open, using a wooden spatula or a spoon wrapped in cloth, and keep this in the mouth while treatment is given. After recovery keep the patient warm and comfortable, and reassure him.

Heatstroke

High ambient temperatures, particularly if accompanied by high humidity, can cause excessive loss of fluids and salt from the body. One of the first symptoms may be cramp due to the salt deficiency, followed by a feeling of weariness and dizziness, perhaps vomiting and even fainting, accompanied by a high body temperature, clammy skin and rapid breathing. Cramp may be quickly relieved by administering a saline drink, in the ratio half a teaspoonful of salt to one pint of water, and by stretching and relaxing the affected muscles manually. If the heatstroke has progressed to the fainting stage, remove the patient to the coolest place available and remove all unnecessary clothing. Reduce his body temperature by covering him with towels soaked in cold water, and keep them wet and cold until the patient's temperature has fallen below 102° F. When he recovers consciousness allow sips of water with a little salt in it.

Insect stings and bites

These are more of a nuisance than a danger, unless the person concerned has an allergic reaction, in which case he will probably be carrying appropriate medication. Remove an embedded sting by means of a sterilized needle, clean the site and apply Anthisan cream or bicarbonate of soda.

Foreign bodies in the eye

If the object has not been washed out by tears it may usually be removed using the moistened corner of a handkerchief, providing that the foreign body is on the white of the eye. Anything lying in the area of the cornea must not be poked or prodded as this could result ultimately in blindness, nor should any matter that is apparently embedded in any part of the eye. In this case cover the closed eye with a soft sterile dressing and bandage and seek medical assistance at once.

CHAPTER TEN

GAZETTEER

ENGLAND AND WALES

Aire and Calder Navigation

This navigation dates from the early years of the eighteenth century and was built to serve the thriving woollen industry of Yorkshire, but later – much enlarged and improved – it was to become the principal transport artery for rapid industrial expansion and the exploitation of the huge Yorkshire coalfield. It is still essentially a commercial navigation, but sadly carries only a fraction of the tonnage that it did in its heyday. For the enthusiast who wishes to see a working commercial navigation at first hand the exploration of the Aire and Calder can be a fascinating experience, but to the pleasure-boater it is mainly important as a link between the tideways of the Trent and the Ouse and the Leeds and Liverpool Canal. Scenically it is uninteresting, as the surrounding countryside is flat and featureless in the parts that are not industrialized.

The main line of the navigation commences at Goole on the lower section of the Ouse tideway and runs through Knottingley, Ferrybridge and Castleford to Leeds, a total distance of thirty-four miles with twelve large locks, only one of which is not mechanized – Leeds Lock, above which access may be gained to the eastern end of the Leeds and Liverpool Canal. About seven miles from Goole the New Junction Canal (five and a half miles, with one lock) branches south off the main line and runs through flat but pleasant farmland to a connection with the Sheffield and South Yorkshire Navigation, thus forming part of the link between the Aire and Calder Navigation and the Trent. At Knottingley, Bank Dole Lock provides access to the lower River Aire, which follows a tortuous course between high banks to

Haddlesey Flood Lock, a distance of six and a half miles with one lock. The Flood Lock marks the entrance to the Selby Canal, which runs on the level for just over five miles and forms part of the through route to the Ouse tideway at Selby Lock.

Just beyond Knottingley the main line enters the Aire at Ferrybridge Flood Lock and passes the huge cooling towers of Ferrybridge A, B and C power stations, thereafter following a winding course to Castleford and a four-way junction of canal and rivers. After the flood lock the route to Leeds turns sharply northwards, and almost dead ahead lies the entrance to the Wakefield section of the navigation, while to the south the weir stream of the Aire loops away towards Castleford. From here to Leeds the navigation passes through desolate surroundings and after Kippax Locks runs in artificial cut until near the city centre, where the river is re-entered.

The Wakefield section begins at Castleford Junction and follows the River Calder for eight miles and through four locks to Wakefield, where it joins the Calder and Hebble Navigation. After the first lock (Woodnock) the waterway runs in artificial cut, crossing the Calder on the Stanley Ferry Aqueduct before re-entering the river on the outskirts of Wakefield at Broadreach Flood Lock. Just upstream of this point the Barnsley Canal at one time joined the river, but has long since been filled in. Fall Ing Lock and the start of the Calder and Hebble Navigation lies a few hundred yards beyond the old junction.

Ashby Canal

Lock-free throughout its length of twenty-two miles, the Ashby Canal runs from the Coventry Canal at Marston Junction to a mile or so beyond the village of Snarestone just south of Ashby-de-la-Zouch. The stop-lock at the entrance to the canal is now disused, so that the Ashby and Coventry canals form a common level, giving lock-free cruising over a distance of about thirty-eight miles, and considerably more if the stop-lock at the entrance to the northern section of the Oxford Canal is discounted.

Although the Ashby Canal does not possess any features of particular note, it is nevertheless a very pleasant waterway and is deservedly becoming more popular with boaters. Hinckley, the only sizeable town nearby, is bypassed by the canal, which remains rural in character throughout almost its entire length, passing through remote farmlands and the occasional small village. Near Shenton the canal skirts the edge of Bosworth Field, where Richard III was defeated. About three-quarters of a mile before the terminus a 250-yard tunnel takes the canal under the village of Snarestone and on to an abrupt end at a concrete wharf and winding hole.

Ashton Canal

Although only just over six miles long, the Ashton Canal forms an essential link in the waterways that comprise the 'Cheshire Ring', a very popular cruising route which takes in parts of Greater Manchester, Cheshire and the north-west fringe of the Peak District via the Trent and Mersey, Bridgewater, Rochdale, Ashton, Lower Peak Forest and Macclesfield Canals. It is urban and industrial in character throughout, and runs from a junction with the Rochdale Canal at Ducie Street near Manchester city centre through eighteen narrow-gauge locks to Ashton-under-Lyne, where it connects with the Lower Peak Forest Canal at Dukinfield Junction.

Avon, River (Warwickshire)

This ancient navigation is extensively used for pleasure-cruising and is very beautiful throughout the whole of its length from the Severn at Tewkesbury to just above Stratford-upon-Avon, a total distance of about forty-six miles. The locks, seventeen in all, are broad-gauge; some are attended by lock-keepers, but the majority have to be worked by boat crews.

At present the river is administered by two separate bodies: below Evesham the navigation authority is the Lower Avon Navigation Trust, and above Evesham it is the Upper Avon Navigation Trust – a situation which originated in the eighteenth century when the two sections of river first came under separate ownership. The navigation forms part of the 'Avon Ring', a superb route comprising the Rivers Avon and Severn, the Worcester and Birmingham Canal and the Stratford-upon-Avon Canal.

At Tewkesbury entry to the Lower Avon proper lies a few hundred yards upstream of the junction with the Severn. Large grain mills and wharves stand close by the first lock, where licences may be purchased from the keeper. From here the river winds through lovely countryside towards Pershore and on to Evesham, about twenty-six miles away by water. Mooring can be difficult as most of the banks are in private ownership and such mooring sites as have been provided by the Navigation Trust are inadequate for the number of boats using the river. Just above Evesham the Bridge Inn at Offenham marks the start of the Upper Avon, which is superb and in places wild and remote, in complete contrast to the busy waterway scene at Stratford-upon-Avon. Here, during the season, the river and waterfront by the Memorial Theatre are thronged with tourists, rowing boats and trip boats. Beyond the theatre lies the entrance to the Stratford-upon-Avon Canal, while straight ahead under the old tramway bridge and Clopton road bridge the river continues for another three miles or so before finally becoming unnavigable below Alveston.

Birmingham Canal Navigations

At the heart of the Midlands waterway system lies an amazingly complex network of canals known as the Birmingham Canal Navigations (BCN) connecting the manufacturing towns of the Black Country with each other and providing outlets to the principal waterways of the Midlands. As a canal system the BCN is unique, encompassing three distinct levels – the Wolverhampton, the Birmingham and the Walsall – situated on the West Midlands plateau, so that all approaches to the navigation entail the passage of considerable lock flights.

The main line of the system runs from Aldersley Junction on the Staffordshire and Worcestershire Canal through Wolverhampton to Gas Street Basin in Birmingham, a distance of about fifteen miles, and features a long flight of twenty-one locks at Wolverhampton (all locks on the BCN are narrow-gauge). From a junction at Tipton the original main line (Brindley's) follows a rather circuitous route, rejoining the 'new' main line (Telford's) at Smethwick. Branches from these two principal through routes include the Wyrley and Essington Canal, which loops round to the north from Wolverhampton towards

Cannock and the vast Chasewater reservoir, finally turning south to Birmingham via the Rushall and the Tame Valley Canals; the Walsall Canal, connecting the 'new' main line to the Wyrley and Essington; the Birmingham and Fazeley Canal, running from Farmer's Bridge in Birmingham to Fazeley on the Coventry Canal; the Dudley Canals, 1 and 2, connected to the main lines by great tunnels at Dudley and Netherton and leading to the Stourbridge Canal, which joins the Staffordshire and Worcestershire Canal at Stourton Junction. Beyond Gas Street Basin the Birmingham Level extends unbroken to the top of the Tardebigge flight of locks on the Worcester and Birmingham Canal, and to Lapworth Locks on the northern Stratford Canal. At Aston a short branch from the Birmingham and Fazeley Canal leads down through Ashted Locks to the northern section of the Grand Union Canal.

For the enthusiast the BCN provides an enormous variety of experience, much of it within an industrial landscape and essentially of an historical nature, for here it is possible to see at first hand that intimate relationship between industry and water transport that nurtured the growth of the Industrial Revolution. Now the once-busy waterways are deserted and still, apart from the occasional pleasure-craft, but surprisingly impressive and endlessly interesting.

Brecon and Abergavenny Canal

The Brecon and Abergavenny Canal is a spectacularly beautiful waterway which follows the valley of the Usk from Brecon to Pontymoile, where it joins the derelict Monmouthshire Canal. It is about thirty-three miles long with six broad-gauge locks (just over nine feet wide) and a 375-yard tunnel. Since the whole of the canal lies within the Brecon Beacons National Park, all building and engineering work associated with the waterway is carefully controlled and thus its essential character is preserved and enhanced; even the towpath is in excellent condition throughout, in contrast to the usual state of affairs.

Although the canal is isolated from the main waterways network and is short in terms of cruising distance, a satisfying holiday can be had by combining boating with exploration of the surrounding countryside of the National Park. Natural history, photography, walking, caving and many other interests may be pursued at leisure in superb surroundings: for instance, industrial archaeology enthusiasts can spend time searching for the remains of the many tramways that once transported stone and minerals to the canal.

Scenically the canal is second to none. For much of its course it contours around wooded hills with splendid views across the Usk valley; the twenty-five-mile pound from Llangynidr Locks to Pontymoile, made possible only by the use of substantial embankments and rock cuts, is an outstanding engineering feat in such hilly terrain.

Bridgewater Canal

Renowned as the enterprise that inaugurated the Canal Era, the Bridgewater Canal spans the Greater Manchester–Cheshire border from Leigh to Runcorn, a distance of thirty-six miles, with a two-and-three-quarter-mile branch to Castlefield in Manchester, where it joins the Rochdale Canal. Another branch, three-quarters of a mile in length, runs from Preston Brook to a connection with the Trent and Mersey Canal just north of Preston Brook Tunnel.

At Runcorn the paired locks which once gave access to the Manchester Ship Canal have long since been filled in, and the canal now ends at a large and rather impressive basin. The canal through Runcorn has not much to offer, but towards Preston Brook the scene becomes rural and continues to improve until it is at its best around the pretty village of Lymm. Beyond Lymm lies the Bollin embankment and aqueduct, scene of a spectacular burst in 1971 and now reinstated in the form of a new piled and concreted channel. The urban landscapes of Altrincham and Sale are somewhat less delightful, and after passing Waters Meeting, where the Castlefield branch joins the main line, the canal enters Trafford Park Industrial estate, at the far side of which lies the Barton Swing Aqueduct. This astonishing structure, pivoted on a central island, carries the Bridgewater Canal over the Manchester Ship Canal and is swung open to allow passage for sea-going ships – a sight well worth seeing.

Beyond the aqueduct the canal again runs through urban surroundings until near Worsley, where it begins a long traverse of the old South Lancashire coalfield. Here the effects of past mining become evident, as the banks are piled and concreted to prevent collapse and are periodically raised to counteract subsidence. Although long since built up, Worsley is a pretty village, with a green through which the canal passes and a boatyard and dry docks. Just beyond lies Worsley Turn and a branch to the Duke of Bridgewater's original coalmines, which were the reason for the canal's construction. Past the turn the canal enters a wasteland of old mine spoil and after a few miles enters the town of Leigh, where it joins the Leigh branch of the Leeds and Liverpool Canal.

The Broads

Although tiny in comparison with the connected system of inland waterways, the Broads have long been acknowledged as Britain's most popular boating area and support a considerable hire-craft industry which, together with private pleasure-boats, amounts to many thousands of craft. The five rivers that constitute the Broads are situated in East Anglia between Norwich and the coast and cover an area of about 350 square miles, most of which lies within Norfolk. The actual 'broads' are small, shallow lakes – in many cases accessible from the rivers – formed by the inundation of ancient peat diggings, and are comparable in nature to the 'flashes' of Cheshire and Lanca-shire, which were caused by subsidence due to salt workings and coal mining. Total length of navigable water is about 125 miles and is lock-free but subject to tides, although the tidal range is not great and is virtually unnoticeable in the upper reaches of the rivers. Con-nections with the North Sea occur at Great Yarmouth and Lowestoft, but hire craft are prohibited from entering these harbours.

The River Yare runs through Great Yarmouth almost parallel with the coast before turning inland for Norwich, about 28 miles away by water. Just behind Great Yarmouth the river enters Breydon Water, a large tidal lake four miles long, at the western end of which the River Waveney branches off to the south. The Yare continues its circuitous course towards Norwich through a typical fenland landscape, flat but not uninteresting, and marked by numerous drainage pumps. At Reedham, where there is a car ferry, the two-and-a-half-mile long Haddiscoe Cut leads off south-east to join with the Waveney, while the Yare gradually swings west and then north-west, meeting the River Chet at Hardley Cross and continuing on by Cantley to Rockland Broad. Above here the river becomes more attractive and wooded, and at Brundall short cuts lead to the pretty Surlingham Broad. Shortly after reaching the outskirts of Norwich the Yare becomes unnavigable, and the city centre is reached by means of the River Wensum. The city itself is both historically interesting and beautiful, with many fine buildings and excellent shops.

The River Waveney forms part of the Norfolk–Suffolk boundary over much of its course. From Burgh Castle, where it meets the Yare, the river traverses marshlands for several miles to the village of St Olave's, and here it is joined by the Haddiscoe Cut leading to the Yare at Reedham. Beyond St Olave's the fenland landscape becomes more wooded, and near the outskirts of Lowestoft a large stretch of open water is reached – Oulton Broad, a major boating centre. About one mile before the entrance to the broad the continuation of the river turns westward and runs through pleasant countryside to Beccles and beyond to Geldeston, the present head of navigation.

The River Bure leads off from the Yare at Great Yarmouth and turns in a great loop to the west through unremarkable scenery until Stokesby is reached. Five miles further upriver the River Thurne enters at Thurne Mouth, and after another two and a half miles the River Ant comes in from the north. Between the two junctions lies South Walsham Broad, reached by means of the old course of the Bure. A navigation cut leads upstream to Ranworth and Honing, the latter a popular boating centre as just a little further on lie several broads including Hoveton Great Broad, Black Horse Broad and Salhouse Broad. Beyond Wroxham Broad lies the town of Wroxham, acknowledged as the 'capital' of Broadland, and thronged with boats and tourists during the season. The river is navigable for only another four and a half miles or so to the lovely village of Coltishall, although at one time craft could reach Aylsham Bridge, ten miles and five locks upriver.

From its confluence with the Bure the River Thurne runs in a roughly north-easterly direction for about five and a half miles to the limit of navigation at Martham Broad, only two miles from the coast, although the restricted dimensions of the famous medieval bridge at Potter Heigham prevent larger craft from reaching this point. Above the village lies the entrance to Hickling Broad, which is the largest of the broads and requires care in navigation on account of its shallowness. It is approached through Heigham Sound, from which a narrow channel – Meadow Dyke – gives access to Horsey Mere.

The River Ant is the northernmost river of the Broads and is at present navigable for about ten miles from its junction with the Bure to Honing, where the now derelict North Walsham and Dilham Canal begins. About halfway along its course the Ant enters Barton Broad, a stretch of water two and a half miles long, and soon afterwards divides, the right-hand fork leading to the very reedy Sutton Broad, while the left-hand channel follows Stalham Dyke, an area of commercial activity with boatyards and holiday chalets. Further upstream lies Wayford Bridge, more boatyards and shopping facilities.

Calder and Hebble Navigation

Among the great works of improvement to river navigations carried out during the eighteenth century, the Calder and Hebble Navigation in Yorkshire is possibly the most outstanding. Engineered by John Smeaton of Eddystone Lighthouse fame, it extends for a distance of twenty-one and a half miles from a junction with the Aire and Calder Navigation at Wakefield to the terminal basin at Sowerby Bridge, where originally it joined the now abandoned Rochdale Canal. The greater part of the navigation consists of artificial cut rather than natural river and there are two distinct gauges of lock: the reconstructed locks on the three-and-a-half-mile section above Wakefield measure 120 by seventeen and a half feet, and the remainder up to Sowerby Bridge have a nominal size of fifty-seven and a half feet by fourteen feet, two inches. An interesting feature of this navigation is the method of paddle operation on the locks above Mirfield: they are worked by wooden handspike instead of the usual windlass.

Between Dewsbury and Brighouse the Huddersfield Broad Canal branches off towards the south-west, ending at Aspley Basin close to the centre of Huddersfield, a distance of just over three miles from the main line. Like the Calder and Hebble Navigation, the Huddersfield Broad Canal at one time connected with a trans-Pennine route to Manchester, the Huddersfield Narrow Canal, now also long since abandoned.

Although the Calder and Hebble system was an industrial navigation and is still heavily industrialized, especially in its lower reaches, the section towards Sowerby Bridge provides pleasant rural stretches of waterway as it passes through the attractive Calder valley. The terminal basin at Sowerby Bridge is impressive, surrounded as it is by eighteenth- and nineteenth-century stone-built warehouses and other buildings. Some of these have been restored and adapted for a variety of uses including a restaurant and bar, a boat centre and boat building workshops and dock. Good moorings are available and the town is within easy reach.

Caldon Canal

The Caldon Canal branches off the summit level of the Trent and Mersey Canal close by Etruria top lock at Hanley and runs to Froghall, a distance of seventeen and a half miles with seventeen narrow-gauge locks. The canal originally continued for another thirteen miles to Uttoxeter, but was abandoned and used in part for a railway line in the middle of the last century. The upper part of the canal is very beautiful, in complete contrast to the urban and industrial surroundings at Etruria and Hanley. Not far from the junction with the main line a two-riser staircase lock lifts the waterway almost twenty feet, and a little further on the shallow Planet Lock marks the start of a long pound which cuts through Hanley Park and enters an area of factories and warehouses before finally approaching open country on the eastern outskirts of the town. The channel, never wide throughout its length, is made even narrower by reed beds in this stretch. From the deep Engine Lock a one-mile pound leads to the flight of five locks at Stockton Brook, which raises the waterway to a summit pound 484 feet above sea level. The canal now passes through rolling green countryside to the pretty Hazelhurst Locks, where the Leek arm branches off to the right and then crosses over the main line on a substantial aqueduct; the arm is navigable through Leek Tunnel (130 yards) as far as the feeder from Rudyard Lake on the outskirts of Leek, and is about two and three-quarter miles long.

The canal to Froghall descends the Hazelhurst flight of three locks and continues along the Churnet Valley through Cheddleton with its fine flint mill, and down a further three locks before entering the River Churnet at Oakmeadow Ford Lock. The river is followed through a very beautiful steep-sided wooded valley for about one mile to Consall

Forge, where the canal, now very narrow, branches off left to Frog-hall. After passing Flint Mill Lock and the curious Cherry Eye Bridge, the canal ends at a basin immediately beyond Froghall Tunnel, which is only seventy-five yards long but has very restricted headroom.

Cam, River

The River Cam is a tributary of the Great Ouse, and from a junction with the latter at Pope's Corner, not far from Ely, the navigable section runs up through three locks to Cambridge, about fourteen miles away. The scenery is typically fenland – flat and bleak. Three miles upriver at Upware lies the entrance lock to Reach Lode, which leads off to the east and provides access to two other small waterways: Wicken Lode and Burwell Lode. All are navigable in craft drawing about two feet. The first lock on the main river – Bottisham – marks the start of the section controlled by the Cam Conservators, and tolls are payable at the two locks further upstream. All locks are manned. About half a mile above Baits Bite Lock the Rule of the Road ('pass on the right') is reversed for several hundred yards as indicated by notice boards at each end of the stretch. Cambridge is entered through a large park, with extensive moorings for visiting craft just below Jesus Lock, although it is possible to lock through into the reach above, which leads to Town Quay and past the famous college 'Backs' to a winding hole. This section of river is often crammed with punts, canoes and skiffs, and visiting craft should navigate with care.

Chesterfield Canal

The original route of the canal ran from the tidal Trent at West Stockwith to Chesterfield, a distance of forty-six miles with sixty-five locks, but abandonment of the upper section has left a navigable length of twenty-six miles with sixteen locks. From West Stockwith to Retford the canal is broad-gauge, and the remainder to Worksop narrow-gauge. It is a rural waterway almost throughout and consequently provides pleasant cruising. However, it suffers from the disadvantage of being cut off from the main network by the Trent tideway, which is out of bounds for most hire craft unless special arrangements can be made with the hire company. Some firms solve the problem by offering pilotage for the tideway, at an extra charge.

Coventry Canal

Built to serve the coalmining regions around Bedworth, and providing an important link in the Midlands canal system, the Coventry Canal runs from Fradley Junction on the Trent and Mersey Canal to Coventry, where it ends in a fine basin not far from the city centre. It is thirty-eight miles long with thirteen narrow-gauge locks, eleven of which are arranged in a single flight at Atherstone, resulting in long, lock-free pounds.

The first five and a half miles from Coventry Basin are mostly through urban and industrial surroundings, and it was on this section of canal that a spectacular burst occurred in December 1978, causing considerable damage to property in the neighbourhood. On the outskirts of the city, where the northern Oxford Canal is joined at the famous Hawkesbury Junction, the landscape is more rural and open, although marred by a conglomeration of electricity pylons. Between Hawkesbury and Nuneaton the Ashby Canal branches off to the east, and shortly after the canal passes through Nuneaton to enter an area of quarry workings and spoil heaps. The surroundings are surprisingly pleasant, however, and there are good views across the valley to the north.

Open country follows to Atherstone, where the long sixteen-and-a-half-mile pound ends at a flight of eleven locks. Below the flight the canal passes through pleasant farmlands to Polesworth, another coalmining area of huge spoil tips and flooded depressions, or 'flashes', caused by subsidence. From here it is only a short distance to the two locks at Glascote near Tamworth, and after crossing the River Tame on an aqueduct the canal enters Fazeley, where it is joined by the Birmingham and Fazeley Canal. The final stretch to Fradley is entirely rural and very pretty in places, particularly around Hopwas.

Erewash Canal

Originally connected at its upper end to the Cromford and Notting-ham Canals – both now derelict – the Erewash Canal is a mere twelve miles in length with fifteen broad-gauge locks. From its terminus in the Great Northern Basin at Langley Mill it runs through rural surroundings towards Ilkeston, crossing the River Erewash on a small aqueduct close to an abandoned railway interchange wharf. At Ilke-ston the landscape becomes decidely urban and then industrial as the large Stanton ironworks are reached just before the canal passes under the M1 motorway.

More built-up areas follow through Sandiacre; just to the south of the town the waterway was at one time joined by the Derby Canal, now derelict. The approach to Long Eaton is marked by lace mills, and for a while the canal passes through rather pleasant urban surround-ings before winding away south to Trent Lock and a junction with the River Trent.

Fossdyke and Witham Navigation

Reputed to be Britain's oldest navigable canal, the Fossdyke was built by the Romans in about AD 120 to connect Lincoln with the River Trent. Since then it has been improved at intervals; it joins the River Witham in Lincoln, thus providing a through route between the Trent and the Wash. From Torksey on the Trent tideway it is forty-three miles to Boston, where the Witham becomes tidal at the Grand Sluice. There are four broad-gauge locks, including the tidal locks at each end of the navigation.

The scenery throughout is unremarkable, consisting of flat farm-lands seen with difficulty over the high banks, and long, straight reaches of waterway add nothing to the interest. Lincoln and its magnificent cathedral are well worth visiting, however. At Brayford Pool the Fossdyke merges with the Witham, which continues on through the 'Glory Hole' under Lincoln High Street. Beyond Lincoln the navigation resumes its course through a flat rural landscape towards Boston, whose location – marked by the famous 'Boston Stump' (St Botolph's church tower) – can be seen from miles away. Just before reaching the town a branch channel leads off through a

lock at Anton's Gowt; this is the entrance to the Witham Navigable
Drains, a fascinating complex of waterways penetrating into Boston
itself, although there is no connection with the Witham in the town
and craft must make the return trip to Anton's Gowt.

Like the Chesterfield Canal, the Fossdyke and Witham Navigation
is separated from the main network by the Trent tideway, and therefore to reach it most hirers will require special permission from the
hire company.

Gloucester and Sharpness Canal

Constructed as a ship canal to bypass a difficult and dangerous section
of the River Severn below Gloucester, the waterway is frequented by
coasters and other vessels up to about 200 feet in length. The provision of manned swing bridges throughout its sixteen miles eliminates headroom problems, and apart from the ship lock giving access
to Sharpness Docks there are no locks. At the other end of the canal
Gloucester Docks, with their fine warehouses and extensive basins,
are entered from the Severn through a lock which has a somewhat
tricky approach from the river. Craft are expected to make the
through passage without stopping and the bridge tenders are informed accordingly, but the visitor would be well advised to make
arrangements to visit the Slimbridge Wild Fowl Trust, established by
Sir Peter Scott.

Grand Union Canal

The Grand Union Canal as it now exists resulted from an amalgama-
tion of several canal companies in the 1920s, and in this respect it
is unique. For the purposes of present-day navigation it may be
conveniently divided into three major sections: Grand Union Canal
(North), extending from Braunston to Birmingham; Grand Union
Canal (South), from Braunston to London; and Grand Union Canal
(Leicester Section), running from Norton Junction, on the main line
south of Braunston, to Leicester. In addition there are several
branches, of which the Paddington Arm and the Regent's Canal

through London provide an important link with the Thames tideway at Limehouse.

The main line of the Grand Union runs from the Thames at Brentford to Birmingham, a total distance of 135 miles with 165 locks, all broad-gauge. From Brentford to Tring summit in the Chilterns the scenery is mostly urban or industrial, but with some surprisingly pleasant stretches. The Paddington Arm leads off six miles above Brentford at Bull's Bridge, and at Cowley Peachey the five-mile-long Slough Arm comes in from the west. Forty-four locks raise the canal to Tring Summit through Uxbridge, Watford, Rickmansworth and Berkhamsted, and at Marsworth a six-mile-long arm descends to Aylesbury through sixteen narrow-gauge locks. From Tring to the southern fringe of Birmingham the canal traverses some lovely open countryside; this section includes the longest main-line tunnel now in use – Blisworth, 3,056 yards long – followed by Braunston Tunnel, which is about 1,000 yards shorter. Just north of Blisworth the Northampton Arm gives access to the River Nene through seventeen narrow-gauge locks, and further north at Norton Junction the Leicester Section is joined.

Braunston Junction marks the end of the southern section of the main line; from here the northern section shares the line of the Oxford Canal for a few miles before turning off at Napton Junction to run down through lock flights to Leamington and Warwick. The spectacular Hatton Flight of twenty-one broad locks lifts the canal towards its final level, which is reached at the top of the five locks at Knowle, just south of Birmingham.

The Leicester Section extends from Norton Junction on the main line to the River Trent at Trent Junction, and includes the River Soar (see p. 265). A narrow-gauge flight of locks at Watford, including a staircase, leads to the twenty-mile summit pound, a beautiful and remote stretch of waterway. This long pound, which has tunnels at Crick and Husbands Bosworth, ends at the Foxton flight of locks consisting of two five-rise staircases. Alongside the flight stand the remains of the famous Foxton Inclined Plane, abandoned about seventy years ago. From the bottom of the locks a five-and-a-half-mile arm leads to Market Harborough, while the line to Leicester runs on to Saddington Tunnel and down through pleasant countryside and numerous broad-gauge locks to the southern outskirts of the city, where the canal section joins the River Soar.

Lancaster Canal

The Lancaster Canal as it now exists is the remnant of an ambitious plan to connect Kendal in South Lakeland with the Bridgewater Canal at Worsley. By the end of the eighteenth century the canal was open between Kendal and Preston and a tramroad connection across the River Ribble joined with the ten-mile southern section, which had been completed between Walton Summit and Wigan. However, the work progressed no further, and the southern section was sold to the Leeds and Liverpool Canal Co.; it now forms part of the Leeds and Liverpool main line between Johnsons Hillock and Wigan top lock.

In the 1820s a three-mile branch to the coast was opened, descending through seven broad locks to the Lune Estuary at Glasson Dock. As a result of the failure to construct a water crossing of the River Ribble the Lancaster Canal has always been isolated from the main waterways network, which can be reached only by making a coastal passage. In recent years the canal was much reduced in length when the M6 north of Carnforth was built, as no provision was made for navigation in the design of the earthworks and the channel is now culverted through the embankments. The navigable line of the canal is about forty-two miles long, from Preston to Tewitfield just north of Carnforth, and it is lock-free as the original eight locks – now converted to weirs – are contained within the abandoned section above Tewitfield.

It is an attractive waterway, winding through the pleasant countryside of northern Lancashire and crossing the River Lune at Lancaster on John Rennie's superb stone aqueduct, 640 feet long. Near Carnforth the canal approaches close to the coast, with good views of the Lakeland hills across Morecambe Bay. It is to be very much regretted that the northernmost section is inaccessible, as it is one of the most beautiful stretches of canal in the country.

Lea and Stort Navigation

The River Lea (or Lee) is navigable from the Thames to Hertford, a distance of about twenty-eight miles with twenty-one broad-gauge locks. Entry to the navigation from the Thames is usually made through Limehouse Basin, whence the Limehouse Cut connects with the Lea at a point where Bow Locks give access to Bow Creek, a tidal tributary of the Thames. All this lower section of the Lea upstream as far as Enfield is urban and industrial in character and carries commercial traffic. At Old Ford – about two and a half miles above Limehouse – the short Hertford Union Canal rises through three locks to join the Regent's Canal.

Passing Hackney Marshes, the river follows a winding course through Tottenham and Edmonton, skirting large reservoirs at Ponders End and finally entering more rural surroundings north of Enfield. The Lea Valley Regional Park Authority has contributed much to the recreational use of this area, including waterspace activities in the old gravel pits that lie alongside the navigation. Near Rye House, Hoddesdon, the River Stort branches off to the east; the Lea continues northward through Ware to the head of navigation at Hertford, where it ends in a basin.

The River Stort is a charming navigation, peacefully rural in character and graced with some very fine ancient buildings. Its total length is about fourteen miles with fifteen broad-gauge locks from its junction with the Lea to the end of navigation at Bishop's Stortford.

Leeds and Liverpool Canal

Of the original three trans-Pennine canals, the Leeds and Liverpool is now the only one open to traffic throughout its entire length. From a junction with the Aire and Calder Navigation at Leeds to the River Mersey at Liverpool the total distance is 127 miles. For almost the whole of its course on the Yorkshire side of the Pennines it follows the valley of the River Aire, eventually crossing into Lancashire at one of the lowest sections of the range, and thereafter traversing uplands between Burnley and Wigan before descending to the Douglas Valley and the Lancashire plain beyond.

The scenery is magnificent in places, specially the Upper Aire Valley in the heart of the Pennines. This section is almost entirely rural, in contrast with the industrial and urban landscapes of the Yorkshire mill towns above Leeds, and includes the beautiful sixteen-mile Skipton pound extending from Bingley to Gargrave. A few miles further on above Bank Newton lies Marton Pool – an astonishing pound which follows a tortuous course through low grassy hills as it approaches Greenberfield and the summit level of 487 feet. Here, at Foulridge, the canal runs in tunnel for 1,640 yards before emerging to begin the long descent on the Lancashire side of the Pennines through Burnley with its massive embankment, Blackburn and Chorley, to the great flight of twenty-three locks at Wigan. Near the bottom of the flight a branch turns away eastwards to connect with the Bridgewater Canal at Leigh, while the main line continues on down the Douglas Valley to Burscough. The Rufford branch leads north from here to Tarleton, where a lock gives access to the tidal River Douglas and the Ribble Estuary. From just above Burscough the remaining section to Liverpool is lock-free, although numerous swing bridges help to relieve the monotony of the twenty-nine-mile pound.

The canal is broad-gauge throughout, with locks measuring just over fourteen feet in width but of two different lengths: sixty-two feet from Leeds to Wigan (and on the Rufford branch), and seventy-two feet from Liverpool to Leigh. There are ninety-one locks in all, including the famous Bingley Five-Rise – a very impressive five-step staircase – as well as several two- and three-riser staircase locks on the section between Bingley and Leeds. Large masonry blocks are used for most of the engineering works, lending an air of enduring solidity to the character of the canal and blending well with both natural features and the stone-built towns and villages along the banks.

Llangollen Canal

Probably the most popular canal for pleasure-boat cruising in Britain, the Llangollen Canal is entirely rural throughout its length of forty-four miles, traversing stretches of remote countryside from Cheshire through the Welsh Marches to Llangollen in the valley of the Dee. Quite apart from its charm, the canal is unique in that it acts as a water feeder from the Horseshoe Falls on the River Dee at Llantisilio to reservoirs at Hurleston, where the canal joins the main line of the Shropshire Union Canal not far from Nantwich.

There are twenty-one narrow-gauge locks in all, most of them situated on the lower reaches of the canal, including a fine three-rise staircase at Grindley Brook near Whitchurch. Above this point there is virtually lock-free cruising, as the remaining stretches are broken only by the two locks at New Marton. Scattered throughout the length of the canal are a number of bascule lift bridges which add to the charm of this beautiful waterway.

The farmlands of the lower reaches are somewhat featureless, but after passing the junction with the old Prees branch at Whixall the canal meanders through a very pleasant countryside of woods and small lakes to the town of Ellesmere, reached by a short arm off the main line. Opposite the arm entrance stands Beech House, once the headquarters of the Shropshire Union Railways and Canal Company. Not far above Ellesmere the Montgomery Canal, now being restored, branches off to the south, and shortly afterwards the canal reaches its summit level at New Marton locks. The Welsh hills are now close, and it is only a short distance to Chirk aqueduct and the quarter-of-a-mile-long tunnel beyond. Another tunnel at Whitehouses now lies ahead, after which the canal turns to contour along the southern slopes of the Dee Valley as it approaches the magnificent structure of Pontcysyllte aqueduct, 126 feet high and slightly over 1,000 feet long. Passage of the aqueduct provides a fitting climax to a cruise on this canal, and the interest is maintained by navigation of the narrow and shallow feeder arm up to Llangollen, with superb views of the Welsh hills across the valley. Llangollen is the effective terminus, as navigation of the final stretch of the feeder to Llantisilio is advisable only on craft of shallow draught and short length.

Macclesfield Canal

This was one of the last canals to be constructed before the Railway Age finally brought all canal-building to an end. It connects the Peak Forest Canal at Marple with the Trent and Mersey Canal at Hardingswood, just north of Harecastle Tunnel, and is twenty-seven miles long with twelve narrow-gauge locks at Bosley and a stop-lock at Hall Green near Hardingswood. Mostly rural in character, it is very pleasant throughout and provides good views of the outlying moors and hills of the Peak District, including the curious Mow Cop with its constructed ruins, and the fine ridge of The Cloud near Bosley. Across the canal from Mow Cop stands Little Moreton Hall, an outstanding example of Elizabethan half-timbered construction, easily reached by a short walk over the fields.

After passing Congleton the canal skirts the northern edge of The Cloud and reaches the splendid flight of locks at Bosley. These contain a curiosity in the form of double mitre gates at the head end instead of the usual single gate, a feature that has given rise to much ingenious explanation. At the top of the flight the canal reaches its summit level of 500 feet, which is maintained all the way to Whaley Bridge on the Upper Peak Forest Canal.

A fairly brief interlude of urban sprawl at Macclesfield is followed by rolling farmlands until the stone-built town of Bollington, where massive embankments and masonry aqueducts bear testimony to the assurance with which the later engineers designed their canals. Above Bollington the countryside becomes more open again as the canal passes through Higher Poynton, and beyond High Lane it is just a short distance to Marple and a junction with the Peak Forest Canal.

Throughout the length of the canal there are a considerable number of very fine masonry bridges, those of the roving type being particularly noteworthy, and a scattering of swing bridges, all worked by boat crews.

Medway, River

The tidal section of the Medway commences at Sheerness on the Thames estuary and runs inland through an extremely broad expanse of waterway busy with commercial shipping, to Chatham. Hire craft are not allowed to enter the tideway, and their limit of navigation is the tidal lock at Allington, two and a half miles below Maidstone. Upstream of the lock lies a lovely section of river, and the town of Maidstone is well worth a visit. The nine locks above Allington are all broad-gauge, and are worked by boat crews. The course of the river continues through East Farleigh and Teston, passing hopfields and orchards and becoming increasingly rural and remote until Tonbridge is reached, almost eighteen miles from Allington. Moorings for visiting craft are available not far from the town centre.

Middle Level Navigations

These form an intricate system of navigable drainage channels situated in the Cambridgeshire fenlands between Peterborough and Downham Market. They are of interest to the boater mainly on account of their use as a through route from the River Nene to the Great Ouse and the River Cam. The total distance from the Nene at Stanground Lock near Peterborough to the tidal Great Ouse at Salter's Lode is about thirty miles with four locks which, although broad-gauge, are very short. Limiting dimensions for craft are given as 46 × 10 × 2½-foot draught, but the acute bend at Whittlesey imposes a severe restriction on the length of any craft with a beam greater than seven feet. Entry to the Middle Level from the Nene is at Stanground Lock, which gives access to King's Dyke leading to Whittlesey and to Ashline Lock. Whittlesey Dyke and the old course of the River Nene are then followed through March to Marmont Priory Lock and through the villages of Upwell and Outwell to Well Creek, at the eastern end of which Salter's Lode Lock allows entry to the Great Ouse tideway. A few hundred yards upstream lies Denver Sluice, where it is possible to lock through into the Ten Mile River and so to the River Cam and the upper Great Ouse. The scenery – such of it as can be seen over the high dyke banks – is typically fenland, and the main interest is really confined to the few settlements through which the route passes. There are several intersections with other navigable drains, but most visitors to the area will probably be making a through passage and will have little time for excursions.

Nene, River

From the main waterways system the River Nene is entered via the Northampton Arm of the Grand Union Canal and runs from Northampton to the Wash, although the limit of navigation so far as hire craft are concerned is Peterborough, about sixty-one miles below Northampton. A notable feature of the river is the use of locks with huge guillotine bottom gates in combination with paired mitre gates at the upper ends of the chambers. The locks play an essential part in flood control; the upper gates are designed to act as weirs when the river is at or above normal level, and are opened completely and fastened back during flood conditions, in which circumstances all river traffic must cease. The guillotine gates are left in the raised position to allow a free flow of water and must therefore be worked twice on each occasion – a very tiring exercise as they are extremely low-geared and have to be wound down as well as up. The thirty-seven locks between Northampton and Peterborough are all broad-gauge, although craft from the main system are restricted to narrow-beam because of the narrow-gauge locks of the Northampton Arm.

The river is mostly rural in character and very pretty in places as it winds down a shallow valley through attractive small towns and villages, and there is an abundance of wild life. For many boaters an additional attraction of the Nene lies in the fact that it provides a route to the Middle Level Navigations, which in turn lead to the Great Ouse, the Cam and their associated rivers.

Ouse, Great

From the tideway at Denver Sluice near Downham Market the old course of the lower Great Ouse follows the Ten Mile River and the Old West River by Littleport and Ely to Earith, where the upper Great Ouse is joined, a distance of about thirty miles. The most direct route from Denver to Earith lies along the twenty-mile New Bedford River – or Hundred Foot Drain – which runs almost dead straight for the whole distance and is tidal. All this area comprises the South Level of the fens, low-lying farmlands largely reclaimed from marshes by great drainage schemes carried out in the seventeenth century. Between Denver and Ely the lower Great Ouse is joined by three navigable tributaries: the Wissey (ten miles long); the Little Ouse, or Brandon Creek (fourteen miles long); the Lark (ten and a half miles long), and at Pope's Corner, three miles above Ely, the River Cam enters from the south.

The upper Great Ouse commences at Earith, and from here to the head of navigation at Bedford is about forty miles with fifteen broad-gauge locks, of which only the first two are manned (the other keeper-operated lock is Hermitage, at the entrance to the Old West River just below Earith). Curiously, most of the locks are fitted with guillotine head-gates and mitre tail-gates, an exact reversal of the gate arrangement on the River Nene. The upper river is much more attractive than the exposed fenlands of the lower reaches, and passes through several old and historic settlements – St Ives, Huntingdon, Godmanchester, St Neots, and Eaton Socon – before reaching Bedford. Above Bedford Lock the river is navigable for another three miles or so to Kempston Mill.

Ouse, River (Yorkshire)

To inland waterways enthusiasts the Yorkshire Ouse is one of the lesser-known rivers, probably on account of its relative isolation and the fact that it is separated from the main system by a tideway. The navigation consists of three distinct sections: the River Ouse, which joins the Humber at Trent Falls and extends up through York to Ouse Gill Beck just above Linton Lock; the Ure, which becomes the name of the river above Ouse Gill Beck; and the mile-long Ripon Canal at the head of navigation on the Ure. The total distance from the tidal lock at Naburn to the top of the Ripon Canal is about thirty-one miles with four broad-gauge locks.

The navigation is less often approached through Trent Falls by pleasure-craft – not surprisingly, as the tideway not only runs strongly but is frequented by coasters and other commercial shipping. A much safer alternative is provided by following a route through the Aire and Calder Navigation and the Selby Canal, at the northern end of which Selby tidal lock permits access to the river. Just upstream of the lock there are two hazardous bridges and a great hairpin bend, after which the Ouse runs uneventfully through flat countryside to the start of the non-tidal section at Naburn Lock, about twelve and a half miles from Selby. A few miles above the lock lies the beautiful and historic town of York, which provides the main focus of interest on this navigation.

Beyond York the river is peacefully rural and very remote in its upper reaches. At Nun Monkton the unnavigable River Nidd joins the Ouse just below a reach containing the notorious Linton Clay Huts – underwater banks of hard shale – which in fact are no danger to the boater providing a little care is exercised. About two miles above Linton Lock the Ouse becomes the Ure, which in turn is joined by the River Swale at Swale Nab. From here it is only a short distance to the Boroughbridge Cut, which takes the navigation through the town and rejoins the river a little way beyond the town centre. Some two miles above Boroughbridge lies the entrance to the Ripon Canal at Oxclose Lock, beautifully situated amid remote farmlands. Unfortunately the canal is no longer navigable into Ripon itself – which is not far away – but it does provide a pleasant conclusion to the river navigation, and in addition has the distinction of being the most northerly point of the connected network of inland waterways.

Oxford Canal

A very popular cruising route, the Oxford Canal runs from Hawkesbury Junction on the Coventry Canal to the Thames at Oxford. The total distance is seventy-eight miles with forty-three narrow-gauge locks. A few miles of the line are shared with the Grand Union Canal, from Napton Junction to Braunston Junction, and the two sections on each side of this point are usually referred to as the Oxford Canal (North) and the Oxford Canal (South).

The Oxford Canal (North) was the subject of considerable improvements in the 1830s which resulted in a shortening of the line by about fourteen miles; the remains of the old loops can still be seen today. This portion of the canal is almost lock-free, for apart from the stoplock at Hawkesbury Junction there are only three locks, grouped together at Hillmorton on the outskirts of Rugby. The northern part of the waterway does not contain any outstanding features, but being almost entirely rural nevertheless provides some very pleasant cruising.

Two miles or so south of Napton Junction, where the northern section of the Grand Union Canal branches off towards Birmingham, the Napton Flight of nine locks lifts the southern Oxford to its eleven-mile summit pound, the tortuous course of which is a remarkable example of contour cutting. Just beyond Fenny Compton the canal enters a long, straight cutting, still known as 'The Tunnel', resulting from the opening-up of two tunnels in about 1870 to reduce traffic delays. The summit pound ends at Claydon, and from here the canal runs down through nine locks to the valley of the River Cherwell at Cropredy, thereafter keeping company with the river all the way to the Thames. For most of its length the southern Oxford Canal is completely rural and very attractive, with charming villages such as

Lower Heyford and Aynho, although its principal town, Banbury, leaves much to be desired from the viewpoint of the waterway. Not far from Oxford the Duke's Cut branches off to the Thames and the main line continues through the outskirts of the city to join the Thames at Isis Lock.

Peak Forest Canal

From a junction with the Ashton Canal at Ashton-under-Lyne the Peak Forest Canal runs south for almost fifteen miles to a terminus at Whaley Bridge on the fringe of the Peak District National Park. It is joined by the Macclesfield Canal at Marple, where the only locks on the canal – sixteen in all and narrow-gauge – raise the level through a total of 210 feet. At the bottom of the flight a superb masonry aqueduct spans the River Goyt and, together with the two short tunnels at Romiley and Woodley, constitutes the main interest on this level, which is referred to as the Lower Peak Forest Canal. After many years of dereliction it was at last reopened, together with the Ashton Canal, in 1974 after a great deal of hard work by voluntary labour organized by the Peak Forest Canal Society and the Inland Waterways Association, later backed by the British Waterways Board and local authorities.

Above the Marple flight the Upper Peak Forest Canal contours along the southern slopes of the Goyt valley at a height of 500 feet above sea level to Whaley Bridge, with magnificent views across the moors towards the great plateau of Kinder Scout. The outskirts of Disley and New Mills are hardly touched, so a rural character is maintained almost throughout. Both swing and bascule bridges occur on this section.

Shortly before reaching Whaley Bridge an arm branches off towards Buxworth, terminating in the Buxworth Basin complex, now being restored, which was an important transhipment point for limestone brought by tramroad from Doveholes quarries. From the junction with the Buxworth Arm a short stretch of canal leads to the basin at Whaley Bridge, which is very conveniently situated for access to the town. The building adjoining the basin once formed the terminus of the Cromford and High Peak Railway, an extraordinary engineering work which connected the Peak Forest and Cromford Canals by a standard-gauge line over the Pennines, rising to a summit level of no less than 1,264 feet and notable for its use of inclined planes operated by stationary steam engines. Most of the route can still be traced, the original road bed having been modified into a cross-country track for use by walkers, cyclists and horse riders.

Regent's Canal

From a junction with the Paddington Arm at Little Venice the Regent's Canal runs through London to the Thames at Limehouse, a distance of eight and a half miles with twelve broad-gauge locks. Formerly the locks were paired and worked by keepers, but now one chamber of each pair has been converted to an overflow weir, and crews are permitted to work the locks unsupervised. Needless to say the canal is entirely urban and industrial in character, although it is not without charm in certain stretches – notably the very attractive area around Little Venice and at Regent's Park, where the canal passes through the zoo. The first locks occur just beyond at Hampstead Road and Camden Town, and drop the canal down through the East End and Islington Tunnel (the only other tunnel is at Maida Hill, near Little Venice) to Limehouse Basin, where a massive ship lock gives access to the Thames tideway. A connection with the Lea and Stort Navigation branches off at Victoria Park through the short Hertford Union Canal, and from Limehouse Basin (formerly Regent's Canal Dock) the Limehouse Cut runs north-east to join with the Lea just above Bow Locks.

Rochdale Canal

As originally built in 1804, the Rochdale Canal provided a line between the Bridgewater Canal in Manchester and the Calder and Hebble Navigation at Sowerby Bridge on the other side of the Pennines, a distance of thirty-three miles with an astounding total of ninety-two broad-gauge locks. The navigable section is now reduced to a mere flight of nine locks spread out through Manchester city centre over a distance of about one and a quarter miles. At the time of writing the navigation is in a critical state of disrepair – a matter of some concern, as closure of the flight would sever the 'Cheshire Ring', a very popular circular route in which the Rochdale Canal forms an essential link between the Bridgewater and Ashton canals.

Severn, River

At one time the Severn had a total navigable length of 128 miles from Gloucester to Welshpool, but nowadays its effective length is about forty-two miles, the decline in waterway traffic having been responsible for the virtual abandonment of the upper reaches above Stourport. There are six broad-gauge locks on the remaining section, all mechanized and with keepers in attendance. Downstream craft should take care near the approaches to the lock channels, especially when the river level is above normal, on account of the large unguarded weirs, and all craft should carry a suitable anchor and cable for use in emergencies. As the river is liable to heavy flooding, particularly in the spring and autumn, no attempt should be made to moor to the banks except at recognized mooring points.

Because of flood danger the Severn has high flood banks which in many places restrict the view from the deck of a boat, but there are several very pretty stretches of river, particularly in the reaches above and below Worcester. There are some important connections with the main waterway system: at Stourport, where the Staffordshire and Worcestershire Canal joins the river; at Worcester, the junction with the Worcester and Birmingham Canal; and at Tewkesbury, where the River Avon enters. Below Tewkesbury the river is tidal to some extent, and further down is affected by the famous Severn Bore, a spectacular series of tidal waves reaching a maximum height of about nine feet. The lowest point downstream which can be reached by hire craft is Gloucester, where entry can be made into the upper end of the Gloucester and Sharpness Canal at Gloucester Docks.

Sheffield and South Yorkshire Navigation

Forming part of the Yorkshire commercial canal system, this navigation runs from a connection with the Trent tideway at Keadby to Sheffield, a distance of forty-three miles and twenty-seven locks. The section from Rotherham to Bramwith, and the New Junction Canal, form part of a modernization programme aimed at creating an upgraded waterway – the South Yorkshire Canal – through to Goole on the Ouse, and able to take 700-ton craft. The remaining unimproved sections (Keadby to Bramwith, and Rotherham to Sheffield) retain their original broad-gauge locks, which have a length suitable only for craft not exceeding about sixty-two feet. The fifteen-mile Stainforth and Keadby Canal has long straight reaches and runs from Keadby through flat and rather uninteresting country before joining with the New Junction Canal at Kirk Bramwith, two miles or so beyond which Long Sandall Lock marks the start of a desolate industrial stretch through Doncaster. More attractive countryside follows to Sprotborough and Conisbrough, but then the navigation once more enters a bleak industrial area through Mexborough and Rotherham and up the Tinsley flight of eleven locks into Sheffield, where the canal ends in an impressive basin.

Shropshire Union Canal

The main line of the Shropshire Union Canal is sixty-six miles long and comprises three distinct sections of waterway: the Wirral Line, from Ellesmere Port on the Mersey to Chester; the old Chester Canal, from Chester to Nantwich; and the Birmingham and Liverpool Junction Canal, as it was originally named, from Nantwich to Autherley Junction on the Staffordshire and Worcestershire Canal near Wolverhampton.

Engineered by Thomas Telford, the Birmingham and Liverpool Junction Canal was completed in 1835 to provide a direct link between the manufacturing towns of the Black Country and the River Mersey, and was the last major undertaking of its type to be built as the Canal Era drew to a close in the face of growing railway competition. The line of the canal is uncompromisingly straight over much of its length, demonstrating the advances that had taken place in canal engineering since the time of Brindley. This canal follows the land contours to a minimal extent, relying on deep cuttings and spectacular embankments to maintain the level ('cut and fill' technique), and the locks are grouped in flights whenever possible. It is rural throughout, with some beautiful sections of wooded countryside and fine views from the embankments across to the Wrekin and the Welsh hills.

Fifteen miles or so from its southern terminus at Autherley the canal traverses Shelmore Great Bank into Norbury Junction, from which the now defunct Shrewsbury Canal at one time led to Newport. The superb Woodseaves Cutting is followed by a very pretty flight of five locks at Tyrley, marking the end of a long seventeen-mile pound and bringing the canal to Market Drayton and the Adderley flight of five locks. A short pound then leads to the fifteen locks at Audlem, which lower the canal to the Cheshire plain. From Audlem to Nantwich the countryside is pleasant but somewhat featureless until the old Chester Canal is joined close by Nantwich Basin, with a change of gauge from narrow to broad. Here too the waterway loses its 'modern' character and meanders around the contours, passing Hurleston Reservoir at the junction with the Llangollen Canal and, a little further on at Barbridge, the entrance to the Middlewich Branch, which descends through four narrow-gauge locks to connect with the Trent and Mersey Canal at Middlewich, ten miles away.

About three miles beyond Barbridge the first of the broad-gauge locks occurs at Bunbury in the form of a two-step staircase, followed by wooded farmlands and magnificent views of thirteenth-century Beeston Castle perched on top of a steep hill overlooking the plain. A succession of spaced-out locks leads to a long pound through Waverton to Christleton on the outskirts of Chester, where further locks lower the canal into a pound which skirts the impressive city walls to Northgate Locks, a three-step staircase cut from the solid rock. At the bottom of the flight the canal enters a nine-mile pound to Ellesmere Port (the Wirral Line), rural for most of the way until the industrial area around the Mersey is reached. At Ellesmere Port the North-West Museum of Inland Navigation houses a fine collection of historic craft in a fine setting of old buildings and canal basins overlooking the Manchester Ship Canal.

Soar, River

The navigable section of the River Soar is twenty-five miles long with eighteen broad-gauge locks, and runs from Leicester, where it joins the Leicester Section of the Grand Union Canal, to the River Trent at Trent Junction. It forms an important part of the 'Leicester Ring', a very interesting circular cruising route comprising the lower part of the Trent and Mersey Canal, the upper River Trent, the Soar, the Grand Union Canal (Leicester Section), part of the Grand Union Canal main line, the Oxford Canal (North) and the Coventry Canal. Mostly rural in character, the Soar follows a meandering course through water meadows and riverside settlements, entering an urban area only occasionally, notably at Leicester, where the surroundings are not at all inspiring, and at Loughborough, which is similarly unimpressive. However, the greater part of the waterway is most rewarding and lovely in places, particularly around Sileby and Barrow-upon-Soar. Lower down the river there is a delightful stretch near Kegworth, and the fine village of Normanton-on-Soar with its thirteenth-century church steeple is well worth visiting.

Staffordshire and Worcestershire Canal

One of the earliest canals to be built, the Staffordshire and Worcestershire Canal was engineered by James Brindley and completed in 1772 as the first of a series of waterways linking the four great rivers: Thames, Trent, Severn and Mersey. It is a narrow-gauge canal forty-six miles long, connecting the Trent and Mersey Canal at Great Haywood with the River Severn at Stourport, and has forty-three locks, few of which are arranged in flights.

The northern half of the canal from Great Haywood to Wolverhampton is mainly rural and very attractive in places. A short distance from the Trent and Mersey Canal the waterway opens out into Tixall Wide, a small but beautiful lake forming part of the canal and now the abode of much wild life. After skirting the town of Stafford the canal passes under the M6 motorway and continues on through Penkridge, finally reaching the summit pound at Gailey, with its curious round tower built on to the lock-keeper's cottage. The summit pound then detours round to the east in the direction of Cannock, which once could be reached by way of the Hatherton Branch, now disused. Near Wolverhampton the canal passes through a narrow rock cutting beyond which lies Autherley Junction, where the Shropshire Union Canal enters from the north. The Wolverhampton lock flight, which gives access to the Birmingham Canal Navigations, is situated half a mile further on at Aldersley Junction, and shortly afterwards the long descent to the Severn begins at Compton Lock.

Leaving the suburbs of Wolverhampton the canal meanders through open country to the Bratch, a picturesque flight of three locks built very close together, and followed by a two-rise staircase lock at Botterham. From here down to Stewponey, where the Stourbridge Canal enters at Stourton Junction, the character of the canal begins to change as it approaches the valley of the Stour; the surroundings crowd more closely upon the waterway, which now seems to possess a secretive air. Two very short tunnels, at Dunsley and Cookley, lead to a superb section of canal overshadowed by a leaning rock face and with sharp bends. Once through Kidderminster the canal traverses pleasant wooded country before entering Stourport, an eighteenth-century canal 'port' built around a complex of basins from which access to the River Severn can be gained.

Stourbridge Canal

The Stourbridge Canal provides a useful link between the Staffordshire and Worcestershire Canal at Stourton Junction near Stewponey and the Birmingham Canal Navigations at Brierley Hill, a distance of just over five miles with twenty narrow-gauge locks. The countryside around the first four locks at Stourton Junction is very attractive, but after Wordsley Junction, where a one-mile branch leads off to Stourbridge town centre, the surroundings deteriorate as the canal ascends a flight of sixteen locks to the industrialized area around Brierley Hill, and at the foot of the Delph lock flight Dudley Canal No. 1 provides access to the main line of the Birmingham Canal Navigations through long tunnels at Netherton and Dudley.

Stratford-upon-Avon Canal

This rural canal extends from King's Norton Junction on the Worcester and Birmingham Canal to the River Avon at Stratford-upon-Avon, a total distance of twenty-five and a half miles with fifty-six narrow-gauge locks. The upper section from King's Norton to Lapworth is referred to as the northern Stratford Canal and the remaining part to Stratford as the southern Stratford Canal. After many years of dereliction a massive restoration scheme reopened the southern section to through navigation in 1964, and was one of the first in recent times to be carried out by the use of largely voluntary labour, thus marking the start of the present enthusiasm for the recovery of disused waterways.

The southern Stratford Canal passes through some very beautiful countryside and features interesting iron aqueducts at Wootton Wawen and Edstone; the latter spans a road, railway and stream, and is 475 feet long. Unfortunately the southern Stratford has been plagued by difficulties over the years, not the least of which is a chronic water shortage caused by leakage from the bed, and dilapidated lock gear, and this in spite of the considerable amount of water piped to the canal from the Grand Union Canal near Lapworth. The approach into Stratford is not impressive, but the final stretch to the river makes up for this as the canal passes under a low bridge and enters a large basin set in lawns and shrubs in front of the Shakespeare Memorial Theatre before joining the River Avon through a broad-gauge lock.

The northern Stratford Canal is pleasant without being particularly interesting, and is lock-free apart from the flight of nineteen locks at Lapworth, although boat crews will find some exercise in working several swing and bascule bridges scattered along the waterway. There is one tunnel, 352 yards long, at Brandwood. At the Lapworth end, where the two sections of the canal meet, access to the northern Grand Union Canal is possible through a single narrow-gauge lock leading to Kingswood Junction.

Thames, River

Without doubt the best known of Britain's waterways through its geographical position and historical connections, the River Thames has long been associated with pleasure-boating. It was once the principal water route across the south of England, with a direct connection to the River Severn via the Thames and Severn Canal, and to Bristol by way of the Kennet and Avon Canal from Reading. Both these canals were abandoned many years ago, but the Kennet and Avon is undergoing a tremendous restoration, now well advanced.

From the point of view of hire craft the navigable length of the river extends from Brentford, where the Grand Union Canal joins the tideway, to Lechlade, a distance of about 128 miles with forty-four locks, all broad-gauge and with a minimum length of about 100 feet. The non-tidal section of the river starts at Teddington Lock. This is reached from Brentford after passing the unique Richmond Half-tide Lock where, at certain states of the tides, vertical sluice gates are raised to permit the passage of craft, thus avoiding the use of the lock itself. All Thames locks are manned, and those up to Godstow above Oxford are mechanized, although boat crews may work the locks manually when the keeper is not on duty. Stringent regulations in respect of navigation and boat equipment and fittings are enforced by the Thames Water Authority.

The Thames Valley is very beautiful and full of historical associations, from Windsor Castle and Hampton Court to the city of Oxford. Henley Regatta, held each year in July, was first established in the earlier part of the nineteenth century. All along the river there are numerous boatyards, many hiring out wide-beam cruisers and other craft, and a number of passenger 'steamers' ply the waterway. A truly excellent circular cruise may be made by way of the Thames and the Oxford and Grand Union canals.

Trent, River

Being one of Britain's major river navigations, the Trent should always be treated with respect by the pleasure-boater. Conditions of hire will permit most hire craft to cruise the non-tidal section, but few will be allowed past Cromwell Lock, about six miles downstream from

Newark, where the tidal reaches begin. In all cases, however, a reliable engine of sufficient power is absolutely essential, and no craft should be without an anchor and adequate cable.

For pleasure-boating purposes the navigable part of the river extends from Derwent Mouth, at the junction with the Trent and Mersey Canal, to Keadby Lock, the entrance to the Stainforth and Keadby Canal, a distance of eighty-four miles, of which about half is tidal. At Derwent Mouth the river is already wide and powerful, and from here to Nottingham the navigation is mostly in artificial cut; first, Sawley Cut leading to the crossroads of Trent Junction, where the Erewash Canal and the River Soar enter on opposite sides of the river; then Cranfleet Cut, which is followed by a pleasant section of river to Beeston Cut and the remaining part of the Nottingham Canal in the city itself. The surroundings here are without interest, to say the least, but there is a considerable improvement once the river is rejoined.

From Nottingham to Newark the Trent runs through pleasant but unremarkable flat countryside relieved by the occasional riverside settlement, and its locks, which are manned and mechanized, are huge by canal standards. A ruined castle rises impressively from the waterside near Newark Town Lock, below which the navigation passes under a fine stone bridge, and just beyond there is a temporary mooring place at Town Wharf. From Newark the river resumes its winding course to Cromwell Lock and the start of the tidal section.

Mooring on the tideway should not be attempted, and craft making a through passage to Keadby are recommended to head for Torksey, where there are safe moorings above and below the tidal lock, or West Stockwith Basin at the entrance to the Chesterfield Canal, depending upon the state of the tide. As this section of the Trent runs mostly between high flood banks little can be seen beyond the next bend (particularly at or near low water), and a keen watch should be kept for commercial traffic. An added hazard is the Aegir, or tidal bore, which can affect navigation as far upstream as Torksey.

Trent and Mersey Canal

From the River Trent at Derwent Mouth to Preston Brook on the Bridgewater Canal the Trent and Mersey Canal follows a ninety-three-mile-long route which is mostly rural, although there is a considerable stretch through urban and industrial surroundings in the area of Stoke-on-Trent. One of the earliest canals, it was engineered by James Brindley as part of a grand scheme to link the Rivers Trent, Thames, Mersey and Severn. It has seventy-six locks in all, most of which are narrow-gauge, although sections at each end of the canal are constructed in broad-gauge.

Near the junction with the Trent stands the village of Shardlow, a splendid example of an early canal 'port'. From here to Burton-upon-Trent the canal is broad-gauge, and passes through pleasant open countryside in the wide valley of the Trent. At Burton the waterway becomes narrow-gauge, and beyond the town enters rural surroundings once again. Following a stretch where the canal and river briefly combine near Alrewas, the route passes through Fradley, at a junction with the Coventry Canal, and after another thirteen miles the Staffordshire and Worcestershire Canal enters from the west at the pleasant junction of Great Haywood. From here the canal bends away to the north through Stone and penetrates the industrial landscape of the Potteries, at which point the slow rise through the widely spaced locks of the lower reaches gives way to lock flights as the valley of the Trent steepens. The final flight at Etruria lifts the canal to its summit at 408 feet above sea level, and just beyond the top lock the magnificent Caldon Canal branches away towards the Derbyshire hills.

The summit level of the main line continues through industrial surroundings to Harecastle Tunnel, 2,897 yards long and unique for its employment of tunnel-keepers at each end to regulate the one-way traffic necessitated by the narrow bore. A short distance beyond the northern portal of the tunnel the Macclesfield Canal is joined at a point where the great Cheshire lock flight commences its long descent to the Cheshire Plain through pleasant open countryside to the old salt town of Middlewich and a junction with the Middlewich Branch of the Shropshire Union Canal. The final three narrow-gauge locks are followed by Big Lock on the outskirts of the town; this lock and the broad-gauge section to Preston Brook were constructed to allow passage for salt barges, but reconstruction of Croxton Aqueduct in narrow gauge now prevents access by wide-beam craft. To the north of Middlewich the canal passes through a mixture of farmland and industry; salt workings have caused extensive subsidence in places and occasionally the canal enters a lagoon, or 'flash', similar to those caused by coalmining in other areas. Near Northwich the canal passes close to the River Weaver at high level and a connection is made between the two by means of the famous Anderton Lift, an impressive nineteenth-century vertical boat lift. Tunnels at Barnton (572 yards) and Saltersford (424 yards) are followed once more by green countryside to Dutton Stop, where a broad-gauge stop-lock marks the approach to the 1,239-yard Preston Brook Tunnel, beyond which the canal ends at a head-on junction with the Bridgewater Canal.

Weaver, River

The navigable section of the river extends from Winsford Bridge at the town of Winsford in Cheshire to Weston Point Docks on the Manchester Ship Canal. It is twenty miles long and has five locks, all of which will take commercial shipping. Above Winsford Bridge lies Winsford Bottom Flash, a pretty lake formed by subsidence due to saltmining, and navigable with care. At its upper end a channel leads to the Top Flash, but this is very shallow and can be reached only by rowing boat and similar light craft. Below Winsford the river is very attractive, but as it skirts around Northwich the green countryside gives way to industry, and opposite the huge ICI works stands the Anderton Lift, by means of which craft may be transferred between the Weaver and the adjoining Trent and Mersey Canal. From Northwich the river meanders westwards through the pleasant Weaver valley to Weston, overlooking the Mersey Estuary and the Manchester Ship Canal.

Wey Navigation

The River Wey was one of the earliest rivers to be canalized. The basic work was done in 1653, though there were later extensions, and it was built in the modern manner with the familiar pound locks. It runs from the River Thames at Weybridge to Godalming, a distance of nineteen and a half miles with sixteen broad-gauge locks. There is a connection at West Byfleet with the abandoned Basingstoke Canal, now being restored.

Entry to the Wey from the Thames is through Thames Lock at the convergence of a number of backwaters and weir streams. Soon after this a long artificial cut is entered which leads pleasantly through New Haw to Newark, above which a beautiful stretch of canal and river leads to Guildford. The upper reaches above Guildford are the finest on the river, and the last lock – Catteshall – heralds the end of the navigation at Godalming, the southernmost point of the inland waterways system.

Windermere

This, the largest lake in England, is ten and a half miles long and about one and a quarter miles wide at its widest point, and lies in the southern part of the Lake District National Park. It is divided into two distinct reaches by a cluster of small islands about halfway down the lake and opposite Bowness, which is the only village of any size on the shores of the lake (Windermere town lies a mile or so distant). South Lake gradually narrows to its outfall at Newby Bridge, near which the Haverthwaite steam railway provides a summer service to Lakeside, the lake 'steamer' terminus. North Lake is a much broader and open stretch of water, and on the east shore not far from Bowness stands the Windermere Steamboat Museum housing an interesting collection of historical craft. Views of the Lakeland fells around the head of the lake are superb, and from Waterhead, the northernmost point, Ambleside is easily reached.

Worcester and Birmingham Canal

This is possibly the most heavily engineered canal in the country. The Worcester and Birmingham was built to provide a direct link between Birmingham and the River Severn at Worcester. In its length of thirty miles there are no less than fifty-eight locks and five tunnels, of which one, Wast Hill (sometimes known as King's Norton Tunnel) is 2,726 yards long. All the locks, with the exception of the barge locks at Diglis Basin in Worcester, are narrow-gauge, and they include the longest flight in the country, the thirty-lock Tardebigge flight, of which the top lock is reputed to be the deepest narrow-gauge lock in Britain, although this is periodically disputed.

From King's Norton Junction on the outskirts of Birmingham to the suburbs of Worcester the canal is almost entirely rural and very pretty in places. Between Wast Hill and Alvechurch lie the Bittell reservoirs, haunt of much interesting wild life and a favourite area for bird-watchers and anglers. All this upper section of the canal is actually part of the Birmingham Level of the Birmingham Canal Navigations, extending from Tipton to the top lock at Tardebigge; in addition to Wast Hill it features tunnels at Edgbaston (105 yards), Shortwood (613 yards), and Tardebigge (580 yards).

Below the upper lock flights stands the canal settlement of Stoke Prior, with its old salt works founded on brine pumping in the earlier part of the nineteenth century. Further lock flights lead down to Hanbury, where the Droitwich Junction and Droitwich Barge canals, now being restored, formerly provided a link with the Severn. From here the surroundings become less interesting; Dunhampstead Tunnel (230 yards) is the last tunnel, and after passing under the M5 and negotiating the Offerton flight of locks, the suburbs of Worcester draw near. The canal ends in Diglis Basin, from which two manned barge locks provide access to the Severn.

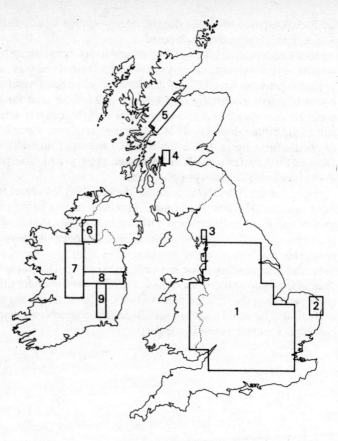

1 The canal and river system of England and Wales
2 Norfolk Broads
3 Windermere
4 Loch Lomond
5 Caledonian Canal
6 Lough Erne
7 River Shannon
8 Grand Canal
9 Barrow Navigation

The principal inland cruising areas of Great Britain and Ireland

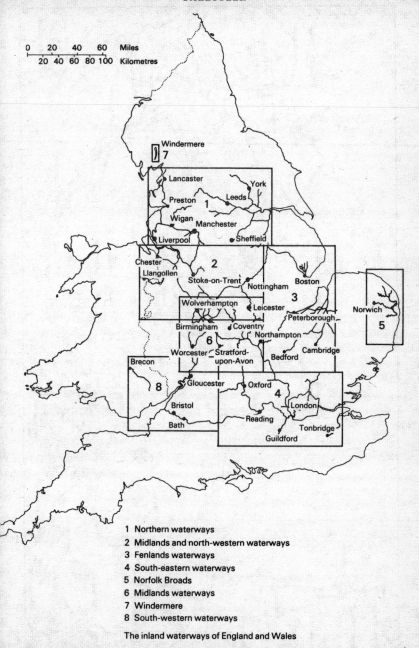

0 20 40 60 Miles
20 40 60 80 100 Kilometres

1 Northern waterways
2 Midlands and north-western waterways
3 Fenlands waterways
4 South-eastern waterways
5 Norfolk Broads
6 Midlands waterways
7 Windermere
8 South-western waterways

The inland waterways of England and Wales

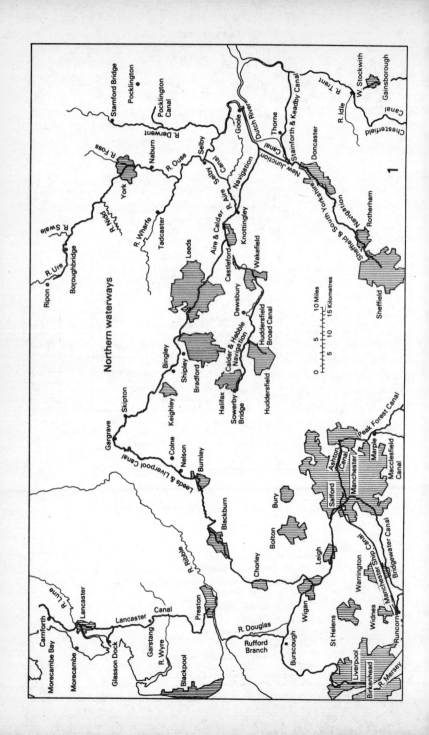

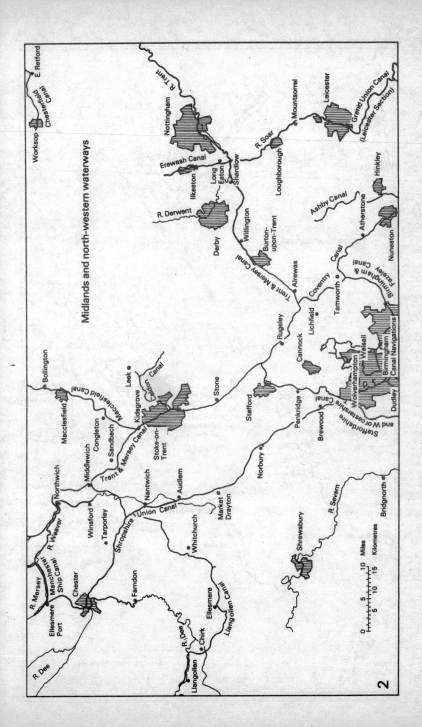

Midlands and north-western waterways

2

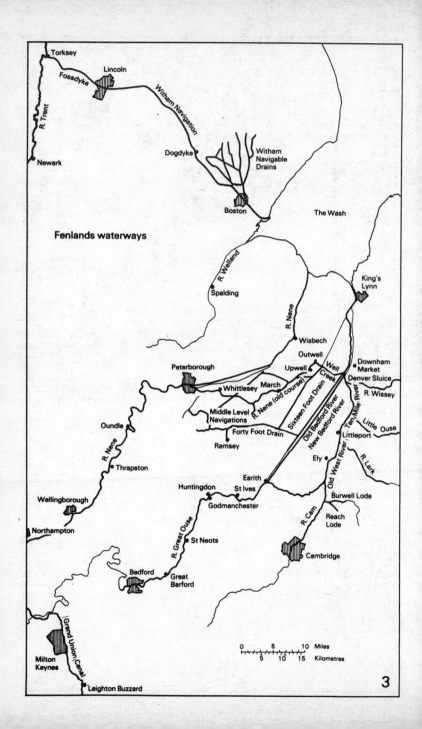

Torksey
R. Trent
Fossdyke
Lincoln
Newark
Witham Navigation
Dogdyke
Witham Navigable Drains
Boston
The Wash

Fenlands waterways

R. Welland
Spalding
King's Lynn
R. Nene
Wisbech
Outwell
Upwell
Well Creek
Downham Market
Denver Sluice
Peterborough
Whittlesey
March
R. Nene (old course)
Sixteen Foot Drain
R. Wissey
Middle Level Navigations
Forty Foot Drain
Old Bedford River
New Bedford River
Ten Mile River
Little Ouse
Oundle
Ramsey
Littleport
R. Nene
Thrapston
Ely
R. Lark
Earith
Old West River
Wellingborough
Huntingdon
St Ives
Godmanchester
Burwell Lode
Northampton
R. Cam
Reach Lode
R. Great Ouse
St Neots
Cambridge
Bedford
Great Barford
Grand Union Canal
Milton Keynes
Leighton Buzzard

0   5   10 Miles
5   10   15   Kilometres

3

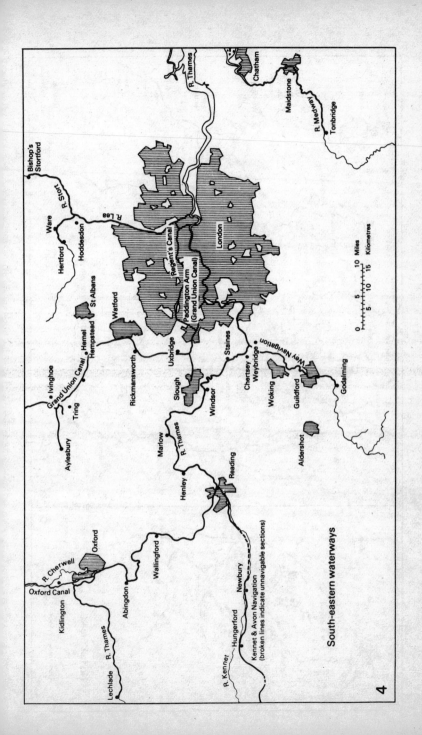

South-eastern waterways

4

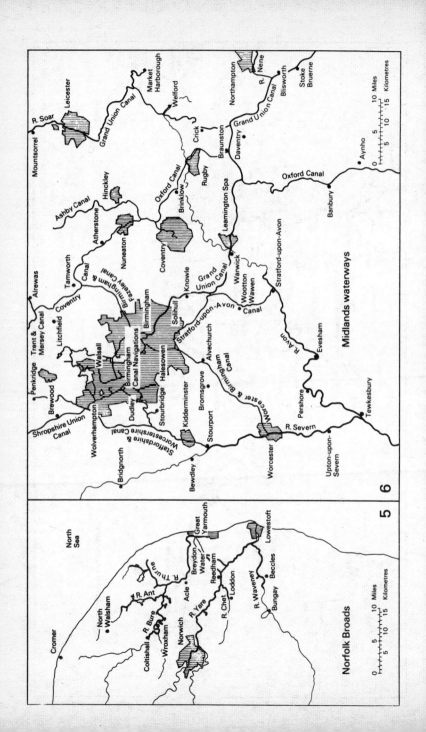

Norfolk Broads

Midlands waterways

5 6

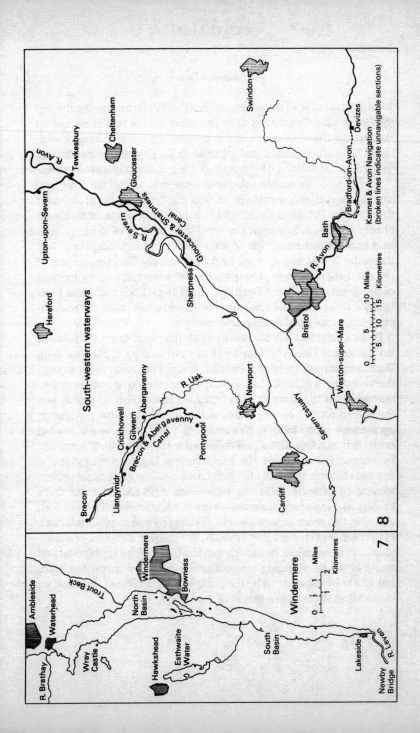

South-western waterways

Kennet & Avon Navigation
(broken lines indicate unnavigable sections)

Swindon

Cheltenham

Tewkesbury

R. Avon

Upton-upon-Severn

Gloucester

Hereford

R. Severn

Gloucester & Sharpness Canal

Sharpness

Bristol

Weston-super-Mare

Bath

R. Avon

Bradford-on-Avon

Devizes

Brecon

Llangynidr

Crickhowell

Gilwern

Abergavenny

Brecon & Abergavenny Canal

Pontypool

Newport

R. Usk

Cardiff

Severn Estuary

Miles
0   5   10
Kilometres
5   10   15

8

Ambleside

Waterhead

R. Brathay

Wray Castle

Trout Beck

North Basin

Windermere

Bowness

Hawkshead

Esthwaite Water

South Basin

Windermere

Lakeside

Newby Bridge

R. Leven

Miles
0   ½   1
Kilometres
1   2

7

SCOTLAND

Caledonian Canal

Taking advantage of the geological fault which forms the Great Glen, the Caledonian Canal runs from Inverness on the east coast to Fort William on the west coast, and is about sixty miles in length, with twenty-nine mechanized and manned locks. Engineered by Thomas Telford – and considered by some to be his greatest single achievement – it was built to enable sea-going vessels to avoid the long and sometimes dangerous passage around the northern tip of Scotland through the Pentland Firth. Within a relatively short time after its opening in 1822, however, the rapid development of steam propulsion and the increasing size of ships made it all but redundant, and thereafter it was mainly used by fishing vessels. The greater part of the navigation consists of four freshwater lochs lying along the axis of the Great Glen – Loch Dochfour, Loch Ness, Loch Oich, and Loch Lochy – which together total thirty eight and a half miles, the remainder being made up of linking artificial cut.

From a tidal lock on the Beauly Firth the canal skirts the town of Inverness and climbs by four locks to a cut leading to the tiny Loch Dochfour, through which a buoyed channel indicates the course to the vast stretch of Loch Ness, twenty-three miles long and about one mile wide. At the western end of the loch stands Fort Augustus and the entrance to a five-mile canal section which takes the navigation up through seven locks to its summit at 106 feet above sea level at Loch Oich, the four and a half mile course through which is marked by buoys. There follows the monumental Laggan Cutting and a descent through two locks to Loch Lochy and the final canal section leading to Banavie. Here the impressive eight-rise staircase flight known as 'Neptune's Staircase' drops the waterway sixty-four feet, and after two more locks sea level is reached by means of the tidal lock at Corpach, not far from Fort William. The scenery throughout is truly magnificent, as might be expected in the heart of the Highlands, and many of the surrounding mountains are well over 2,000 feet high, but all are overshadowed by the great bulk of Ben Nevis, which rises behind Fort William to a height of 4,406 feet.

Situated amid superb mountain scenery a few miles north of Dumbarton on the River Clyde, Loch Lomond is twenty-four miles long and up to five miles wide, although for the greater part of its length it is no more than one mile in width. Scattered throughout its southern section are about thirty islands, some of which are inhabited, and from its eastern shores rises the impressive peak of Ben Lomond, 3,194 feet high. The largest town of any note is Balloch at the southernmost point of the loch, although there are also facilities for boaters at Luss, Tarbet and Rowardennan.

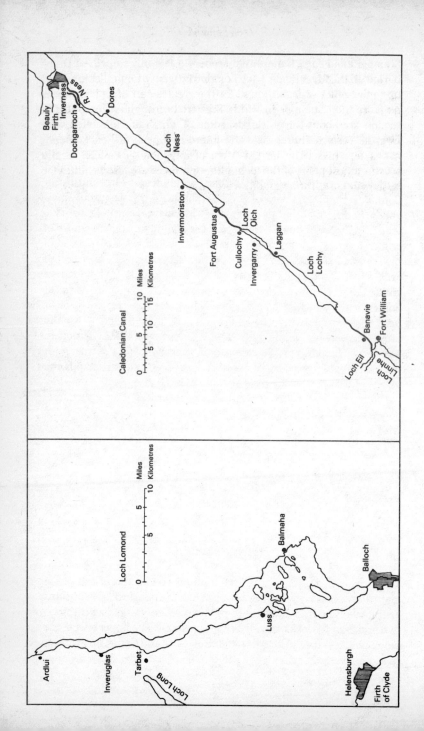

NORTHERN IRELAND

Erne Navigation

The navigable section of the Erne is about fifty-three miles long and essentially consists of two extensive lakes, Upper and Lower Lough Erne, which together cover about 300 square miles and are situated astride the border between Northern Ireland and Eire, mostly in County Fermanagh. Part of the fascination of this beautiful navigation is due to the large number of islands – some 154 in all – scattered throughout both loughs and providing an endless choice of cruising routes. All the main channels are well marked. The head of navigation is at Belturbet in Eire, at the southern tip of Upper Lough Erne, where good facilities for boaters will be found. At the opposite end of the lough a winding river section leads to public moorings at Enniskillen, an excellent and convenient place for shopping. Below here is sited the only lock on the navigation, although it usually proves no obstacle as the gates at both ends are normally left open. The Lower Lough is a vast expanse of open water, in contrast with the island-packed Upper Lough, and at its northern end stands the village of Belleek, the downstream limit of navigation, approached by way of a four-mile stretch of river. There are several other settlements dotted around the shores of both loughs, most of which are provided with good moorings.

EIRE

Barrow Navigation

The Barrow Navigation runs from a junction with the Grand Canal main line at Lowtown near Robertstown to the tidal lock at St Mullins just above New Ross, a distance of about seventy miles with thirty-two broad-gauge locks, mostly keeper-operated. The upper part of the navigation is actually the Barrow Line of the Grand Canal, an artificial cut connecting the main line with the River Barrow at Athy, twenty-eight miles and nine locks to the south. From Lowtown the canal traverses bogland for a few miles to Rathangan, but further on the countryside becomes more attractive, and after Monasterevin the valley of the Barrow is entered and followed on a long pound to Athy, where the river is joined. Care is needed in navigating the river section on account of shallows and unguarded weirs, and craft should keep strictly to the channel (known as the 'boat-stream') as beyond its confines the river is neither dredged nor cleared of obstructions. After passing Levitstown Lock about four miles below Athy, the navigation enters its most beautiful section, which extends all the way down the Barrow Valley to the estuary. In places the river runs at some speed, and a sharp look-out should be kept for shallows and rocks. Four miles or so above St Mullins the river enters a superb wooded gorge as it approaches the town of Graiguenamanagh, which is splendidly situated amid magnificent mountain scenery. The tidal lock at St Mullins is the limit of navigation for hire craft, although the tideway is navigable to the estuary at Waterford Harbour.

Grand Canal

The main line of the Grand Canal, opened in 1805, connects Dublin with the River Shannon, and is about eighty miles long with thirty-six broad-gauge locks. In theory the locks are all manned, but because a keeper is sometimes responsible for more than one lock boat crews may occasionally have to work through themselves, as on the Barrow Navigation. In Dublin the four-mile Circular Line takes the canal around the southern part of the city centre to join the River Liffey, but this section and the remaining urban stretches of main line are not recommended for cruising because of the strong risk of vandalism. From the outskirts of Dublin the canal rises steadily through attractive countryside to its summit, 279 feet above sea level, at the western end of which, just beyond Robertstown, the Barrow Line branches off to the south. Hereabouts the canal enters the Bog of Allen, a vast and remote area of peatland, which now provides machine-cut peat for fuelling power stations. Two long pounds lead through Edenderry to Ballycommon, where the locks cluster more closely together and drop the waterway to Tullamore, the only sizeable town on the main line other than Dublin, and one which offers good facilities for boaters.

Between the town and the Shannon lies another great stretch of bogland, but the scenery becomes more attractive as the canal approaches Shannon Harbour and a junction with the river. At one time the canal continued across the river to the fourteen-mile Ballinasloe branch, now derelict.

Shannon, River

This is a superb navigation, very beautiful and remote in many places, and encompasses a whole range of cruising environments, including narrow backwaters, wide river sections and the huge sea-like expanses of its inland loughs. Navigable length is about 130 miles, but this may be increased considerably by excursions into various branches, and there are five large broad-gauge locks, all manned. The head of navigation, at one time Battlebridge, has now been extended by the reopening of the Lough Allen Canal as far as Acres Lake, a distance of four miles with two broad-gauge locks. A few miles below Battlebridge the Boyle River enters from the west and is navigable for ten miles through Lough Drumharlow to Lough Key, an extremely attractive lake with numerous wooded islands. At Carrick-on-Shannon there are hire-craft bases and good facilities for boaters, and from here to Termonbarry, some twenty-two miles distant, the navigation consists mainly of intricate reed-fringed loughs. The first of the large loughs, Lough Ree, which is about eighteen miles long and over four miles wide in places, is entered at Lanesborough. Safe navigation of these vast expanses of open water requires some experience, not least in the use of charts and binoculars in order to follow the marked channel. On the river south of Lough Ree stands Athlone, the only town of any size on the entire navigation, a few miles below which is situated Clonmacnoise, one of Ireland's most important religious settlements. After passing Shannon Harbour at the entrance to the Grand Canal, the river winds southwards to the wide horizons of Lough Derg, twenty-four miles in length and dotted with numerous islands. The southernmost section of the lough is set in mountainous surroundings and is particularly attractive; one of its extensive arms leads to Killaloe, the present limit of navigation.

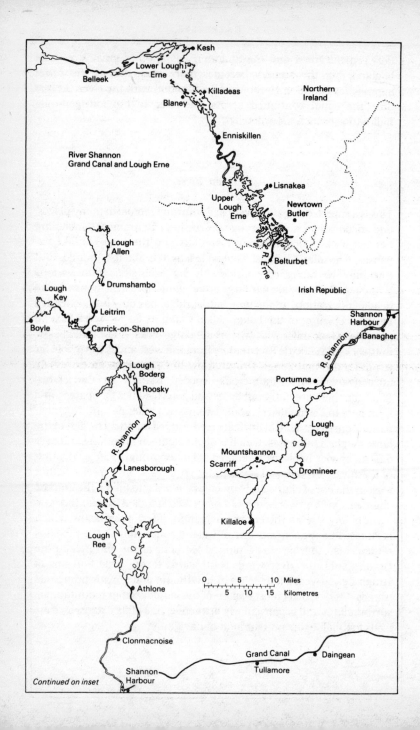

Kesh

Lower Lough
Erne

Belleek

Killadeas

Blaney

Northern
Ireland

Enniskillen

River Shannon
Grand Canal and Lough Erne

Lisnakea

Upper
Lough
Erne

Newtown
Butler

Belturbet

R. Erne

Irish Republic

Lough
Allen

Lough
Key

Drumshambo

Leitrim

Boyle

Carrick-on-Shannon

Lough
Boderg

Roosky

R. Shannon

Shannon
Harbour

Banagher

R. Shannon

Portumna

Lough
Derg

Mountshannon

Scarriff

Dromineer

Lanesborough

Killaloe

Lough
Ree

0   5   10 Miles

5   10   15 Kilometres

Athlone

Clonmacnoise

Grand Canal

Daingean

Tullamore

Shannon-
Harbour

Continued on inset

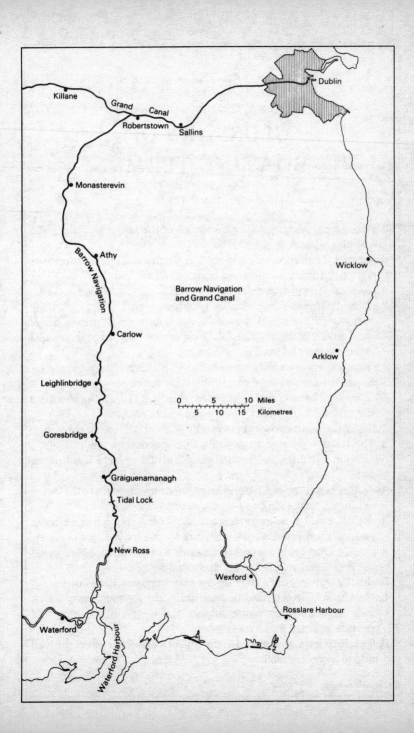

Killane

Grand Canal

Robertstown

Sallins

Dublin

Monasterevin

Barrow Navigation

Athy

Wicklow

Barrow Navigation
and Grand Canal

Carlow

Arklow

Leighlinbridge

Goresbridge

Graiguenamanagh

Tidal Lock

0   5   10 Miles
    5   10   15 Kilometres

New Ross

Wexford

Rosslare Harbour

Waterford

Waterford Harbour

GLOSSARY OF
BOATING TERMS

Abeam At right-angles to the mid-point of the fore-and-aft line of a vessel.

Abutments The supporting and retaining walls of a brick, concrete or masonry structure, such as a bridge or a lock.

Aft or Abaft Towards the stern of a vessel.

Aground With the vessel's hull – or any part of it – resting on the bottom of the channel; the traditional canal term is 'stemmed-up'.

Ahead Directly in front of a vessel. Engines with forward gear engaged are sometimes referred to as 'running ahead'.

Air draught The overall height of a vessel measured from the water-line to the highest fixed part of the superstructure.

Air drawing The action of a propeller when it draws air bubbles from the surface of the water, resulting in loss of efficiency.

Amidships A point midway between the stem and the stern of a vessel. The helm is referred to as being in the *amidships* (or 'midships') position when the rudder is aligned with the vessel's fore-and-aft line.

Anchor A metal device for providing temporary mooring to the bed of a channel, or the sea-bed.

Aqueduct A bridge across which a canal is carried in a trough; more generally, any engineering structure for the conveyance of water.

Astern Directly behind a vessel. Engines with reverse gear engaged are sometimes referred to as 'running astern'.

Backwater Any part of a river off the main navigation channel.

Balance beam The extended beam forming the top member of a lock gate, used both to counterbalance the weight of the gate and provide leverage for its movement.

Ballast Heavy weights placed in the hull of a vessel to correct the trim and to increase stability.

Barge A wide-beam (that is, over seven feet) commercial craft, usually flat-bottomed, and used on inland waters.

Bascule bridge A drawbridge consisting of a hinged deck connected to counterbalanced overhead arms.

Basin A partly enclosed area of water situated off a navigation channel and usually provided with wharves and moorings.

Beacon A fixed guiding mark to assist navigation.

Beam The width of a vessel at its widest part; the term 'on the beam' refers to the direction at right-angles to the fore-and-aft line viewed from a position amidships.

Bearing A direction described with reference to the fore-and-aft line of a vessel: for example, *on the beam* is one such bearing. A 'compass bearing' refers the direction to the compass meridian.

Berth A bunk or bed in a vessel; two-tiered bunks are sometimes referred to as 'Pullman' berths. Also used to indicate the place where a vessel moors.

Bight A loose loop in a rope; also used to describe a pronounced bend in a river.

Bilge The lowest internal part of a vessel's hull; also the lowest curved section of hull between side and bottom in a round-bottomed vessel.

Bilge pump A pump for removing water that has accumulated in the bilges.

Boat-hook A light shaft, usually of wood, with a metal hook at one end.

Boat lift A mechanically or electrically powered structure for transferring craft between different levels of a waterway, usually by means of water-filled tanks in which the craft are contained.

Bollard A short post securely fixed into the ground near the edge of a waterway to provide an attachment point for mooring lines.

Bore A tidal wave, or succession of waves, associated with certain estuaries and rivers; it may vary in height from a few inches to several feet. In the Humber region it is called an 'Aegir'.

Bottom The underwater part of a vessel's hull.

Bow or Bows The foremost part of a vessel's hull; the traditional canal term is 'fore-end'.

Bow-haul To tow a vessel manually from the bank.

Bowline A knot forming a fixed loop at the end of a rope. 'Bow line', written as two separate words, is a line attached to the bow of a vessel.

Bow wave The wave created at the bow of a vessel by the passage of the hull through the water.

Bridge guards Curved steel rails fastened between the forward outer edge of the cabin roof and the fore-deck of a canal boat to protect the superstructure from damage.

Broad The East Anglian term for a lake.

Bulkhead Upright partitions dividing a vessel into compartments.

Buoy A floating marker, usually permanently moored, used as an aid to navigation; buoys are often provided for mooring purposes.

Buoyancy aid Any article – often in the form of a sleeveless jacket – specifically designed to increase the buoyancy of a person in the water.

Butty An unpowered commercial narrowboat, usually towed by a powered narrowboat, the two together being known as a 'pair'.

By-wash A weir-stream, which may be either open or culverted, situated by a canal lock and passing excess water from the upper to the lower pound.

Cable A length of rope or chain attached to an anchor; in connection with small craft the rope is called a 'warp'.

Cavitation Formation of water vapour bubbles on the surface of a propeller blade caused by a drop in water pressure due to the excessive velocity of some part of the blade, resulting in a marked loss of efficiency.

Centre of gravity The point of resolution of the total weights distributed throughout a vessel.

Centre of lateral resistance The balancing point of the immersed profile of a vessel's hull.

Channel The deepest area of a navigable waterway.

Chine The angle between the side and bottom of a vessel's hull constructed with flat side and bottom surfaces.

Cleat A deck fitting, usually having two opposed arms, to which ropes may be secured.

Coachroof The raised top of a cabin.

Coaming A raised edging around a well or hatch.

Cockpit An open area in a vessel, the deck of which is below gunwale level; also called a 'well'.

Composite A term used to describe the construction of a vessel's hull when two different materials are employed – for example, a wooden skin on an iron frame, or iron sides and a wooden bottom.

Contour canal An artificial waterway that follows as much as possible the natural contours of the land.

Counter The curved part of a vessel's stern; sometimes used to refer to the aftermost part of the stern-deck.

Course The track followed by a vessel between two given points, usually expressed in compass degrees; not to be confused with the vessel's 'heading', which may or may not correspond with its course due to the influence of wind and currents.

Crabbing The forward movement of a vessel when the vessel's heading does not correspond with the course being followed.

Cross-sectional effect The relationship between the underwater cross-sectional area of a vessel's hull and that of the waterway in which it is moving (the 'cross-sectional ratio') with reference to the retarding effect of this relationship upon the vessel's progress.

Cut An alternative term for 'canal', or any artificial channel.

Cut and fill An engineering technique used to obtain a level bed by excavating cuttings and using the spoil – if suitable – for the construction of embankments.

Dayboat Any vessel not provided with sleeping accommodation.

Deck Any 'floor' in a vessel.

Deckhead The underside of a deck; the roof of a vessel's cabin.

Dinette An arrangement of facing seats on two sides of a table; usually the table may be lowered to form, in conjunction with the seats, a single or double bed.

Dinghy A small open boat, often used as tender to a cruiser; also a small sailing boat.

Dipstick A graduated rod for measuring the amount of liquid in a container.

Displacement The amount of water in units of weight displaced by the underwater volume of a vessel's hull.

Dolly An upright cylindrical metal deck fitting to which ropes may be secured.

Dolphin A staging for mooring not usually connected to the bank or shore, and supported on massive timber or metal piles.

Draught Strictly speaking, *water draught*, as distinct from *air draught*: the maximum underwater depth of a vessel's hull.

Dredge To clean out and deepen a channel.

Ebb A falling tide.

Eddy A local disturbance of water, often caused by an underwater obstruction.

Engine compartment That part of a vessel in which the engine is situated.

Fairlead A metal deck fitting to control the direction of a rope and to prevent chafe.

Fairway A navigable channel.

Fender A shaped cushion or pad of resilient material – typically woven rope or plastic – attached to a vessel's hull as protection from damage or chafe.

Fend off To deflect, push off, push away.

Fiddle A raised lip or rail around the edge of a horizontal surface to prevent objects from sliding off.

Flake, to To coil a rope down in layers free for running.

Flash A sudden flush of water; in the north-west of England it is the name given to a sheet of water filling a depression caused by mining subsidence.

Flash flood A sudden rise in river levels together with an increased current speed, caused by heavy rain and, occasionally, melting snow; also called a 'spate'.

Flash lock A crude type of lock providing a navigable channel through a weir; craft proceed through the weir on a *flash*, hence the name; also known as a 'staunch'.

Flat A type of barge indigenous to the area around the River Mersey; also applied to the small rectangular swim-ended craft used for canal maintenance purposes.

Flight Two or more locks spaced fairly close together – usually not more than about 400 yards apart.

Flood A rising tide; a marked rise in river levels.

Flood lock A lock situated at the upstream end of a canal section of a river navigation to protect water levels in the canal during flood conditions.

Fore Forward; towards the bow of a vessel.

Fore-and-aft In line with the longitudinal axis of a vessel.

Fore-deck The decked area in the bows of a vessel at or about gunwale level.

Fore-foot The lowest part of the *stem*.

Forepeak The extreme forward volume of a vessel's hull, immediately abaft the *stem*.

Fore-well A well situated in the bows of a vessel, immediately abaft the *fore-deck*.

Forward Towards the bows of, or looking ahead of, a vessel.

Freeboard The height of the hull measured from water level.

Galley The kitchen of a vessel.

Gangplank A footboard used to bridge the gap between bank and vessel.

Gates The watertight doors of a lock chamber.

Gauge The *gauge* of a waterway refers to the water level width of the channel at engineering structures such as locks, bridges, tunnels and aqueducts; 'narrow-gauge' waterways will only pass craft not exceeding seven feet in beam; all other waterways are 'broad-gauge'.

Gearbox A device mounted between the engine and the propeller shaft for altering the direction of rotation of the propeller; in effect, to move a vessel *ahead* or *astern*.

Gear lever A hand lever connected to the *gearbox* for selecting forward or reverse gear; when the same lever also operates the throttle it is referred to as *single lever control*.

Grab-rail A rail, usually fixed to the *coachroof*, to provide a secure handhold when moving along the deck or gunwale of a vessel.

Guillotine gate A vertically sliding lock gate.

Gunwale The top edge of a vessel's side.

Hatch A horizontal opening with a movable cover in the deck or superstructure of a vessel.

Heading The direction in which the bow of a vessel is actually pointing; not to be confused with *course*.

Heel post The 'hinge' post of a lock gate.

Helm The *tiller* or *wheel* of a vessel by which it is steered.

Helmsman The person steering a vessel; the traditional canal term is 'steerer'.

Hollow quoin The recess in the wall of a lock chamber into which the *heel post* of the gate fits.

Hull The main body of a vessel, excluding superstructure, masts, rigging, and other fittings.

Hydrostatic drive A type of transmission whereby power is delivered from the engine to the propeller by means of oil-filled pipes (that is, hydraulically) instead of through a conventional *gearbox*.

Inboard Within the confines of a vessel's hull; towards amidships.

Inboard motor An engine mounted within a vessel's hull.

Inclined plane A slope fitted with rails upon which wheeled containers are raised and lowered by means of gravity, a winding engine, or a combination of both.

Invert The lowest point of an inverted arch.

Kedge A lightweight *anchor*.

Keel The lowest fore-and-aft member of a vessel's hull; a structure projecting from the bottom of a hull to provide stability; also a type of vessel indigenous to the north-eastern waterways.

Knot The nautical unit of speed: one nautical mile (6,076 feet) per hour.

Land water Drainage water from the land.

Lanyard A small-diameter rope or light line used for lashing and attachment.

Lay When used of a rope, the direction in which the strands are twisted – that is, right-handed or left-handed. A laid rope is one in which the strands are twisted together, as distinct from being woven or plaited.

Leeward In the direction away from the wind; downwind.

Leeway The angle between a vessel's *heading* and her *course*; the effect of being moved sideways through the water by wind and current.

Legging Propulsion of a vessel through a tunnel by thrusting with the legs against the walls or roof.

Let go To drop *anchor*.

Level A long *pound* in an artificial waterway, sometimes given a distinguishing name – for example, 'Birmingham Level'.

Life-buoy A buoyancy aid in the form of a ring or collar to be thrown to a person in the water.

Lift bridge A movable bridge, the deck of which is either hinged or moves vertically upwards.

Lighter A type of unpowered barge, usually with swim ends, used in the Thames area.

List Tilt of a vessel to one side due to a change in *trim*.

Lock A structure comprising a chamber with watertight gates at each end, by which a vessel is able to move from one level to another in a waterway; also known as a 'pound lock'.

Lockwheel To prepare or 'set' a lock ahead of a vessel.

Log book A day-by-day detailed record of a vessel's cruise.

Main line The principal navigation channel in a waterway system.

Mitre posts The vertical members at the outer edges of a pair of lock gates, the meeting surfaces of which are mitred to make a water-tight fit.

Mooring Securing a vessel by tying to the bank, shore, or mooring *buoy*, or by dropping *anchor*; a vessel's *berth*.

Mooring line A rope used to moor a vessel.

Mooring ring A metal ring securely fixed to a bank, wharf, or quay to receive a *mooring line*.

Mud weight A heavy weight attached to a *warp* and used instead of an *anchor* in certain circumstances.

Narrowboat A vessel with a *beam* of seven feet or less; the term was originally applied to seventy by seven-foot commercial canal craft, but now tends to cover all narrow-beam steel or wooden-hulled boats built on lines similar to those of the commercial narrowboat.

Navigation The act of conducting a vessel efficiently and safely from one point to another; a navigable waterway, either artificial or natural.

Neaps The tides having least range in a tide-cycle – that is, lowest high water and highest low water.

Outboard Beyond the confines of a vessel's hull; away from *amidships*.

Outboard motor A combined engine and propeller unit mounted externally on the *transom* of a vessel by means of a swivel attachment; steerage is effected by movement of the entire unit.

Outdrive An arrangement whereby an *inboard motor* drives a *propeller* unit mounted *outboard* on a vessel's *transom* through a system of shafts and bevel gears; also called a 'Z-drive', 'sterndrive', or an 'inboard–outboard' drive.

Overboard Over the side of a vessel.

Overfalls Steep breaking waves caused by strong currents and shoals, often in combination with contrary winds.

Overflow weir A *weir* set in the bank of a canal to take away excess water and prevent flooding.

Paddle The sliding cover of a sluice, the opening, or 'drawing', of which allows the passage of water.

Paddle gear An inclusive term for the mechanism by which a *paddle* is operated.

Paddle post The upright member to which the winding mechanism of a *paddle* is attached, and by which it is supported.

Painter The line used to secure a small boat.

Part (of a rope) The 'standing part' of a rope is that section towards the fixed end or the coils; the 'running part' is that section towards the free end.

Pennant A small flag, often triangular; also called a 'burgee'.

Piling Long heavy sections of metal, reinforced concrete or timber driven into the ground to provide a secure foundation. 'Sheet' piling is used in the construction of coffer dams and for retaining earth; it is also used extensively for bank protection on inland waterways.

Pipe cot A *berth* made up of canvas slung between a tubular frame.

Pitch As applied to a propeller, the theoretical forward distance through which it would travel during one revolution, assuming no slip.

Pitching Rocking of a vessel in a *fore-and-aft* direction.

Port On the left-hand side of a vessel when facing *forward*.

Pound An unbroken stretch of water on a canal.

Propeller Also called a 'screw' or 'fan'; shaped metal blades mounted on a central boss and angled in such a manner as to propel a vessel through the water when revolved.

Propeller shaft The metal shaft on which a *propeller* is mounted.

Puddling A mixture of clay and water worked up to a waterproof consistency and used for lining the bed of a canal, and to repair leaks.

Quadrant A metal frame shaped as a segment of a circle and fixed to the *rudder stock*, around which the steering cables from the *wheel* pass.

Quarter With reference to a vessel, halfway between *on the beam* and dead *astern*.

Ram's head The Z-shaped steel member attached to the upper end of a narrowboat's *rudder stock*, and to which is fitted the *tiller*.

Reach A stretch of water between locks or bends on a river; known in the Trent area as a 'rack'.

Rolling Rocking of a vessel from side to side.

Round turn One complete turn of a rope around anything.

Roving bridge A fixed bridge over a waterway at which the *towpath* changes from one side to the other; also called a 'turnover' or 'changeline' bridge.

Rubbing strake A longitudinal reinforcing strip attached to the hull of a vessel to reduce damage to the sides.

Rudder A vertical flat plate of metal or wood mounted at the *stern* of a vessel by which the vessel's direction is controlled.

Rudder stock A vertical metal shaft connecting the *rudder* with the *tiller* or the *ram's head*.

Saloon The main living cabin of a vessel.

Shackle A shaped metal fitting with securing pin, used as a connector.

Shaft (or long shaft) A long pole used for manoeuvring a vessel when not under power; sometimes called a 'quant'.

Sheer The fore-and-aft curve of a vessel's *gunwale* when viewed from the side.

Shoal A more or less pronounced lessening of water depth.

Side paddle The *paddle* situated in the culvert connecting a lock chamber and a *side pond*.

Side pond A brick- or masonry-lined reservoir alongside a lock chamber and used for the temporary storage of water which would otherwise run to waste as the lock is worked.

Sill The ledge under a lock gate, rebated to provide support to the bottom of the gate in resisting water pressure.

Single lever control A hand lever combining the functions of both gear operation and throttle control.

Skeg A short member running *fore-and-aft* beneath the *propeller*, for which it provides some protection; also functions as a housing for the lower end of the *rudder stock*.

Slack water A period when no tidal movement occurs – that is, at the top of the *flood* and the bottom of the *ebb*; the relatively still water outside the main current in a river.

Snub To check suddenly.

Sound signals A code of signals sounded on a vessel's hooter to indicate the helmsman's immediate intention.

Splice The interweaving of the strands of a rope, commonly to join two ropes together, or to form a permanent eye.

Springs The tides having greatest range in a tide-cycle – that is, highest high water and lowest low water; mooring ropes placed diagonally between vessel and bank, additional to *bow* and *stern* lines.

Squall A sudden gust of wind, often of some violence.

Staging A jetty of lightweight construction, usually timber.

Staircase lock An arrangement of two or more lock chambers, each of which leads directly into the next without an intervening *pound*.

Starboard The right-hand side of a vessel when looking *forward*. (Note: on inland waterways the terms 'right' and 'left' are generally used instead of *starboard* and *port* respectively.)

Stem The *forward* meeting point of a vessel's sides.

To 'stem-up': see *Aground*.

To 'stem the tide': to breast a tidal current without losing ground.

Stem-head The topmost part of the *stem*; on canal craft taken above *fore-deck* level and rounded to prevent the *bow* jamming under projections.

Stern The aftermost part of a vessel's *hull*.

Stern gland An arrangement – usually by means of greased packing – whereby water is prevented from entering a vessel at the point where the *propeller shaft* passes through the *hull*.

Stern-gland greaser A device for introducing grease under pressure into the *stern gland*.

Stern rail An enclosing safety rail around the *stern* of a vessel.

Stern wave The wave created at the *stern* of a vessel by the passage of the *hull* through the water.

Stern way Movement of a vessel through the water, *stern* first.

Stop-gate A gate, or gates, positioned at a narrow place in a canal and used for shutting off a section in the event of a burst, or when water is drained off for maintenance purposes.

Stop-lock A lock with a small rise in level and sited at the junction of two canals, originally constructed to prevent loss of water from one canal to the other.

Stop-planks Stout planks, by means of which a temporary dam may be constructed across a narrow place in a canal by slotting them into vertical grooves cut into each side of the channel; the dam fulfils the same function as a *stop-gate*. A section thus dammed is said to be 'stanked off'.

Strake A side plank of a vessel's *hull*.

Summit level The highest *pound* in a section of canal.

Superstructure The upper works of a vessel above *gunwale* level.

Swim The afterpart of a *narrowboat hull* below the *waterline*, which is curved and tapered to allow an easier flow of water to the *propeller*. A hull that moves easily through the water with a minimum of disturbance and has good manoeuvrability is said to 'swim well'.

Swim-ended A vessel's *bow* or *stern*, usually rectangular on plan, with an outward taper from the *waterline*; the Thames *lighter* provides a typical example.

Swing bridge A movable bridge which pivots horizontally on some form of turntable.

Tender A small boat or dinghy used in connection with a larger 'parent' vessel.

Throttle A device – often a hand lever – for controlling the speed of an engine.

Tide The cyclical rise and fall of the sea caused mainly by lunar and solar influences.

Tiller A horizontal bar connected to a *rudder* by means of which a vessel is steered.

Toggle A small wooden crosspiece fixed in the end of a rope and intended to engage with an eye.

Topsides All that part of a vessel above water level.

Towpath The path built alongside a waterway from which unpowered vessels may be towed.

Transit To establish a vessel's position in one direction by lining up two known fixed points.

Transom The flat stern-member of a square-sterned vessel.

Trim A vessel's balance in the water.

T-stud A metal T-shaped deck fitting to which ropes may be secured.

Tumblehome Inward slope of the sides of the superstructure to reduce a vessel's *beam* above *gunwale* level.

Under way Movement of a vessel through the water, usually with the connotation of being under power.

Veer To let out or pay out a rope or *cable*; to alter *course*.

Wake The disturbed water *astern* of a moving vessel.

Warp A mooring rope; a towing rope; the rope cable attached to an *anchor*.

Wash Waves created by a vessel's movement through the water.

Waterline The continuous horizontal line around a vessel's *hull* on the level at which she floats.

Way The momentum of a vessel's movement through the water, often with the connotation of not being under power.

Weather The *windward* side of a vessel.

Weed hatch A watertight compartment with removable lid, situated in the *stern* of a vessel and providing access to the *propeller* from *deck* level, mostly for the purpose of removing fouling.

Weir An overspill dam placed across a river for the purpose of regulating the depth and flow of water; generally, any similar arrangement for the purpose of water regulation.

Well-deck The floor of a well or *cockpit*.

Wharf A substantial canal or riverside structure built of brick, concrete, masonry or timber, for cargo transhipment; in some areas called a 'staithe'.

Wheel A spoked wheel used for steering a vessel instead of a *tiller*.

Whipping Binding at the end of a rope to prevent it from fraying.

Winch A mechanical device for obtaining an increased pull on a rope or cable.

Windage The wind resistance offered by the *topsides* of a vessel.

Winding The act of turning a vessel right round in a waterway, especially when the vessel is large relative to the width of the *channel*, as may commonly happen in a canal.

Winding hole A bay in one bank of a canal to provide sufficient room for larger craft to turn right round.

Windlass The cranked handle used for operating the *paddle gear* of locks, and sometimes for operating movable bridges; also called a 'lock key'.

Windward In the direction towards the wind; upwind.

Work a vessel, to To handle or manoeuvre a vessel.

Yaw A side-to-side swinging movement of a vessel's *bow*.

APPENDIX ONE

WATERWAYS
MAPS AND GUIDES

MAPS

Stanford's Inland Cruising Map of England**
Maps by Doug Smith** A series of very detailed cruising maps to
a scale of two miles to one inch:
*Upper Thames; London Waterways; From Avon to Thames; Grand
Union; Warwickshire Ring; Black Country Canals; Avon Ring; Four
Counties Ring; East Midland Canals; Cheshire Ring; Chester and
Llangollen; Nottinghamshire's Waterways; Stourport Ring; Pennine
Waters West; Pennine Waters East; Trent Waters; Upper Trent Valley;
South Yorkshire Waterways*

Other rivers and canals:
Caledonian Canal**
River Cam and Lower Great Ouse**
Upper Great Ouse**
Middle Level Navigation**
River Nene**
River Thames (Lechlade to Teddington)**
River Thames (Teddington to Southend)**
River Wey**
River Medway*

Tidal Waters of the River Trent; Tidal Waters of the Yorkshire Ouse
Detailed charts, updated by the Trent Boating Association and
affiliated clubs. Obtainable from: T. R. Pattison, Trent Boating
Association, 16 Baker Avenue, Arnold, Nottingham NG5 8FU

1:50 000 Series Ordnance Survey Maps Obtainable from book-sellers and stationers. Very useful when used in conjunction with cruising maps and guides.

GUIDES

Inland Waterways Guide** A general guide to holiday hire listing hire companies throughout the country, including the Broads, Thames, English Canals, Scotland and Ireland. The book gives brief descriptions of routes, navigation information, cruising hints, addresses of boatyards, chandlers and services.

The Canals Book** Provides navigational details of more than 2,000 miles of inland waterways.

The Thames Book* Provides navigational details of the River Thames from Lechlade to the sea, including tide tables.

Waterways World Guides* ** A series of navigation guides, spiral-bound for easy use, clear maps and route descriptions: *Llangollen Canal*; *Shropshire Union Canal*; *Staffordshire and Worcestershire Canal*; *Oxford Canal (South)*; *Oxford Canal (North)*, *Coventry Canal, and Ashby Canal*; *Trent and Mersey Canal (North)*; *Trent and Mersey Canal (South)*

Birmingham Canal Navigations*
Dudley and Stourbridge Canals**
Stratford Canal (South)**
Upper Avon (Stratford to Evesham)**
Gateway to the Avon (Evesham to Tewkesbury)**
Guide to the Rivers Great Ouse and Nene**
Bridgewater Canal**
Cheshire's Waterways**
Lancashire's Waterways**
Calder and Hebble**
Chesterfield Canal**

Yorkshire Waterways**
Braunston to Brentford (Grand Union Canal South)**
Aylesbury and Wendover Canals**
London's Waterways Guide**
Wey and Godalming Navigations**
Caledonian Canal**
Guide to the Barrow**

Publications marked * are obtainable from:
Waterways World Book Service, Kottingham House, Dale Street,
Burton-on-Trent DE14 3TD
Publications marked ** are obtainable from:
The Inland Waterways Association (Sales) Ltd, 114 Regent's Park
Road, London NW1 8UQ

The Inland Waterways Association (IWA) was founded in
1946, is registered as a charity and campaigns for the restoration,
retention and development of inland waterways in the British Isles
and their fullest commercial and recreational use. It receives no
financial support from government or other official sources, but
derives its finances from membership subscriptions, private
donations and fund-raising schemes generally, including national
events such as the annual rally of boats, local rallies, sponsored
walks and so on. Membership inquiries should be sent to the
address given above.

Maps and guides to the Broads are obtainable from:
Blake's Holidays, Publications Service, 29 Tenby Avenue, Harrow
HA3 8RU, and Hoseasons Holidays Ltd, Sunway House,
Lowestoft, Suffolk NR32 3LT

For details of cruising facilities and guides to the waterways of
Northern Ireland, apply to
Northern Ireland Tourist Board, River House, 48 High Street,
Belfast BT1 2DS Tel. Belfast (0232) 46609

For details of cruising facilities and guides to the waterways of
Eire, apply to:
Irish Tourist Board, Baggot Street Bridge, Dublin 2, or ITB offices
in London, Birmingham, Manchester and Glasgow.

BRITISH WATERWAYS BOARD GENERAL CANAL BY-LAWS 1965

The British Waterways Board By-laws apply to all canals and inland navigations in England and Wales administered by the Board with the exception of the Gloucester and Sharpness Canal, the River Severn Navigation from Gloucester to a point about half a mile upstream of the bridge at Stourport. The Lea and Stort Navigation, formerly subject to the River Lea General By-laws 1908, was included in the Board's General By-laws by an amendment dated 1966.

Some of the By-laws do not apply to, nor are the concern of, pleasure-boat hirers, although they may affect the hire company. In this respect the definition of 'owner' under *Interpretation, By-law 2: Definition of Terms* is interesting, as 'owner' is defined as including 'in relation to any vessel the master or hirer', and all hirers should bear this in mind if they wish to keep strictly to the letter of the law.

It is worth noting that the By-laws define a 'canal' as 'any canal or inland navigation belonging to or under the control of the Board', a definition which clearly includes all rivers under BWB jurisdiction. *By-law 3* says 'No person shall bring use or leave in any canal any vessel which is not in every respect fit for navigation on the canal or part thereof where it is intended to be used.' This requirement is mainly the responsibility of the hire company, but there are instances where the onus is on the hirer to ensure that his craft is free from defects that might place it at risk in certain circumstances – for example, continuing to navigate with an inoperative reverse gear.

By-law 6: Vessels to have fenders ready for use – 'Every vessel navigated on any canal shall have ready for immediate use proper fenders of suitable material and in good condition and the master of such vessel shall use such fenders whenever there is a risk of the vessel striking against any other vessel or against any wall, lock-gate, bridge or other thing.' This requirement is usually met by the provision of fixed bow and stern fenders made of woven rope.

By-law 7: Stowage of equipment – 'Every vessel navigated on any canal shall have her goods and equipment stowed so that nothing except necessary fenders and spars shall project over the sides thereof whereby injury might be caused to any vessel or to the works of the Board, or to any person or persons on such vessel or works and such goods and equipment shall be secured so that no part thereof can be washed or otherwise fall into the canal . . .'. This is a common-sense by-law; the hirer should make sure that nothing projects outboard (including the crew's arms and legs) at any time.

By-law 8: Stowage of inflammable spirit intended for use of vessel – 'The owner of any vessel navigating on any canal shall take proper steps to ensure that inflammable spirit taken on to or carried on such vessel and intended for use on the vessel shall be loaded stowed and used in such a manner as not to be or to become a danger or a nuisance to persons or property and shall have available at all times adequate equipment and materials for fighting fire.' In this connection the By-laws define 'inflammable spirit' as including 'petroleum spirit, diesel oil, paraffin and gas contained in a bottle or other receptacle'. This requirement is the responsibility of the hire company in most cases, as all diesel-engined hire craft are provided with sufficient fuel tank capacity for all normal purposes, and with enough bottled gas. However, petrol-engined boats will have to be refuelled during the course of a holiday, and the hirer should observe all common-sense precautions during this and any other operations involving the handling of inflammable liquids by switching off the engine, not smoking, turning off gas appliances and so on.

By-law 9 is interesting, as it requires that 'Every vessel navigated on any canal shall have in attendance an adequate and competent crew.' Crews made up entirely of novices may or may not be competent, depending upon circumstances; the hirer would therefore be wise to err on the side of caution, bearing in mind that *he* may be held responsible in the event of an accident (see pp. 111–13, Conditions of Hire, and Insurance).

By-law 10: Displaying of lights and visual signals (I) states 'Subject as hereinafter provided, a power-driven vessel (other than a narrow canal boat) when under way at night shall carry:
(a) On or in front of the foremast, or if a vessel without a foremast then in the forepart of the vessel, and in either case at a height above the hull of not less than four feet, a visible white light so constructed as to show an unbroken light over an arc of the horizon of twenty points of the compass (225°) so fixed as to show the light ten points (112½°) on each side of the vessel that is, from right ahead to two points (22½°) abaft the beam on either side; and (b) in addition to the above light, at her stern a visible white light so constructed as to show an unbroken light over an arc of the horizon of twelve points of the compass (135°) so fixed as to show the light six points (67½°) from right astern on each side of the vessel.'

Paragraph (2) of the same By-law states: 'A power-driven vessel, being a narrow canal boat, under way at night shall display in the forepart of the vessel, where it can best be seen and at a height above the deck or gunwale of not less than one foot, a visible white light.' All canal hire craft are fitted with a tunnel light, usually fixed to the forward bulkhead, but carry no other navigation lights and would in consequence be prohibited from cruising at night even if the Conditions of Hire allowed this – which they do not. The requirement for canal hire craft under way at night, and in restricted visibility, to carry full navigation lights was introduced in 1980 when the *Standards for Construction and Equipping of Pleasure Boats on the Board's Waterways* came into force, and will ultimately be extended to all craft using the Board's waters, at which time By-law 10(2) will cease to have effect.

The relevant paragraph (A15) of the *Standards* states that: 'Every boat to be navigated between sunset and sunrise or in restricted visibility shall have navigation lights installed to comply so far as is practicable with the Final Act of the International Conference on the Revision of the Regulations for Preventing Collisions at Sea, 1972 as amended from time to time. (*Note*: Although the range of visibility and height of the lights required by this Standard may be departed from because of the physical limitations of the navigation, their number and character must be adhered to.)' These requirements are identical to those given in By-law 10(5). Note that the By-laws define a 'narrow canal boat' as 'a vessel having a beam of less than seven feet six inches', and 'night' as 'the period between sunset and sunrise' (*NOT* 'lighting-up time').

By-law 10 goes on: (5) 'On the Trent Navigation, the Weaver Navigation, the Aire and Calder Navigation, the New Junction Canal and the Sheffield and South Yorkshire Navigation (below Doncaster) a power-driven vessel shall in addition to the lights prescribed in paragraphs (1), (2) ... as the case may be of this By-law display:

(a) On the starboard side a visible green light so constructed as to show an unbroken light over an arc of the horizon of ten points of the compass (112½°) so fixed as to show the light from right ahead to two points (22½°) abaft the beam on the starboard side.

(b) On the port side a visible red light so constructed as to show an unbroken light over an arc of the horizon of ten points of the compass (112½°) so fixed as to show the light from right ahead to two points (22½°) abaft the beam on the port side.'

By-law 10(8) deals with mooring on a commercial waterway: 'On the Trent Navigation, the Weaver Navigation, the Aire and Calder Navigation, the New Junction Canal and the Sheffield and South Yorkshire Navigation every vessel aground in the fairway or mid-channel and every vessel moored at any place (including vessels comprised in a composite craft) shall by night display a visible white light of such a character as to be capable of being seen from all directions.' Note that 'visible', when applied to lights described in the By-laws means 'visible on a dark night with a clear atmosphere at a distance of at least one mile'. As mooring lights are not provided by hire companies the onus is upon the hirer to supply a suitable light and wiring in accordance with the provisions of By-law 10(8), but only with the consent of the hire company and after agreement has been reached regarding mooring arrangements – always assuming, of course, that this is likely to be necessary.

With regard to lights in tunnels, *By-law 10(9)* requires that: 'Any vessel passing by day or by night through a tunnel exceeding 440 yards in length shall display in the forepart of the vessel a visible white light.' This requirement is met by provision of a headlamp, as previously mentioned.

By-law 10(10) states: 'A vessel while actually engaged on work of dredging, piling, diving, or other works of repair or construction on any canal shall display:

(a) by day, at right angles to the keel, and in a position visible to vessels approaching from any direction, on that side of the vessel on which work is proceeding or on which obstructions may be present and on which vessels must not pass, a red metal square of cruciform construction (a side of which measures not less than eighteen inches) and on that side of the vessel which is clear of obstruction and on which vessels may pass a white square similar in construction and size to the said red square ...'

Approach all dredging and construction operations with extreme caution, and slow right down and wait for signals before proceeding if the channel is obstructed by plant or machinery. In practice the requirements of paragraph (10) (a) are adhered to only on the major commercial waterways, and hand and voice signals are normally given in other situations. On rivers watch out for large dredgers moored by cables to both banks; the dredger will carry visual signals as described above indicating which mooring cable will be slackened to allow passage of craft. Watch out too for any additional hand signals from the dredger, and navigate with caution.

Construction work obstructing the channel should be marked by signs as provided for in *By-law 11*: 'Where and so long as works in progress on or near a bank of any canal involve the projection of any works into the navigable channel:

(a) By day, the extremities from the bank of the projecting works shall be marked by the placing thereon of metal squares 18 inches by 18 inches of cruciform construction painted red and notice boards with the words "CAUTION – WORK IN PROGRESS" in red letters on a white background shall be exhibited on the bank on both sides of the works at distances of both 100 yards and 200 yards therefrom.

(b) By night, the said extremities shall be marked by the placing thereon of two red lights situated side by side about one foot apart.'

The *sound signals* to be used on the Board's waterways (and which also apply to other inland navigations) are described in *By-law 12*:

(1) 'Every power-driven vessel navigating on any canal shall be furnished with an efficient whistle.'

'Whistle' is defined in the By-laws as 'any appliance capable of producing the prescribed short and prolonged blasts'. 'Short blast' is defined as 'a blast of about one second's duration' and a 'prolonged blast' as 'a blast of from four to six seconds' duration'.

(2) 'When vessels are in sight of one another the master of a power-driven vessel under way in taking any of the courses hereinafter referred to in this By-law shall indicate that course by the following

signals on such whistle, namely: One short blast to mean "I am altering my course to starboard", two short blasts to mean "I am altering my course to port", three short blasts to mean "My engines are going astern", four short blasts to mean "I am about to turn or to turn round". This signal shall be followed after a short interval by one short blast if turning to starboard or two short blasts if turning to port and shall be repeated to any approaching vessel, whereupon such approaching vessel shall take action to avoid collision.

(3) In fog, mist, falling snow, heavy rainstorm or any other conditions similarly restricting visibility whether by night or day, the following signals shall be used:

(a) A power-driven vessel making way through the water shall sound, at intervals of not more than two minutes, a prolonged blast.

(b) A power-driven vessel under way but stopped and making no way through the water shall sound, at intervals of not more than two minutes, two prolonged blasts with an interval of about one second between them.

(c) A vessel when towing and a vessel under way which is unable to get out of the way of an approaching vessel through not being under command or unable to manoeuvre as required by these By-laws shall sound, at intervals of not more than one minute, three blasts in succession, namely, one prolonged blast followed by two short blasts.

(d) Every vessel aground in the fairway or mid-channel shall, so long as she remains aground, signify the same by sounding five or more blasts in rapid succession at intervals of not more than one minute.

(4) When the view of the canal ahead is obstructed by a bend in the canal and until such view is no longer obscured, a power-driven vessel making way through the water shall sound, at intervals of twenty seconds, a prolonged blast.

(5) The master of a power-driven vessel approaching a lock which is operated by staff provided by the Board for that purpose and requiring the lock to be opened shall sound one prolonged blast, except that on the Weaver Navigation when navigating downstream he shall sound one prolonged blast followed by one short blast.

(6) The master of a power-driven vessel intending to pass a movable bridge, which is operated by staff provided by the Board or other authority, and requiring the bridge to be opened shall sound one prolonged blast, except that on the Weaver Navigation when navi-

gating downstream he shall sound one prolonged blast followed by one short blast.' Note that the signal consisting of four short blasts may also mean 'I am unable to manoeuvre'.

In my opinion pleasure-boaters do not make anything like sufficient use of the official sound signals – not even the obvious common-sense long blast sounded when approaching a blind bend or a bridge-hole. Perhaps for some this reluctance to use the 'whistle' arises from car-driving habits, where the horn – if used at all – seems to be mostly employed as a means of expressing annoyance. Properly used, sound signals tend to reduce the chance of collision (which is why they were devised in the first place) and thus maintain a certain orderliness in matters of navigation; to understand a signal and respond to it correctly should be second nature to any boater who considers himself competent. Hand signals, which seem to be used much more often than sound signals, are not only frequently ambiguous, but can only hope to be effective when craft are in sight of each other – when it may be too late for appropriate responses to be made. In the interests of safety, boaters venturing on to the commercial navigations *must* know the whole range of sound signals given above as they are always used by commercial vessels, the masters of which expect all other craft to understand their signalled intentions.

The manner in which craft are to be navigated, and speed limits, are laid down in By-laws 13 and 14 respectively.

By-law 13: 'Every vessel navigating on any canal shall at all times be navigated with care and reasonable consideration for all persons using the canal or being on the banks thereof and in particular in such a manner as will not obstruct the passage of any other vessel using the canal or involve risk of collision or endanger the safety of other vessels or their moorings or cause damage thereto or to the banks of the canal or to any part of the Board's property.'

By-law 14: 'No person shall navigate a power-driven vessel on any canal at a speed over the bed of the canal greater than the following:
(a) On the Trent Navigation (except between Averham Weir and Newark Nether Lock and between Beeston Lock and Trent Lock, Nottingham), a speed of 6 miles per hour upstream and 8 miles per hour downstream.
(b) On the Aire and Calder Navigation (except the Selby Canal), the New Junction Canal, the Sheffield and South Yorkshire Navigation, the Grand Union Canal (from the junction with the River Trent at

Soar Mouth to West Bridge, Leicester), the Weaver Navigation and the Witham Navigation a speed of 6 miles per hour.

(c) On any canal or part thereof other than those to which paragraphs (a) and (b) hereof apply, a speed of 4 miles per hour. Provided that no person shall be convicted of any offence under this By-law upon proof by him that the speed at which he navigated the vessel was necessary for safe navigation in conditions of flood tide or strong ebbtide or flood water.'

These are straightforward requirements to prevent increased collision risk due to excessive speed, and to minimize damage to banks through wash from craft. The four miles per hour speed limit on the main canal system is misguided in the opinion of many, and should be replaced by the criterion of absence of a breaking wave at the banks (although this is covered by By-law 13).

By-law 16 states: 'No vessel shall overtake or pass another vessel on any part of any canal without observing due precautions to avoid danger or risk to either vessel or the canal or to any works, person or property.'

The rules for deciding who has right of way, and when, and the procedures to be followed when deviating from the 'Rule of the Road' are laid down in By-laws 17–21.

By-law 17: 'Except as provided in By-law 19 where two vessels meet in any part of the canal where they cannot pass in safety the master of the vessel which is nearest to that part of the canal where the vessels can pass in safety shall navigate his vessel back to such passing place and allow the other vessel to pass. Provided always that:

(a) a vessel which is not towing another vessel shall give way to a vessel which is towing another vessel or vessels;

(b) vessels which are unladen shall give way to vessels which are laden;

(c) on the Aire and Calder navigation, the Sheffield and South Yorkshire Navigation, the Trent Navigation and the Weaver Navigation, a vessel which is proceeding against the tide or stream shall give way to a vessel which is proceeding with the tide or stream.

By-law 18: 'Without prejudice to the generality of By-law 16 the following By-law shall apply to vessels passing or overtaking other vessels on any canal:

(1) Except as hereinafter mentioned where two vessels proceeding in opposite directions meet the master of each vessel shall steer his vessel to its starboard side in such a manner that such vessels pass freely

with the port side of each vessel nearest to the port side of the other vessel.

Provided always that:

(a) where one but not both of such vessels is a hauled vessel the masters of such vessels shall steer the vessels in such a manner that the vessels pass freely with the hauled vessel between the towing path and the other vessel; ...

(c) on the Aire and Calder Navigation, the Sheffield and South Yorkshire Navigation, the Trent Navigation and the Weaver Navigation, where circumstances render it impracticable for vessels to pass port side to port side a power-driven vessel proceeding with the tide or stream shall have the right of way and must indicate to the other vessel by two short blasts on her whistle in ample time to prevent collision, her intention to pass starboard to starboard. The approaching vessel shall immediately reply by a similar sound signal and pass accordingly, stopping, if necessary, until the other vessel has passed clear.

(2) Except as hereinafter mentioned the master of a vessel overtaking another vessel proceeding in the same direction shall steer his vessel in such a manner that his vessel shall pass with her starboard side nearest to the vessel overtaken and the master of the vessel overtaken shall steer his vessel to her starboard side so as to permit the overtaking vessel to pass in safety on the port side of the vessel overtaken. Provided that:

(a) where a vessel which is not a hauled vessel is overtaking a hauled vessel the masters of such vessels shall steer their vessels in such a manner that the vessels pass with the vessel overtaken between the towing path and the overtaking vessel and the master of the vessel overtaken shall slacken his hauling line and keep his vessel as near as possible to the towing path whilst the other vessel is passing: ...'

'Hauled vessel' is defined as '... any vessel which is being hauled or towed from the towing path or which has ropes from time to time or continuously passed to the towing path to assist in the navigation of such vessel'.

By-law 19 specifically refers to pleasure-boats:

(1) 'A pleasure-boat when meeting, overtaking or being overtaken by a power-driven vessel other than a pleasure-boat shall as far as possible keep out of the main navigable channel.'

(3) 'When two pleasure-boats one of which is a sailing vessel are

proceeding in such directions as to involve risk of collision, the pleasure-boat not being a sailing vessel shall keep out of the way of the sailing vessel.'

By-law 20: 'Vessels turning in or into any canal shall do so in such a manner as not to cause any obstruction or interference to any other vessel using the canal.'

By-law 21: 'Every vessel approaching any ferry shall reduce speed, and if necessary stop, and thereafter navigate so as not to obstruct or interfere with the effectual working of the ferry.'

The procedures to be followed at locks and movable bridges are detailed in By-laws 23–7.

By-law 23(1): 'The master of any vessel approaching, entering, passing through or by or leaving any lock or movable bridge shall cause his vessel to be navigated at such speed and controlled in such a manner as not to strike, imperil, damage, obstruct or run foul of the lock or movable bridge or any part thereof or any other vessel approaching, entering, passing through or by or leaving the lock or movable bridge.

(2) At any lock or movable bridge which is operated by staff provided by the Board for that purpose the lock-keeper, bridge-tender, or other authorized officer in charge shall regulate the vessels approaching, passing through and leaving such lock or movable bridge and the masters of all vessels in the vicinity of such lock or movable bridge shall obey the directions of the said lock-keeper, bridge-tender or other authorized officer.

(3) Where a signal light is in operation to indicate when a lock or movable bridge is open for vessels to pass the master of a vessel approaching such lock or movable bridge shall not permit his vessel to proceed beyond the said signal light unless it is showing green and shall not permit his vessel so to proceed whilst such light is showing red.'

The operation of locks by boat crews is dealt with in By-laws 24 and 25.

By-law 24: 'Any person operating a lock which is not operated by the Board's staff shall do so in accordance with the following procedure:

(1) The gates and the sluices astern of a vessel in such a lock shall be closed before the sluices and the gates ahead of such vessel are opened.

(2) When a lock which has a side pound is being filled the upper sluice

of such lock shall not be opened or drawn until as much water as possible has been drawn from the side pound and the sluices thereof have been closed.

(3) When a lock with a side pound is being emptied the lower sluices of such lock shall not be opened or drawn until as much water as possible has been drawn into the side pound and the sluices thereof have been closed.'

By-law 25: 'No person shall:

(a) Open or close or attempt to open or close the gate of any lock except by the means provided for that purpose or before the water is level on both sides of the gate.

(b) Draw or operate any sluices until the lock-gates are closed.

(c) Operate or leave open any sluice so as to waste water.

(d) Operate any sluice otherwise than by means of the handle or other device normally used for that purpose.

(e) Fill or empty any lock of water for the admission of any vessel to the lock when there is another vessel approaching the lock from the opposite direction and within 200 yards thereof and the level of the water in the lock is suitable for such approaching vessel to enter the lock.

(f) Cause or allow any vessel to remain in a lock longer than is necessary for the convenient passage thereof.'

'Sluice' is defined as 'any sluice, clough, clowe, valve, paddle, penstock or other device for controlling the passage of water through weirs, dams, lock-gates, the walls of locks, or through the banks of a canal or any works connected therewith.'

By-law 26: 'The master of any vessel intending to navigate the vessel under any bridge shall take all steps necessary to ensure that his vessel can pass such bridge without touching or damaging the same.'

By-law 27(1): 'The master of every vessel intending to pass any movable bridge which is not operated by staff provided by the Board for that purpose shall close or cause to be closed any protection gate or other barrier provided for the safety of users of the roadway before the bridge is moved from the closed position and shall unless there is another vessel within 200 yards of such bridge and intending to pass the same close or cause to be closed the bridge immediately his vessel has passed the same and open or cause to be opened such protection gate or other barrier immediately the bridge is closed.

(2) Any person being on a movable bridge and any person in charge

of any animal, vehicle or thing on any movable bridge shall leave such bridge and remove such animal, vehicle or thing from such bridge immediately on being warned that the bridge is about to be opened. No person shall go upon or permit any animal, vehicle or thing under his control to go upon or to drive any animal, vehicle or thing on to a movable bridge after receiving warning that the bridge is about to be opened until the bridge has been closed after such opening and no person shall pass or attempt to pass any protection gate or other barrier provided for the safety of users of the roadway until such gate or other barrier is fully opened so as to permit the passage of road traffic.

Provided that for the purpose of this By-law a movable bridge shall be deemed to be closed only when it is secured in position to allow persons and traffic to pass in safety over the canal by means of the bridge.'

By-laws 28 and 29 lay down certain rules governing mooring.

By-law 28: 'Any vessel (other than a dredger or other vessel engaged in works of maintenance of the canal) moored at any wharf or elsewhere in any canal shall be securely moored head and stern with good and sufficient ropes or other efficient apparatus and shall be laid as close to and along the side or in front of such wharf or other mooring place as conveniently may be and shall be moored in such a manner and in such a position as not to cause any obstruction to the navigation of other vessels.'

By-law 29: 'No mooring rope shall be affixed to any sluice lock-gate, bridge or other work of the Board not provided for the purpose of mooring.'

The remainder of the By-laws deal generally with matters other than navigation.

By-law 31(1): 'No person, unless authorized by the Board or otherwise legally entitled so to do shall:

(a) Ride or drive any animal or vehicle over any towing path.

(b) Obstruct any towing path or interfere with the authorized use thereof.

(c) Leave open any gate or rail used as a fence or part of a fence alongside across or on any way leading to a towing path.

(2) No person shall wilfully, wantonly or maliciously damage or otherwise interfere with any hedge, post, rail, wall or other fencing the property of the Board alongside a towing path or on any way leading to a towing path.'

Note that 'vehicle' in this context includes bicycles.

By-law 32: 'No person using the towing path on any canal shall obstruct, interfere with or hinder the towing or navigation of any vessel on the canal and such person shall permit any person engaged in towing or navigating any vessel and any horse or vehicle used for such purpose to pass on the side of the towing path nearer to the canal.'

By-law 36: 'No person shall wilfully or negligently suffer any vessel to run aground or sink in any canal. The master of any vessel running aground or sinking in any canal shall forthwith inform the Board of the said running aground or sinking and of any danger to navigation caused thereby and shall also forthwith inform the masters of any vessels navigating at any time in the vicinity of such running aground or sinking.'

By-law 37: 'No person shall turn any vessel adrift upon any canal or shall unnecessarily cast off, cut loose, or interfere with any mooring or rope or fastening of any vessel.'

By-law 38: 'No person shall unless so authorized by the Board turn or cause to be turned the propeller or propellers of any vessel while such vessel is moored alongside any wharf, wall, bank or other work of the Board except as may be necessary for the proper navigation of the vessel.'

By-law 39: 'No person shall commit any nuisance in or on any canal.'

By-law 40: 'No person shall throw or discharge into or on to any canal any animal (whether alive or dead) or any rubbish, stones or other material of any kind whatsoever or deposit such materials so as to be washed or carried into any canal by floods or other means, or in any wise cause obstruction in any canal.'

By-laws 41–3 prohibit: bathing of persons or animals; obstruction of any officer of the Board in the execution of his duties and disobedience of his lawful orders; abusive and offensive language on or near any canal. By-law 44 sounds a note of warning for those who navigate mainly by the *Real Ale Guide*: 'No person shall navigate any vessel on any canal or take part in the navigation, mooring or handling of any vessel on the canal whilst under the influence of drink to such an extent as to be incapable of having proper control of the vessel.'

By-laws 46 and 48 prohibit: throwing of stones and other missiles and shooting into or over the canal; damage to the Board's property. By-laws 50 and 56 forbid operation or interference with the Board's works, plant and machinery without due authorization; getting over any wall, fence, or hedge belonging to the Board.

An Amendment to the By-laws dated 1972 prohibits unauthorized water-skiing: 'No person shall carry on water-skiing on any canal without the consent of the Board which consent may be subject to conditions.'

An Amendment to the By-laws dated 1976 deals with licensing: 'No person shall knowingly cause or permit to be brought, kept, let for hire or used on any canal (not being a river waterway) any pleasure-boat unless there is then in force in relation to the pleasure-boat a pleasure-boat licence.'

'The owner of a pleasure-boat shall not knowingly cause or permit to be used on a canal (not being a river waterway) any pleasure-boat in respect of which a pleasure-boat licence has been issued unless the licence for the time being in force is displayed on the pleasure-boat in such a manner and position as to be clearly visible from outside the pleasure-boat at all times.'

'No person shall knowingly cause or permit to be concealed a pleasure-boat licence or commercial vessel licence required to be displayed on a pleasure-boat or commercial vessel in accordance with this By-law.'

NOTE: GLOUCESTER AND SHARPNESS CANAL AND RIVER SEVERN NAVIGATION

The By-laws governing these navigations were drawn up in 1962 (under the authority of the British Transport Commission, since transferred to the British Waterways Board), and in most respects are similar to the General Canal By-laws, but with the addition of the following specific clauses:

By-law 11(1): 'No powered vessel shall navigate upon the River Severn Navigation within a distance of thirty feet from the water's edge on either bank thereof except when proceeding into or out of any lock, or under any bridge, or when mooring. PROVIDED ALWAYS that this By-law shall not apply to

(a) any vessel in distress or engaged in maintenance works;

(b) vessels navigating in the Eastern Channel of the River Severn Navigation from the Lower Parting to the Upper Parting; or

(c) vessels navigating within thirty feet of the west bank of the River Severn Navigation between the following places:

(i) in the parish of Hasfield in the County of Gloucester for a distance of 190 yards between the map reference point SO.846258 and the map reference point SO.847260;

(ii) in the parish of Forthampton in the County of Gloucester for a distance of 330 yards between the map reference point SO.871310 and the map reference point SO.873313;

(iii) in the parish of Hanley Castle in the County of Worcester for a distance of 290 yards between the map reference point SO.845417 and the map reference point SO.845420;

(iv) in the parish of Hanley Castle in the County of Worcester for a distance of 250 yards between the map reference point SO.852428 and the map reference point SO.853430.

(2) No powered vessel shall overtake or attempt to overtake another powered vessel whilst either of such vessels is navigating any of the sections of the River Severn Navigation described in sub-paragraph (1)(c)(i), (ii), (iii), and (iv) of this By-law.

(3) In this By-law a map reference point shall mean the point ascertained in accordance with the National Grid on the Ordnance Survey Map drawn to a scale of six inches to one mile.'

By-law 21(1): 'No person shall navigate a vessel upon the River Severn Navigation at a speed exceeding six miles per hour over the bed of the said Navigation when travelling in the upstream direction or eight miles per hour over the bed of the Navigation when travelling in the downstream direction. Provided that no person shall be convicted of any offence against this paragraph of this By-law upon proof by him that the speed at which he navigated the vessel was necessary for safe navigation in conditions of flood tide or flood water.

(2) No person shall navigate a vessel upon the Gloucester and Sharpness Canal at a speed exceeding six miles per hour over the bed of the Canal.'

By-law 27(1): 'No vessel shall be moored

(a) on the Gloucester and Sharpness Canal or in the Gloucester

Docks or Sharpness Docks without the authority of a duly authorized officer;

(b) on the River Severn Navigation to any property owned by the Commission without the authority of an authorized officer.'

THE PERFORMANCE
OF VESSELS
IN CONSTRICTED CHANNELS

The performance of any vessel, whether sail- or power-driven, is governed by a combination of factors, all of which must be taken into account if the behaviour of the vessel in a given set of circumstances is to be understood. Some of the factors, such as wind, tide, current, wave action and frictional and wave-making resistances, are clearly external forces to which the vessel may be subject, but the vessel's response to these influences is governed by her overall design in the way of hull form and draught, superstructure, sails and rig, and propulsion unit, in appropriate combination. This interaction between a vessel and the external forces acting upon her is further complicated in the case of craft navigating inland waterways by certain effects associated with channel constriction. In considering the influence of these effects upon a single-screw vessel it is convenient to ignore, for the sake of clarity, the forces of wind, tide and current.

RESISTANCE THEORY

The performance of a vessel in a waterway is critically governed by *the size of the vessel (more specifically, its cross-sectional area below water level) relative to the cross-sectional area of the channel which the vessel is navigating.* This relationship between vessel and channel may be explained by reference to a theorem dealing with fluid dynamics. Bernoulli showed that in a fluid flow the total energy in its various forms – kinetic energy, potential energy, and pressure energy – must be a constant; from which it follows that an increase in flow velocity (increase in kinetic energy) entails a corresponding decrease in pressure energy.

Water being an incompressible fluid, its density remains almost constant, varying only slightly with temperature, while its pressure increases with depth. A stationary vessel displaces a volume of water equal to its own weight, and is supported by pressure acting on the submerged portion of the hull such that the sum of the forces involved equals zero, and the vessel remains at rest. If, however, a propulsive force is applied to the vessel through the medium of a screw propeller, then the equilibrium of forces is disturbed, and redistributions of velocities and pressures begin to occur in the water immediately surrounding the vessel.

SKIN FRICTION RESISTANCE

At relatively low speeds the major part of the resistance encountered by a vessel is due to friction at the hull surface, for water does not act as a perfect fluid, but has viscosity. The magnitude of the surface friction depends upon the length and area of hull surface in contact with the water, degree of hull roughness and speed of the vessel through the water. Particles of water in actual contact with the hull adhere to it and are carried along, with no slip. At small distances from the hull surface the velocity imparted to the surrounding water is quite low, producing a shearing effect (and thus frictional drag) together with a noticeable degree of turbulence. The width of this belt, known as the *boundary layer*, increases somewhat towards the afterpart of the vessel, where it leaves the hull and encloses the propeller, producing an important effect upon the axial thrust. The shed boundary layer is known as the *viscous wake*.

WAVE-MAKING OR RESIDUAL RESISTANCE

Part of the energy required to move a vessel is expended in the creation of pressure waves, which form a resistance to the forward motion of the vessel. Three wave systems are involved: a bow divergent system, a stern divergent system, and a transverse system.

As the vessel moves forward it displaces water, which flows beneath and around the sides of the hull, eventually returning to the undisturbed state some distance behind the vessel. In consequence of the vessel's movement, the surrounding water beyond the boundary layer may be considered to have a *relative* velocity equal and opposite to the velocity of the vessel. The advancing bow of the vessel presents a resistance to this water flow and thereby reduces its velocity, causing a corresponding increase in pressure, and thus a *bow wave*. As water flow velocity at the bow wave equals zero, the wave assumes a constant form and height and travels with the vessel so long as uniform speed is maintained.

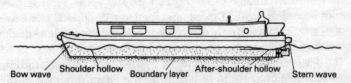

Bow wave   Shoulder hollow   Boundary layer   After-shoulder hollow   Stern wave

Fig. 52 Movement of water around vessel's hull

Abaft the stem the water flow passing down each side of the hull increases in velocity, with decrease in pressure, to the *shoulder hollow*, followed by a small pressure rise to almost constant velocity as the flow proceeds down the hull. Some distance ahead of the stern flow velocity again increases, then decreases, forming the *after-shoulder hollow*, following which rising pressure results in the formation of a *stern wave*, culminating at the central stream line in zero velocity. Astern of the vessel, at first fairly rapidly then more gradually, the values of flow velocity and pressure tend to return to those obtaining for the undisturbed water.

The wave system generated by the vessel's passage is mainly controlled by the relatively large and sudden pressure increases at bow and stern; to a lesser degree by the pressure decreases at the fore- and after-shoulders.

Secondary wave-making occurs once the vessel's speed exceeds 0.233 m/sec (0.764 ft/sec, or 0.52 mph); it is prevented at lesser speeds by the prevailing surface tension of water. At practical speeds gravity waves form within an angle of about twenty degrees on both sides of the hull in a pattern of slightly curved divergent and transverse waves. Further increase of speed (or decrease in water depth) causes the wave group angle to increase steadily until it approaches ninety degrees at a certain critical speed, while the transverse waves show a corresponding contraction.

At the *critical speed*: $C_s = \sqrt{g \cdot W_d}$ for unrestricted breadth, where $C_s =$ critical speed (and also the speed of a wave in very shallow water)

$g =$ gravitational constant

and $W_d =$ water depth

the transverse waves have massed into two large waves called *waves of translation*, concentrated respectively at the bow and stern of the vessel. At speeds exceeding the critical (or with decreasing depth) these waves are unable to keep pace with the vessel because they cannot exceed the critical speed, and therefore disappear. The wave system now comprises only divergent waves, whose angle with the axis of moment decreases steadily with increasing speed.

The disappearance of the waves of translation is accompanied by a considerable decrease in resistance to the forward motion of the vessel, which, as speed increases, trims more heavily by the stern, while at the same time the fore-foot tends to lift clear of the water. At still higher speeds the vessel rides up on to a single large wave and is supported only by the afterpart of the hull – a condition known as *planing*, and attainable solely by craft of suitable design and power/weight ratio.

THE APPLICATION OF RESISTANCE THEORY TO VESSELS NAVIGATING CONSTRICTED CHANNELS

As previously mentioned, the *cross-sectional ratio*

$$\frac{\text{sectional area of channel below water level}}{\text{area of submerged midship section of vessel}}$$

is crucially important, and should not be less than 4.5, increasing with speed.

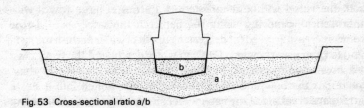

Fig. 53 Cross-sectional ratio a/b

A vessel moving up a constricted channel may be compared to a loose-fitting plunger acting in a water-filled tube; resistance to the plunger increases proportionately to its speed, in spite of water loss round the sides. A vessel at speed may heighten the 'plunger effect' to the point where a discernible head of water is pushed ahead of the bow, with rapid increase in frictional resistance and decrease of pressure along the hull, causing a large rise in water flow velocity relative to the speed of advance.

Surface-water flow along the hull forms a downward gradient from stem to stern, and as resistance increases the trim of the vessel undergoes a change. The bow and stern waves become transverse waves of considerable height, and the vessel moves up against the

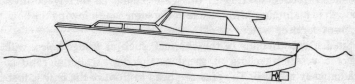

Fig. 54 Vessel encountering slope-resistance

bow wave slope, creating *slope-resistance*. At the critical speed the wave system is compressed into single large transverse waves at bow and stern, there is a greater surface drop near the midship section and the trim aft reaches its maximum, while wave-making resistance rises rapidly. Because of the heavy trim aft, wider parts of the stern become immersed, thus greatly increasing *eddy-resistance*.

The effect of this combination of factors upon the vessel is known as *squat*.

The wave system created by a vessel at or near critical speed can be very destructive to a waterway. If the water is relatively deep at the banks the changes in pressure distribution travelling outwards from the vessel will be manifested as a series of large waves with unbroken tops moving along the banks at the same speed as the vessel. Increasing speed (or decreasing depth of water at the bank) will tend to raise wave height relative to water depth, and the wave crest will break due to greater frictional resistance at its base. In these conditions the bow and stern waves are often united into a single large wave breaking at the bank with considerable force, and keeping pace with the vessel on a transverse line just abaft the stern, accompanied by a marked increase in surface gradient.

STEERING IN CONSTRICTED CHANNELS

At practical speeds a vessel's steering may be influenced by the cross-section of the channel bed, especially if the deeper part takes the form of a relatively narrow V-shape with pronounced shoulders. As the vessel moves forward the bow wave tends to thrust the fore-end away from the shoulder towards deeper water – an effect particularly noticeable if the deepest part of the channel (the 'slot') meanders about. Corrective steering in this case should be merely positive enough to maintain control, while at the same time allowing the bow to 'hunt' for deep water.

Sudden constrictions of the channel, such as bridge-holes, will affect a vessel travelling at speed as the cross-sectional ratio is dramatically reduced. The pressure head in front of the bow is first compressed and then subjected to an abrupt pressure increase by entry of the bow into the narrows. The fore-end rises and the vessel moves up against the bow wave with loss of speed, while the stern trims down and water flow velocity along the hull sides increases markedly. Momentum and screw-thrust together force the vessel through the narrows; as the bow reaches the far side the pressure head is suddenly reduced and the bow drops while the stern lifts, giving rise to the slightly odd sensation of 'going over the hump'. This situation is not without hazard: if the vessel is noticeably off the centreline of the narrows there will be greater constriction of the water flow on that side of the hull nearest the bank, resulting in – according to Bernoulli's Theorem – an increased flow velocity and therefore fall in pressure on that side as compared with the other; the differential pressure acting on the hull will then tend to draw the vessel against the nearer bank, possibly with some force.

The tendency for a vessel to be drawn towards a bank may occur in any situation where water depth is sufficient for the vessel to approach the bank. If, for instance, a vessel is allowed to move too close to the side of a tunnel or an aqueduct trough, the resulting differential pressure will draw the vessel into the side and hold it there.

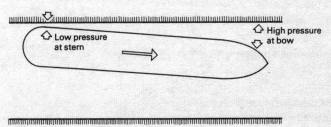

Fig. 55 Vessel drawn against tunnel wall by differential water pressure

Attempts to break the deadlock by applying more power, or by very positive steering, will merely worsen matters; in the former case by increasing flow velocity and therefore differential pressure, and in the latter by urging the stern more strongly into the side. Instead, reduce flow velocity by reduction in power, and use very small rudder angles to coax the vessel towards the middle of the channel.

NEGOTIATING BENDS

Bernoulli effects may also influence a vessel's steering at acute bends, where the deeper part of the channel often lies towards the outer radius and a shallow shoulder marks the inside of the bend. Cutting the corner will perhaps run the bow in too close to the shoulder, in which case the bow wave will tend to thrust the fore-end into deeper water at the outside of the bend, thus maintaining the vessel on a more or less straight course. Resistance to turning is further augmented by the effects of differential pressure as the afterpart of the hull is drawn towards the shoulder, and any attempt to counter loss of steerage by large rudder angles is likely to prove ineffectual, as the forces generated at the rudder are insufficient to overcome the forces acting on the hull. Nor will increased power solve the problem, but only worsen it by adding to the speed, thus reinforcing the likelihood of a severe collision with the outside of the bend – if not something even more drastic. On the contrary, the situation may only be recovered by going hard astern the moment steerage is lost, for the first priority must be to avoid the possibility of collision.

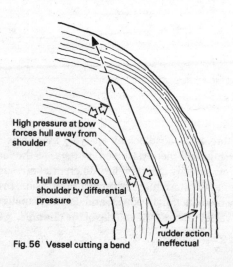

High pressure at bow forces hull away from shoulder

Hull drawn onto shoulder by differential pressure

rudder action ineffectual

Fig. 56 Vessel cutting a bend

VESSELS PASSING AND OVERTAKING

The effects of differential pressure are noticeably apparent when two vessels meet and pass in a constricted channel, and when one vessel is overtaking another.

In meeting and passing, the respective bows with their high-pressure heads will tend to be thrust away from each other towards the banks. As the hulls draw level, differential pressures are largely cancelled out, but when they have partly passed each other their bows will be drawn towards the middle of the channel as high pressure at the bow of one meets low pressure at the stern of the other. It is unwise to correct this sometimes abrupt change of course (unless circumstances dictate otherwise), for as the vessels' sterns pass they

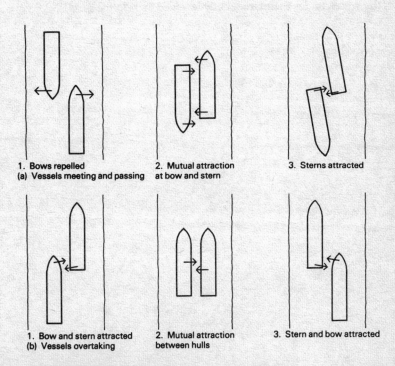

1. Bows repelled
(a) Vessels meeting and passing

2. Mutual attraction at bow and stern

3. Sterns attracted

1. Bow and stern attracted
(b) Vessels overtaking

2. Mutual attraction between hulls

3. Stern and bow attracted

Fig. 57 Effects of differential water pressure on vessels passing and overtaking

are attracted towards each other by the coincidence of their low-pressure zones, with danger of possible collision.

In the case of one vessel overtaking another, the risk of collision tends to be greater unless the overtaken vessel is given a wide enough berth, for as the bow of the overtaking vessel approaches the stern of the other there is a mutual attraction between their respective high- and low-pressure zones. When running side by side the water flow velocity between the hulls will rise considerably, thereby lowering pressure to such an extent that the hulls will be drawn together with some force and held there by differential pressure. As the stern of the overtaking vessel draws level with the bow of the other there will again be an attraction between the two, though of lesser magnitude.

In these situations, as with others likely to be encountered in navigating constricted channels, the danger of collision and unwanted effects such as squat is roughly proportional to the speed of the vessel, and is therefore greatly lessened by *reducing speed*.

THE ACTION OF PROPELLERS AND RUDDERS

SCREW PROPELLER (OR SCREW)

A screw propeller consists of a boss to which usually two, three or four separate blades are attached symmetrically. The unit thus formed derives its name from the characteristic motion of a screw: that is, uniform translation combined with uniform rotation in a plane at right-angles to the direction of advance, and in this respect may be compared with an aircraft rotating wing, or an aerofoil section. To achieve this form the face of the screw blade (the *face* is the surface viewed from aft and the reverse surface is the *back*) is shaped as part of a helicoidal surface.

The common characteristics of a screw propeller are usually defined by:

(a) the number of blades;
(b) the diameter – that is, the diameter of the circle traced by the tips of the blades;
(c) the pitch, a term describing the axial advance per revolution (often referred to as the *nominal pitch*, a term independent of blade contour, thickness, and shape of sections).

Figure 58b illustrates a screw blade of suitable section, together with the various forces responsible for, and generated by, its rotation in a fluid medium.

An aerofoil advancing through a fluid with a constant speed V and an angle of attack α produces a lift A normal to the direction of advance together with a relatively much smaller resistance or drag W in the direction of advance. The relative speed V is equal, but opposed to, the resultant of a speed of advance v_e in the direction of thrust and a rotative speed u, which together may be considered typical for this propeller type. The resultant of the lift and the drag

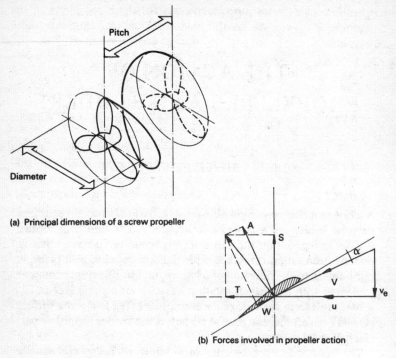

(a) Principal dimensions of a screw propeller

(b) Forces involved in propeller action

Fig. 58 Screw propeller

can be resolved into a longitudinal component S – which is identical with the thrust acting on the vessel – and a transverse component T, which has to be exerted in the form of a torque. The ratio of u to v_e is usually large, so that the force T to be applied is small as compared with S.

From this it becomes clear that a screw propeller produces its effect (which, of course, is transmitted to the vessel through the propeller boss) not by somehow pushing against the water, but by converting the rotational force (or *torque*) of the screw into a longitudinal force (or *thrust*) through the *lift* generated by the aerofoil section of the screw blades.

Distribution of pressure around a blade section is of crucial importance to the efficiency of the screw; negative pressure on the back of the blade is greater than the positive pressure on the driving face and therefore contributes more to thrust, but there are limits to the reduction of pressure on the blade back which, with increasing revolutions, can be supported without a breakdown in efficiency.

CAVITATION AND OTHER CAUSES OF EFFICIENCY LOSS

Such a breakdown is known as *cavitation*, and is the result of modification of the flow around the screw, characterized by the fact that in certain regions of the velocity field the pressure drops until it reaches the vapour pressure of the fluid (in this case water), accompanied by change of some of the fluid into saturated vapour, forming cavities or bubbles which coincide with regions of maximum velocity. The consequent fall-off in thrust is marked by vibration due to the sudden collapse of the cavities acting like a hammer on the screw blade surfaces.

A somewhat similar effect may be produced if the screw is positioned too close to the water surface – as may happen, for instance, if the vessel is insufficiently ballasted – when there will be a tendency to draw air into the screw race, thus reducing lift and, consequently, thrust. For this reason the screw ideally should be located as low down as possible and *under* the stern of a vessel.

A further source of thrust loss is *blade slip*, which may occur under a variety of conditions and is due to the fact that the screw is acting in a fluid medium.

AXIAL DISPLACEMENT OF THRUST

As mentioned previously (see Appendix III), a vessel in motion drags along with it a large mass of water – the *boundary layer* – with a forward velocity less than the speed of the vessel. It therefore follows that the screw, operating in that part of the boundary layer shed from the hull – the *nominal wake* – has a speed through the latter which

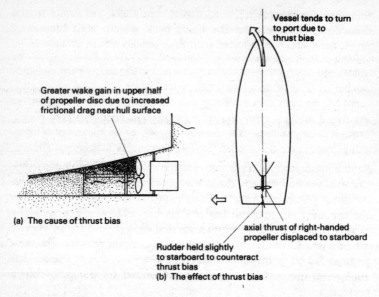

Greater wake gain in upper half
of propeller disc due to increased
frictional drag near hull surface

Vessel tends to turn
to port due to
thrust bias

(a) The cause of thrust bias

axial thrust of right-handed
propeller displaced to starboard

Rudder held slightly
to starboard to counteract
thrust bias

(b) The effect of thrust bias

Fig. 59 Axial displacement of thrust

is less than the speed of the vessel. The resulting gain in efficiency due
to this fact is referred to as the *wake gain*. However, the gain is not
uniform over the whole screw disc area due to increasing frictional
drag nearer the hull surface, giving rise to variations in torque
between the upper and lower halves of the screw disc and consequent
displacement of the axis of thrust in the direction of rotation.

Thus vessels equipped with a single, right-hand turning screw (a
right-hand screw rotates clockwise as viewed from aft) will have their
axis of thrust displaced to the right, and to the left if the screw rotation
is left-handed. Therefore if a vessel with a single right-hand screw is
to follow a straight course, the rudder must be held at a slight angle
to starboard. This problem does not arise in the case of twin-screw
vessels as the screws revolve in opposite directions, thereby cancelling
out bias.

RUDDER ACTION AND STEERING

Although now designed in a variety of forms, a rudder consists basically of a hinged vertical plate attached to the stern of a vessel and capable of being rotated through a lateral arc of dimensions sufficient to provide control of the vessel's course. Rudder movement is usually effected by either a steering wheel connected to the rudder through a mechanical or hydraulic system, or by means of a tiller acting directly on the rudder stock. The steering action of a rudder is achieved by exerting a lateral thrust at the vessel's stern through the hydrofoil lift effect of the rudder acting in the water flow. In the absence of water flow over the rudder surfaces no hydrofoil effect is possible, hence a vessel usually must have *steerage way* – that is, movement relative to the water – to enable steering control to occur.

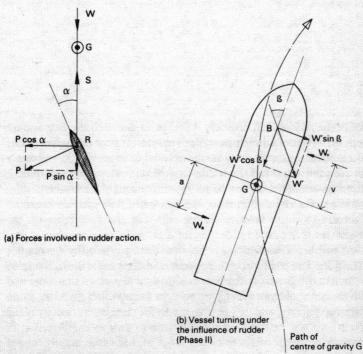

(a) Forces involved in rudder action.

(b) Vessel turning under the influence of rudder (Phase II)

Path of centre of gravity G

Fig. 60 Rudder action and steering

As the effectiveness of a rudder is related to the velocity of water flow over its surfaces, rudders are positioned whenever possible so as to act in the screw race. and vessels equipped with steering gear so designed are capable of being steered from rest. In the case of unpowered craft, compensation for the absence of the screw race may be brought about by increasing the rudder area.

The forces acting on a rudder would be quite inadequate to turn a vessel entirely of their own accord; what a rudder does is to push the vessel slightly off its heading – in other words, to start a yaw. Thus what is known as *drift angle* is first established, and the vessel is then turned in the same direction as the initial yaw by large hydraulic cross-forces acting on the hull as a result of the yaw. In fact it is the underwater hull itself which turns the vessel in a circle, the rudder only rotating the vessel in yaw.

Figures 60a and b illustrate in diagrammatic form the various forces involved both in rudder action and turning effect on the hull of a vessel.

RUDDER ACTION

With the rudder held centrally – that is, in line with the fore-and-aft axis of the vessel – any athwartships or lateral forces are balanced out because of symmetry (assuming the vessel to be moving in still water of adequate depth). If the rudder is now put over, say, to starboard, the fore-and-aft flow due to its motion through the water is augmented by a circulation flow. The combined flow systems cause an increase in water velocity on the port side and a decrease on the starboard side of the rudder; hence a pressure decrease on the port side and a pressure increase on the starboard side, by Bernoulli's Theorem. The resultant of these pressure differences is the *rudder force*, which in this case is directed from starboard to port. At the upper and lower edges of the rudder free vortices form which give rise to an induced velocity, and this, together with the circulation velocity of the bound vortex, causes the so-called *induced drag* in the direction of motion. A further loss of efficiency is due to *profile drag*, mainly caused by frictional resistance.

The rudder force P causes a tendency for the vessel to rotate about three mutually perpendicular axes, only one of which – rotation about the vertical axis – is desired, the others being unwanted additional results.

A vessel turning under the influence of rudder does so in three distinguishable phases:

Phase 1

With the rudder central and the vessel on a straight course, the only forces acting upon the vessel are the thrust S and the resistance W. When the rudder is put over to starboard, rudder force P is generated which, for the sake of simplicity, is assumed to act normal to the centreline plane of the rudder (an approximation only, but sufficient for all practical purposes), and to have its point of application located in the centreline of the rudder stock R. The fore-and-aft component of the rudder force $P\sin\alpha$ acts in the same direction as W and retards the forward motion of the vessel. The lateral component $P\cos\alpha$ imparts to the vessel a sideways motion and also causes a turning moment about the vessel's centre of gravity by virtue of the couple $P\cos\alpha \cdot RG$ which, however, must first overcome the mass moment of inertia of the vessel augmented by the surrounding water before any turning about the vertical axis through G can take place. During the first moments after putting the rudder over the force $P\cos\alpha$ predominates so that the vessel drifts away bodily to port, without any appreciable turning about the vertical axis. This situation exists for only a short time and merges with the gradual swinging of the vessel's bow to starboard under the influence of the couple $P\cos\alpha \cdot RG$ as the second phase commences.

Phase 2

As a consequence of the sideways drift in the first phase and the turning which begins in the second, the vessel's resistance W – originally acting along the fore-and-aft axis – gradually changes into a resistance W', which acts at an angle β to the fore-and-aft axis on the port side. The fore-and-aft component $W' \cos \beta$ together with the force $P \sin \alpha$ retards the vessel, and the lateral component $W' \sin \beta$ opposes the force $P \cos \alpha$ so that the drift to port of the first phase is arrested. At the same time the turning moment of the couple $W' \sin \beta$ $.BG$ assists the couple $P \cos \alpha . RG$, and consequently the angular velocity of the turning motion increases. Under these influences the vessel now follows a curved path whose radius of curvature decreases as the angular velocity increases. As W' acts at a point between G and the stem, the vessel advances with bow inside and stern outside the path of the centre of gravity. In swinging, the vessel meets with a water resistance W_v forward on the starboard side acting at a distance v from G, and a corresponding resistance W_a aft on the port side acting at a distance a from G.

Throughout the first and second phases the various forces and motions are changing, but the variations merge at the end of the second phase into the constant conditions of the third phase, due to several causes. First, B (the point of application of resistance W') travels aft as the drift angle increases, so that the turning moment induced by the couple $W' \sin \beta . BG$ decreases. Next, the turning motion alters the flow of water around the vessel in such a way that the true angle of attack of the rudder becomes less than the rudder angle α. In consequence, P and the couple $P \cos \alpha . RG$ are both decreased but, on the other hand, the couples due to the resistances W_v and W_a both increase.

Phase 3

Evidently a position of equilibrium must be attained at a particular drift angle, at which point the centrifugal forces and the water forces acting on the vessel are balanced, and the radius of curvature of the turn becomes constant. In this state the centre of gravity of the vessel will describe a turning circle, although to an observer on board the vessel *appears* to turn about a point situated between one-sixth and one-third of the vessel's length abaft the stem, called the *pivoting point*. During the first and second phases the speed of the vessel diminishes due to increased water-resistance and rudder force, but in the third phase remains constant.

REFERENCES

W. P. A. Van Lammeren, L. Troost and J. G. Koning, *Resistance, Propulsion and Steering of Ships*, 1948

A. Roorda and E. M. Neuerberg, *Small Seagoing Craft and Vessels for Inland Navigation*, 1957

J. Anthony Hind, *Background to Ship Design and Shipbuilding Production*, 1965

(For advice and assistance in compiling the information contained in Appendices III and IV I am much indebted to Dr R. L. Townsin, Senior Lecturer in the Department of Naval Architecture and Shipbuilding, University of Newcastle upon Tyne)

INDEX

Bold page numbers refer to illustrations